AC⚡DC 1973–1980

THE BON SCOTT YEARS
JEFF APTER

A GENUINE JAWBONE BOOK

AC/DC
1973–1980
The Bon Scott Years
Jeff Apter

Also by Jeff Apter
Never Enough: The Story Of The Cure
The Dave Grohl Story
Together Alone: The Story Of The Finn Brothers
A Pure Drop: The Life Of Jeff Buckley
Tragedy: The Ballad Of The Bee Gees
High Voltage: The Life Of Angus Young
AC/DC's Last Man Standing
www.jeffapter.com.au

ISBN

Jacket design

Printed in China

This one's for Elizabeth.

A Jawbone book
First edition 2018
Published in the UK and the USA by
Jawbone Press
Office G1
141–157 Acre Lane
London SW2 5UA
England
www.jawbonepress.com

978-1-911036-41-8

Mark Case

1 2 3 4 5 22 21 20 19 18

INTRODUCTION

"In the AC/DC scheme of things, I've been really fortunate. I was a music-loving teen growing up in Sydney in the 1970s, an amazing time for live music. An impressive array of rock bands emerged from that sweaty era: Midnight Oil, The Angels, Rose Tattoo, Cold Chisel, Sports, Australian Crawl, and, crucially, AC/DC. Some great pop bands, too, such as Split Enz, Flowers (aka Icehouse), Skyhooks, and Dragon.

On a good week, I could see any of these acts playing in a pub in or around Sydney; then, on Sunday night, many of them would turn up on *Countdown*, the ABC TV show that provided a splash of pop madness at the end of the weekend. It was the best of times, it was the loudest of times.

My first encounter with AC/DC outside of *Countdown* was at the Haymarket in Sydney, in late January 1977—a gig that I've covered in some detail in the following pages. My underage buddies and I couldn't talk our way into the gig—even though someone had slipped us the name of the guy on the door—so we soaked up AC/DC's rock'n'roll firestorm while slouching around on the street outside the venue. Fortunately, they played so loud that it didn't really matter. My ears rang for days afterward; the brick wall that separated me from the band hardly softened the blow.

It was enough to convince my mates and me to see them pretty much wherever they played—and this was a band who, as this book goes to show, took the old adage 'weddings, parties, anything' to a whole new level. Town halls, school dances, civic centres, flatbed trucks rolling down the main street of Melbourne during peak hour: where there was a stage, some kids, and something resembling a PA, you'd usually find AC/DC during the 1970s.

Fast-forward many years and I got to write about the band quite a bit when I was on staff at **Rolling Stone** *and found myself drawing on memories I'd acquired from more than twenty years of watching and listening.*

It was a time when a lot of the 'garage revival' bands, such as The Vines and Jet, and The Hives—as well as Metallica, Foo Fighters, and many others—were name-checking AC/DC as a major influence. I recall an interview I did with Angus Young where he spoke fondly of Bon and the man's thing for 'swimming with the sharks'. I thought he was speaking metaphorically, until I learned that Bon, when he was growing up in Fremantle, actually had a job that involved swimming with white pointers—or around them, ideally. It hardly came as a shock. When it came to life, unlike the sharks with whom he swam, Bon Scott took very large bites.

My understanding of the band deepened even further when I worked on two AC/DC-related books as ghostwriter. The first was *Dirty Deeds: My Life Inside & Outside AC/DC*, Mark Evans's ripping yarn of his fast times as the band's bassist during what I believe to be the glory years, 1975 to 1977. Mark played on what to me remain the band's best songs: 'Dirty Deeds' and 'High Voltage' and 'Long Way To The Top' and 'T.N.T.'

and the rest of them. I also helped AC/DC's former manager Michael Browning with his memoir, *Dog Eat Dog*, a bullshit-free account of his years spent steering the band from the bacterial barns of Australia to the stadiums of America—a book that sets the record straight on a lot of key events in the making of AC/DC.

Both books provided me with a rare insider's glimpse of life in the bubble of AC/DC—and both were a blast to work on. I then wrote my own book, *High Voltage: The Life Of Angus Young*, a few years later.

Yet still my most vivid memory of AC/DC is standing on that street corner in the Haymarket in Sydney in the summer of 1977, soaking up the blitzkrieg happening on the other side of the brick wall, wondering what kind of madness was going on inside. Hopefully, this book will stir up similar memories for you.

AUTHOR'S NOTE

The mother lode of dates, locales, venues, chart positions, sales numbers, etc. quoted in this book are derived from a wide range of good sources, including reliable websites (cited in the bibliography) and numerous publications, interviews, and articles (also cited in the bibliography). However, as is the nature of projects such as these—and memories being the flexible thing they can sometimes be—these facts and figures can vary from source to source, so I have relied upon only the most reliable, including, in some instances, the band work ledgers maintained by former manager Michael Browning.

This book's title, *AC/DC 1973–1980: The Bon Scott Years*, may give the well-informed reason to pause—Bon Scott didn't actually join the band until 1974—but my publisher and I agreed this was the best way to sum up the era.

Nonetheless, if anyone reading the book spots what they think is a genuine error, and has the data to support it, feel free to contact the author and/or the publisher at bonscottyears@jawbonepress.com.

Most of all, enjoy the book.

JEFF APTER WOLLONGONG, NSW, AUSTRALIA, AUGUST 2018

ANGUS YOUNG, MARK EVANS, AND MALCOLM YOUNG AT WORK INSIDE ALBERTS STUDIOS, SYDNEY, RECORDING THE LP *DIRTY DEEDS DONE DIRT CHEAP*, JANUARY 1976.

The Young family relocates from Glasgow to Oz; George Young and Harry Vanda form The Easybeats and 'Easyfever' erupts in Australia; 'Friday On My Mind' becomes a huge international hit while Malcolm and Angus Young look and learn.

EARLY
YEARS

June 22 1963 The Young family, formerly of 6 Skerryvore Road, Cranhill, Glasgow—father William (b. 1911), mother Margaret (b. 1913), children Angus (b. 1955), Malcolm (b. 1953), George (b. 1946), Stephen (b.1933), and William Jr (b. 1940)—arrive in Sydney as part of the Assisted Passage Migration Scheme, known locally, and colloquially, as the 'Ten Pound Pom' scheme. (It costs ten quid to sign up; children travel free.) Also travelling is sister Margaret (b. 1935), whose married name is Horsburgh; she arrives with her husband, Samuel, and their son, Samuel Jr. Another Young sibling, John (b. 1937), is already in Australia, while Alex Young (b. 1938) has remained in the UK.

The Youngs have been enticed to leave Glasgow by a combination of the big freeze of 1963—the coldest winter in the UK for 200 years—and a TV ad that announced, 'Come over to the sunny side now: Australia, a great place for families—opportunity for you, fine for your wife, great for your children—you could be on your way over to a sunnier future in the new year, on your way to Australia, a great place for families.'

'Me dad couldn't get work up in Scotland,' Angus Young will tell a reporter from *Sounds* in 1976. 'He found it impossible to support a family of our size … so he decided to try his luck Down Under.'

Angus has retained a few memories of Glasgow. 'All I remember,' he recalls much later, 'was being hit by a car and playing football in the streets near the housing estate where we lived.'

On a Commonwealth of Australia Department of Immigration form, William records his 'usual occupation' as spray painter (semi-skilled) and prior occupations as 'wheel boy' at Todd & Sons, a rope work factory; 'machine operator' at Turner & Newall, a Clydebank manufacturer of cement (and asbestos); flight mechanic engineer while in the RAF during World War II; press assistant; and postman. 'No police trouble,' notes his interviewer on the form, which no doubt helped secure the Youngs passage as Ten Pound Poms, along with one million fellow immigrants during the life of the scheme. At fifty-two, William doesn't meet the exact criteria (preferred applicants are under forty-five), but as a parent (with quite the brood), he has been granted permission.

The Youngs and Horsburghs, along with a mixture of British and German immigrants, travelled from London on Qantas flight QF738064, registration VH-EBG. On arrival at Sydney Airport, eight-year-old Angus, the youngest of the Young clan, throws up as soon as he disembarks. Travelling by air is uncommon; most of their fellow Ten Pound Poms come by sea. (Among the better-known are Ronald Belford 'Bon' Scott, Olivia Newton-John, the Gibb family of Manchester, notorious 'Bodyline' cricketer Harold Larwood,

Hugh Jackman, Kylie Minogue, and two future Australian prime ministers, Julia Gillard and Tony Abbott.)

At the time of the Youngs' arrival in Australia, the local Top 10 is an Anglophile's wet dream, featuring Gerry & The Pacemakers' 'How Do You Do It?', The Shadows' 'Atlantis', and Cliff Richard's 'Summer Holiday'. It is the most vanilla of times in the pop charts. Music made available to the masses is first scrutinised closely by various nosey government departments. Leading Sydney DJ Bob Rogers will later write of the time, 'All recorded foreign music had to first go through a public service cleansing bath in case it might contain anything that would contaminate us.' On the small screen, British soap *Coronation Street* is immensely popular, while Prime Minister Robert Menzies is a self-confessed Pom-lover. 'I'm British to my bootstraps,' he crows. When Queen Elizabeth II visited Australia, Menzies almost melts. 'I did but see her passing by,' he gushes, quoting poet Thomas Ford, 'and yet I love her 'til I die.'

In some ways, Australia is just like home for immigrants like the Youngs.

Upon landing in Sydney, the family travel by bus directly to the Villawood Migrant Hostel on the suburban outskirts of Sydney, forty kilometres to the west of the city, a camp populated entirely by fellow 'new Australians'. Fifteen hundred people reside at Villawood; twenty such camps are scattered across New South Wales. Life inside the fence at Villawood isn't vastly dissimilar to life in Cranhill, the housing estate the Youngs lived in back in Glasgow: several times a week, the local police are called in to investigate the latest break-in, usually the work of a resident, while the ambulance service also does a lively trade, as the combination of dodgy food, confined quarters, the frustrating search for full-time work, and invasive weekly checks by hostel staff manifests itself in violent flare-ups. Fortunately, booze is banned at Villawood, or the situation could get a whole lot uglier.

Years later, Angus will sometimes joke that his family first settled at Tasmania's Port Arthur, a much-feared convict site, and the last port of call for many of the first wave of Brits sent to Oz. Villawood isn't that dire—the sight of green, open land and vast trees is a pleasant surprise for Angus and his kin, although the ever-present snakes come as a bit of a shock—but it is hard going, a tough introduction to life in Oz. All the talk of sea and sun in the TV ad that lured them now seems like a terrible con.

Within months, however, the Youngs relocate to 4 Burleigh Street in Burwood, a blue-collar suburb ten kilometres to the west of Sydney. There, William gets some work, the kids start school, and their lives gain some stability.

'TEN POUND POMS' LIKE THE YOUNGS OF GLASGOW WERE ENTICED TO POSTWAR AUSTRALIA AS PART OF THE ASSISTED PASSAGE MIGRATION SCHEME.

11

June 11 1964 The Beatles arrive in Sydney for their only Australian tour. Despite a wild rainstorm, thousands of screaming fans turn up, hoping for a glimpse of their new idols. The Fab Four (well, three, if you exclude stand-in drummer Jimmy Nicol, deputising for an ill Ringo) try to take cover beneath some flimsy umbrellas given to them by airline staff, but the wind swiftly despatches them.

The group then travel on to Adelaide, where 250,000 people line the route from the airport to their hotel in the city. It's a crowd more in keeping with a visit from royalty—which it is, in some ways. A night later, they pack Adelaide's Centennial Hall for the first of a week of wildly received Australian shows, all for the outrageously low fee of £2,500 for the week—a fraction of their current asking price of £25,000 *per show*. The promoter, Kenn Brodziak, secured the band's services in 1963, just before they exploded internationally.

'You got us for the old fee, didn't you?' John Lennon says with a chuckle to Brodziak, who may well be the luckiest man on earth.

On June 18, the Fab Four play on a revolving stage at the Sydney Stadium, the first of six gigs over three days (with more than 70,000 fans attending the shows). After each song, Ringo, who's returned to the band, is forced to pick up his drum kit and manually shift it to face another part of the audience—all while doing his best to dodge the Jelly Babies being thrown toward the band by over-eager fans.

Local daily the *Sun-Herald* captured the craziness. 'Thousands of girls under sixteen, who occupied the most expensive seats,' the paper reports, 'seem to be in a state of delirium … laddering stockings and losing their shoes. Many were hurried off to the first aid room, too excited to stand anymore.'

In the midst of the Sydney Stadium mayhem are Malcolm, George, and Margaret Young. Angus insists he was also at the show, though that seems unlikely. Later, when he boasts to a future bandmate that tickets for the concert 'cost a couple of bucks', it is pointed out to Angus that decimal currency wasn't introduced to Australia until 1966. (The best tickets actually went for 37/-.)

The importance of The Beatles' tour of Australia can't be understated. It inspires the rise of The Easybeats and The Bee Gees, among dozens of other bands. The Gibb brothers, upon seeing the Sydney show, immediately go out and buy Beatle boots and updated their sound, while The Beatles help The Easybeats find a name and a style. They will soon enough be referred to as the 'Antipodean Beatles'.

Malcolm Young also becomes a huge fan, if not so much his younger sibling. 'I used

IN THE EARLY PART OF THIS BOOK, ALL CURRENCY QUOTED IS IN AUSTRALIAN DOLLARS, UNLESS OTHERWISE NOTED. LATER, AS THE BAND MAKE INROADS IN THE UK AND THE USA, BRITISH POUNDS AND US DOLLARS ARE USED. FOR COMPARISON, IN 1973, WHEN THE MAIN ACTION OF THIS BOOK BEGINS, $10 AU EQUATED TO AROUND $15 US AND £5.80 IN THE UK; AT THE TIME OF BON SCOTT'S DEATH IN 1980, $10 AU WAS WORTH $11 US OR £4.90.

to listen to The Beatles and the Stones,' he will later tell a reporter, 'whereas Angus was more into the heavier stuff.'

Winter 1964 George Young (guitar), Harry Vanda (guitar), Dick Diamonde (bass), Gordon 'Snowy' Fleet (drums), and vocalist Stevie Wright form The Easybeats, first jamming in the laundry room at the Villawood Migrant Hostel in suburban Sydney and in a shed at the rear of Diamonde's parents' home. (*Australian Musician* magazine later cites the meeting of Vanda and Young at Villawood as 'the most important moment in local music history'.) Australia's first internationally successful rock group comprises five immigrants—two Dutchmen, a Scot, and a pair of Poms—yet they proudly refer to themselves as an Aussie band.

November 1964 One Sydney concert a youthful Angus Young definitely does catch (with his sister Margaret) is Louis 'Satchmo' Armstrong at the Sydney Stadium.

While there might not seem to be much common ground shared by a trumpet-playing African-American with balloons for cheeks and a nine-year-old budding guitarist, Angus will later insist that Armstrong was a massive influence. 'There was an aura about him. It's amazing to hear his old records and hear the musicianship and emotion, especially when you consider that technology, in those days, was almost non-existent.'

Angus's other key early influences are a tad more relatable: he's mad for 1950s rockers. He will one day tell *Countdown*'s Molly Meldrum, 'From when I was pretty young, old rock'n'roll songs, Little Richard'—whose 'Tutti Frutti' was a hit the year Angus was born—'and Buddy Holly … it was always being played in the house, so I picked up on that.'

While they were still living in Glasgow, his sister Margaret would bring home records of classic-era rockers, which were on high rotation Chez Young. That has continued in Australia. Chuck Berry is a particular favourite of Angus's—so much so that he'll 'borrow' Berry's 'duck walk' when he eventually begins playing live.

March 1965 Having signed to Albert Music—a Sydney family business that made its fortune selling sheet music and the very popular Boomerang harmonica—The Easybeats

> **"Chuck Berry brought together blues, country music, folk music, a bit of jazz, and blended it all into this thing that we called rock'n'roll. He's the one that inspired most. And he was a great entertainer, so he had a lot of elements. He was a pure talent and an inspiration."**
>
> ANGUS YOUNG TO MOLLY MELDRUM, COUNTDOWN, 1976

release their debut single, 'For My Woman'. It's produced by twenty-eight-year-old Ted Albert, a scion of the Albert dynasty. The Easybeats find a live home at a venue called Beatle Village, having been turfed out of another Sydney venue for being 'too loud and too filthy'.

May 1965 'She's So Fine' (co-written by George Young and singer Stevie Wright, a huge influence on Bon Scott) becomes The Easybeats' first Oz #1, and 'Easyfever' erupts all over the country.

Angus Young returns home from school one day to find his home at Burwood surrounded by hundreds of screaming female fans—on the lookout for his brother, George—and a handful of police, struggling to maintain order. Someone had found Easybeat George's home address.

'Let me in,' Angus demands, 'I live here.'

'That's what they're all saying,' a copper replies.

Angus is forced to jump the back fence to get inside.

Malcolm Young, however, is very impressed. 'Those were great days,' he would later recall. 'I was just going into puberty and we were getting all these screaming girls, a couple of hundred of them, hanging outside our house for a glimpse of The Easybeats, who were like Australia's Beatles. [Angus and I] used to hang out there with them thinking, *This is the way to go!* That planted the seed for us and made us play more, try harder.'

Angus is impressed by the sound of The Easybeats, especially the interplay between guitarists Vanda and Young. 'They had a very good sound, a unique thing going between [George] and Harry,' he remarks, many years later.

September 1965 The Easybeats' debut album, *Easy*, is released, while their next single, 'Wedding Ring', becomes an Australian Top 10 hit. Despite their success, the band members survive on a wage of just five quid each per week.

October 1965 West Australian group The Spektors, featuring Bon Scott on vocals and drums, record three tracks for Perth TV show *Club 17*—tracks that won't surface until 1992, when they're released under the name Bon Scott & The Spektors. The songs are all covers: The Beatles' 'Yesterday', Chuck Berry's 'On My Mind', and Them's 'Gloria'.

One of Bon's bandmates is singer Al Collins, a fellow Scot, whose mother refers to

ANGUS YOUNG AS PART OF BURWOOD PRIMARY'S CLASS OF 63 (FRONT ROW, FAR RIGHT); EASYBEATS GEORGE YOUNG, STEVIE WRIGHT, AND DICK DIAMONDE OUTSIDE THE YOUNGS' HOME IN SUBURBAN BURWOOD; GEORGE YOUNG AND HIS SISTER MARGARET.

Bon as 'Wee Ronnie'. While driving to a gig, Collins's car runs out of petrol, so Scott milks another car and they drive on. ('He was a rough little bastard,' Collins recalls in 2011, 'but you couldn't wish for a better friend.')

Scott, who was born in Scotland in 1946, moved to Australia in 1952. He was one of four siblings, although the firstborn, a boy named Sandy, died shortly after birth. His father, Charles, is known as Chick; his mother, Isabelle, is Isa. The Scotts initially lived in the Melbourne suburb of Sunshine, before moving to Fremantle in Western Australia, where Scott joined the Fremantle Scots Pipe Band, playing the drums. He left school at fifteen and soon began to stray, spending time in the Fremantle Prison assessment centre, and nine months at the Riverbank Juvenile Institution, on charges that included escaping custody, having unlawful carnal knowledge, and stealing. He was rejected by the Australian Army, having been deemed 'socially maladjusted', thereby avoiding the dreaded national service (and, quite possibly, Vietnam).

Scott's home was once raided, he will later insist, for 'pornographic photos', resulting in the cops unearthing some pictures of Scott and a lady friend *in flagrante delicto*. When he was being booked by the sergeant on duty, Scott said, 'I bet you'll show them to every bloke on the force.' The cop shook his head; no, of course not, that would be irresponsible. Seemingly within minutes, some other coppers walked past Scott, stopped, pointed, and declared, 'You stud!'

December 1965 At the 4BC Sound Spectacular at Brisbane's Festival Hall, The Easybeats' set is halted after just seventeen minutes when a riot erupts among the 5,000-strong crowd. Dozens of fans are injured in the crush. The band members make their escape in a taxi, but are set upon when the driver stops at a red light; the cab is almost overturned by rabid fans (and the odd angry boyfriend). 'That's where all the bullshit started,' George Young tells *Rolling Stone* in 1976. 'We weren't really playing anymore, we were just satisfying demand. From then on, the gigs became a chore.'

Mid-1966 The Spektors morph into The Valentines, with Scott sharing vocal duties with Vince Lovegrove. The Valentines wear cute matching red suits and sing the hits of the day: everything from The Who to The Spencer Davis Group and Wilson Pickett, and even such standards as Gershwin's 'It Ain't Necessarily So' (which was given a rock treatment by local star Normie Rowe in April, and hit #1 in Melbourne). But Scott's biggest inspirations are Little Richard and legendary American rocker, Chuck Berry.

According to Angus, 'Bon always said, when it comes to rock'n'roll, you have to go back to Chuck Berry, Little Richard, and the other pioneers. He judged all singers by comparison with them.'

In an interview with acdccollector.com in 2001, Lovegrove describes The Valentines' various inspirations as 'a mixed bag: Sam & Dave, The Beatles, Small Faces, Santana, Traffic, Easybeats.'

July 10 1966 The Easybeats are set to leave Australia for the UK, seeking the pop pot of gold, when Harry Vanda's wife, Pam, commits suicide. 'Tragedy struck The Easybeats on the eve of their departure for England,' the *Australian Women's Weekly* reports, 'when the wife of guitarist Harry Vanda died of an overdose of sleeping tablets. Few people knew that Harry was married.' (They also have a son, Johan.)

The band carry on, and when their flight reaches Perth, a brief performance is hastily arranged—on the tarmac, no less, alongside a Lancaster bomber. But the surge of the 4,000-strong crowd prevents the show from taking place. 'At one stage,' the *Canberra Times* reports, 'several hysterical girls were being carried away or led off the tarmac, displaying bare midriffs and thighs as they struggled with police.'

When the band finally board their London-bound 707, there is a bomb scare, and they are rushed by police wagon to a remote part of the airport, away from the screaming teens who'd assembled to see them off. Just before they are finally able to depart, singer Stevie Wright, showing a deft gift for understatement, tells the press that the reception 'was better than we have received elsewhere'.

Soon after reaching London, George Young begins writing with Harry Vanda, rather than Stevie Wright, and a legendary musical partnership is born. The duelling guitars of Vanda and Young will become a massive influence on Malcolm and Angus Young. 'Harry was doing the same thing I'd do with Malcolm,' Angus states in the documentary *Blood & Thunder*. 'George had that very high rhythm and Harry provided the highlights, the colour.'

November 1966 'Sorry' becomes The Easybeats' second Australian #1 single. Meanwhile, 'Friday On My Mind', the band's working-class anthem, falls into place for Vanda and Young after they watch a film featuring the Swingle Singers, who inspire the distinctive opening notes of the song. The record is produced by Shel Talmy—who's already struck gold with The Kinks and The Who—and reaches #6 in the UK charts.

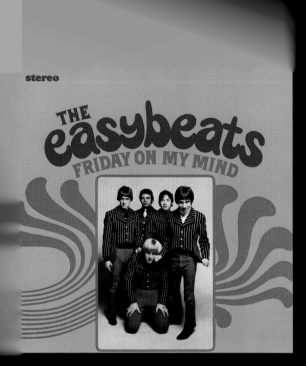

stereo

THE easybeats
FRIDAY ON MY MIND

THE EASYBEATS
FRIDAY ON MY MIND
REMEMBER SAM • PRETTY GIRL • MADE MY BED

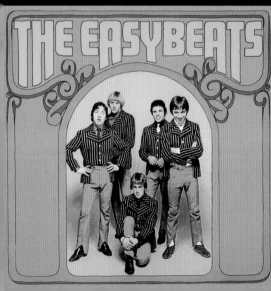

THE EASYBEATS

easy
THE EASYBEATS

PLUS 8 BONUS TRACKS

The Easybeats are the first Australian rock band to achieve this level of international success. Their chart-mates at the time include The Beach Boys' 'Good Vibrations', Tom Jones's 'Green Green Grass Of Home', 'Gimme Some Lovin'' by The Spencer Davis Group, and The Four Tops' 'Reach Out, I'll Be There'. In May 1967, 'Friday' enters the US charts, too, reaching a peak of #16.

The Easybeats' relationship with Talmy, however, is a fractious one; a later song, 'Do You Have A Soul?', is allegedly directed at the producer.

'Friday' will later be covered by David Bowie, on his *Pinups* album, and by Peter Frampton, Richard Thompson, Gary Moore, and Blue Öyster Cult—there are more than forty recorded covers of the song in all. Even today, Bruce Springsteen sometimes covers it live. In 2001, 'Friday' will be voted the 'Best Australian Song Of All Time' by the Australian Performing Rights Association (APRA), and in 2007 it is added to the registry of the National Film and Sound Archive of Australia.

January 21 1967 Malcolm and Angus attend a Yardbirds show at the Sydney Stadium—the same venue The Beatles played three years earlier. (The Yardbirds' 'I'm A Man' is one of the first records Angus ever bought.) It's a stellar bill: also playing are Roy Orbison and The Walker Brothers, plus an assortment of local talent, including pop star John Young (no relation).

Angus is particularly impressed by the sight of Jimmy Page playing his guitar with a bow. 'It was just a great atmosphere,' he later recalls of the show. 'They came on, they played, they were really short and sweet. I thought, this is very flash.'

Yardbirds singer Keith Relf also impresses him. 'He didn't dazzle you with his hips—he concentrated on what he was there for: to make a bit of rock'n'roll.'

May 13 1967 The Easybeats return to Australia for a national tour, but by now they are unravelling even quicker than the Carnaby Street gear they wear, struggling to repeat the success of 'Friday', and deep in debt.

June 1 1967 The Australian magazine *Good Neighbour* reports that 'five young immigrants known as The Easybeats have made a million dollars in the past year'. (It's not made clear how this figure has been arrived at—bad business decisions haunt The Easybeats throughout their career, and they make very little real money.) A civic reception is held for the band in Sydney, attended by the lord mayor of the city. 'Three years ago,'

THE EASYBEATS, ON THE STRENGTH OF THEIR 1966 SMASH SINGLE 'FRIDAY ON MY MIND', ARE THE FIRST AUSTRALIAN ROCK BAND TO ACHIEVE GLOBAL SUCCESS. LOU REED AND DAVID BOWIE ARE AMONG THEIR MANY ADMIRERS.

a reporter at the event notes, 'the boys were playing in a laundry at Villawood Hostel—only for their own amusement.'

As they leave the reception, The Easybeats are mobbed by female fans—now standard procedure at any public event the band members attend.

August 1967 In a classic mismatch, The Easybeats tour America as the support act for pop warbler Gene Pitney, whose 'Just One Smile' was high in the UK charts when 'Friday On My Mind' was a hit. In New York, they are introduced to the Warhol/Max's Kansas City crowd by influential writer (and expat Aussie) Lillian Roxon, who becomes their den mother and a very handy contact. In print, she calls George Young 'a genius'. Lou Reed is in awe of Vanda & Young's 'Falling Off The Edge Of The World', which he plays repeatedly on the jukebox at Max's. 'This is one of the most beautiful songs in the world,' he tells Roxon.

April 1968 'Hello, How Are You?' is the next UK Top 20 hit for The Easybeats. It's clearly not George Young's favourite Easybeats moment however; he later dismisses it as 'cornball schmaltz shit'.

June 1968 The Easybeats song 'Good Times'—featuring piano by Rolling Stones sidekick Nicky Hopkins—hits Paul McCartney like a thunderbolt. Immediately upon hearing it on the radio, he pulls off to the side of the road and calls the BBC, demanding they play it again. Despite his support, it's not a hit.

July 1968 Now based in Melbourne, Bon Scott and The Valentines record their own version of The Easybeats' 'Peculiar Hole In The Sky', but it fails to chart nationally. A few months earlier, they cut another Vanda & Young track, 'She Said', which scaled the lower reaches of the Perth Top 40 but didn't chart elsewhere.

Regardless, The Valentines have begun building a profile, readily admitting to *Go-Set* that they're 'not afraid of being commercial'. (In concert, they cover such hits as 'Build Me Up Buttercup' and 'To Know You Is To Love You'.) Bon shaves three years off his age, telling the magazine he's only nineteen. On stage, he applies foundation to conceal his tattoos (the domain of bikers, sailors, and ex-cons) and straightens his hair with sticky tape, although the heat of the stage lights usually means his disguise doesn't last beyond the first number. In a profile, Bon lists his likes: 'My room (painted red), long blonde hair, sex, showers, swimming.' His favourite music? 'Scottish pipe band music, soul, worried jazz.'

July 7 1968 The Easybeats appear at the *Sounds 68* concert at the Royal Albert Hall, alongside The Move, The Byrds (with Gram Parsons), Joe Cocker, Bonzo Dog Doo-Dah Band, and The Alan Bown Set.

February 14 1969 The Valentines—having recently spruced up their stage act with smoke bombs and sparklers, acquired matching scarlet outfits, and begun proudly promoting themselves as heart-throbs ('Be My Valentine In 69' is their slogan)—cover yet another Vanda & Young song, 'My Old Man's A Groovy Old Man', which was also covered, a year earlier, by British act Dr Marigold's Prescription (Billy Fury's backing band).

At a Valentines gig in the working-class Melbourne suburb of Prahran—home of future AC/DC bassist Mark Evans—the mainly female audience drags Scott and Lovegrove onto the dance floor; Scott emerges from the melee minus his pants and jacket. They draw 2,000 screaming teens to another gig in suburban Melbourne, then play to 7,000 at a free gig, part of Melbourne's annual Moomba festival.

Around this time, a roadie named John Darcy joins their crew. After a gig, Bon asks him if he's interested in some female company. Scott then directs him to a room in the house where a party is taking place with a few very welcoming female guests.

A few minutes later, as Darcy's needs are being seen to, Scott wanders into the room. 'How do you think you'll like this job?' he asks.

'Well,' says Darcy, briefly coming up for air, 'I suppose I can try to adapt.'

August 1969 The Easybeats final single, the classic 'St Louis'—one of their best-ever songs—makes it into the Australian Top 20; it even brushes the US Top 100.

September 20 1969 The Valentines become the first Oz group to be publicly busted for marijuana possession, the cops apparently acting on a tipoff from a fellow pop star who'd turned informant after also being busted. According to a report in *Go-Set*, which has already had The Valentines as cover stars, 'The pop world was rocked last week when the police raided the practice hideaway of top pop group the Valentines and found them in possession of the drug marijuana.' The band's counsel, William Lennon,

“*Female fans of The Easybeats … will be dismayed to find out that three of their idols will soon cease to be bachelors.***”**

AUSTRALIAN WOMEN'S WEEKLY, OCTOBER 1969

relates to the court their belief that 'under the influence of marijuana they become more perceptive to musical sounds'. All five band members are fined $150 and given a 'good behaviour' bond.

Rather than atone for their 'sins', Bon Scott and Vince Lovegrove speak openly about pot, with the latter insisting it should be legalised. Scott, meanwhile, says that the law should worry about more important matters. '[Cops] should realise that what we do is right for us,' he tells a *Go-Set* reporter. 'They shouldn't persecute whole groups of people just for being different.'

'The Australian government deserves a few ripples,' he says in another interview. 'They'll be the last to legalise homosexuality, and pot will be the same.' (These are prescient words: same sex marriage will not be made into law in Australia until late 2017, while, at the time of writing, pot has yet to be decriminalised in any state or territory.)

Controversy is clearly good for business, because 'My Old Man's A Groovy Old Man' will go on to stay in the charts for twelve months, reaching the Top 10 in Brisbane and Melbourne and #19 in Sydney. But their next single—a cover of the children's nursery rhyme 'Nick Nack Paddy Whack', cut as a possible theme for a TV series and never intended for release—will prove an embarrassment and a flop. The flipside, though, features Bon Scott's first co-writing credit: a song called 'Getting Better'.

October 15 1969 The Easybeats return to Oz for a five-week, thirty-five-date tour. Harry Vanda announces his engagement to a twenty-one-year-old Melbourne local, Robyn Thomas, while at the same time it's made known that Stevie Wright has been engaged to his fiancée, Gail Baxter, since the time they left for London. Bassist Dick Diamonde is also engaged. The *Australian Women's Weekly* reacts with due shock: 'Female fans of The Easybeats … will be dismayed to find out that three of their idols will soon cease to be bachelors.'

On the tour, The Easybeats are supported by The Valentines; the parents of the musical Youngs, William and Margaret, attend a reunion party at a Kings Cross hotel. The band, meanwhile, don't respond when asked if they're set to split, but they will do soon after, some $85,000 in debt. Vanda & Young decide to return to the UK to work as

OPPOSITE: THE EASYBEATS PLAY SYDNEY IN 1969 AS PART OF THEIR FINAL TOUR. ABOVE: THE VALENTINES, FEATURING BON SCOTT (SECOND FROM LEFT).

a songwriting/production team, hopefully to wipe out some of their debt. Here they will fine-tune the studio skills they'll later exploit when producing AC/DC. They also agree that whomever they work with in the future will not make the same business mistakes as The Easybeats, who committed such rookie errors as signing conflicting record deals in the same country.

Early 1970 Back in Burwood, Angus Young graduates from playing a banjo—restrung with six strings—to his first Gibson SG, which he buys second-hand from a local music shop. He'll continue to use this guitar until 1978. He also owns a Hofner—a Malcolm hand-me-down—but finds the relatively lightweight Gibson a much better fit. (Angus will go on to play SGs for the bulk of his career, and even design his own signature model for the company.)

'I got out and got a Gibson SG that I played until it got wood rot because so much sweat and water got into it,' he later recalls. 'The whole neck warped. It had a real thin neck, really slim, like a custom neck. It was dark brown.' His favourite players include Leslie West (from Mountain), Jimmy Page, and Eric Clapton—particularly during his stint with John Mayall's Bluesbreakers.

Malcolm develops an early liking for Gretsch guitars—his first guitar is a Gretsch handed along by Harry Vanda, from his time with The Easybeats—eventually settling on a Jet Firebird model. (He, too, will go on to design his own guitar, the 'Salute Jet'.)

Malcolm gives Angus some rudimentary guitar lessons. 'Don't tickle it,' he tells his younger brother. 'Hit the bugger.' (Malcolm always plays this way.) It might be the best advice Angus ever gets—from here on, he is convinced that the best way to get a good guitar sound is to hit the strings hard.

When they come to play together, Angus is awestruck by the precision of his brother's rhythm-guitar work. 'He's like a friggin' human metronome,' he later tells a reporter. 'It's all in the right wrist, you know.'

April 1970 The Valentines release their final single, 'Juliette'. Their timing is unfortunate, because there is currently an ongoing 'pay for play' dispute between commercial radio stations and the six largest record labels, who are demanding payment for music played on air, which has not been the norm. This results in British and Australian songs being refused airplay. The controversy rages for six months, and 'Juliette' barely grazes the Oz Top 30.

By August, the band have split. In a letter to a girlfriend, Scott hints at his next musical move. 'We're going to add an electric piano and organ and a new drummer and go into hiding for a few months.' He predicts the result will be a 'shit hot' band.

September 1970 A bearded Bon Scott re-surfaces in Fraternity, an Adelaide-based group heavily influenced by The Band. He sings and plays the recorder, like an Aussie Ian Anderson. They appear on the new ABC TV music show *GTK*, and tour with The 1910 Fruitgum Company and Jerry Lee Lewis.

October 17 1970 Billed as 'Australia's only group with a completely original repertoire', Fraternity appear on Channel 9 Adelaide's new music show, *Move*. Former Valentines co-vocalist Vince Lovegrove, now a *Go-Set* journalist, pours on the praise when they play Adelaide venue Headquarters. 'They came, they played—they CONQUERED!' he writes.

The band are approached by a fledgling booker, Hamish Henry, who convinces them to establish themselves in a secluded property in the Adelaide hills named Hemming's Farm—their very own Big Pink! Henry covers their rent, pays them a wage, and manages them—he's their very own patron.

The members of Fraternity talk a big game; they even hint at a move to America, as early as next year. Scott continues writing, but none of his material is thought suitable for the band, who, despite the name, are more of an autocracy: bassist Bruce Howe runs things. As a new recruit, Scott is very low in the hierarchy.

> **"Fraternity worked on a different level to me. They were on the same level and it was way above my head."**
>
> BON SCOTT TO ED NIMMERVOLL, *JUKE*, JUNE 1975

December 1970 At the urging of Stevie Wright, former frontman of The Easybeats, seventeen-year-old Malcolm Young is recruited as a guitarist for a jobbing Sydney band named The Velvet Underground. 'His brother is George Young from The Easybeats,' Wright tells the group, which is all the recommendation they need.

When the other members of The Velvet Underground—Herm Kovac, Les Hall, Ronnie and Stephen Cruthers—arrive at the Young home at 4 Burleigh Street, Burwood, they are greeted at the door by a pint-sized terror with a shaved head and bovver boots. His rarely brushed teeth are an interesting shade of green. Thankfully, it's not the dude they're searching for.

'Hi, I'm Angus,' this vision tells the visitors. 'You want Malcolm.'

Big sister Margaret introduces herself and warms to drummer Herm Kovac, who is a little older than the others—and a regular churchgoer, she learns. Margaret christens him 'Uncle Herm'. Over time, he'll become Angus's guardian at gigs when the underage rocker goes to check out his brother playing with the band. A deal is set in place: in exchange for Kovac's supervision, Angus will serve the band cups of Ovaltine after each gig, along with a local delicacy—vegemite on toast. He's the accidental caterer.

Kovac also owns a pristine copy of Jeff Beck's 1968 single 'Hi Ho Silver Lining' (with 'Beck's Bolero' on the B-side), which Angus craves. Angus offers him two dollars for the record, and, in order to sweeten the deal—quite literally—ensures that an extra scoop of sugar makes its way into every cup of post-gig Ovaltine he makes him. Kovac finally relents and sells the record, which Angus still owns, forty-odd years later.

A novice artist, Kovac paints a portrait of The Easybeats, which takes pride of place in the Youngs' Burwood home. Again inspired by Kovac, Angus also takes up painting.

April 1971 Malcom Young finally makes his debut with The Velvet Underground at a gig in the Sydney suburb of Parramatta, at a venue named the Rivoli. Around the same time, the band are profiled in *Go-Set* by a writer going by the peculiar byline of Aunty Agnes.

'Act Two [of The Velvet Underground] begins in April 1971,' she writes. 'There are now five happy-looking faces on stage, and rock music is driving from the wall of amps situated at the back of the stage. Velvet Underground is rocking again; the line-up has changed slightly with Andy Imlah now doing the vocals and the addition of a second guitarist, Malcolm Young.'

Their setlist includes such covers as The Rolling Stones' 'Brown Sugar' and Blues Image's 'Ride, Captain, Ride', but they have also begun writing original songs. 'It's a better, stronger Velvet than ever existed,' says lead guitarist Les Hall.

'Velvet Underground have changed,' Aunty Agnes concludes, 'for the better.'

April 27 1971 Fraternity perform a note-perfect cover of The Band's 'The Shape I'm In' on ABC TV's *GTK*. A frightfully earnest Bon Scott sports a beard that wouldn't have been wasted on the Amish. As one YouTube commenter will later note, with some justification, 'I just can't fathom Angus and Malcolm approaching Bon and saying, We want you to be lead singer of our tough-sounding rock band.'

FRATERNITY—LEFT TO RIGHT: BON SCOTT, 'UNCLE' JOHN AYERS, MICK JURD, JOHN FREEMAN, AND JOHN BISSET—CIRCA 1971.

May 20 1971 Malcom and Angus are among 30,000 punters to attend a show at Sydney's Randwick Racecourse. The brothers are there to see British blues-rockers Free (the Youngs will have business of their own with the band's guitarist, Paul Kossoff, in the not too distant future). They're both hugely impressed by what they see: a band playing no-holds-barred rock'n'roll, raw and sweaty, with a hefty dose of the blues.

Also on the bill are Manfred Mann's Earth Band; Deep Purple are the headliners. The paths of that particular supergroup and the Youngs would eventually intersect—truth be told, it'll be more like a collision. Angus will one day describe Deep Purple as a 'poor man's Led Zeppelin'.

June 1971 Go-Set runs a profile of Fraternity (written again by Bon's buddy, Vince Lovegrove). '[Fraternity] live like no other band in Australia, in a house in the hills seventeen miles from Adelaide,' he writes. 'It's surrounded by seven acres of bushland. They're away from everything but nature. What a buzz! Once a week they come into the city to have a meeting with their management and collect their pay. They only leave their pad to play gigs.'

Scott, Lovegrove adds, 'is constantly in a dream world of his own, but he's having a ball. He says, "The point is, the dollar sign is not the ultimate. We want to try and help each other develop and live. So that the thing inside of us, whether it be creative or not, is satisfied. Something makes us tick, and it's up to people to satisfy that something. We are satisfying ourselves and others by creating an environment."'

July 1971 Bon Scott and Fraternity win Hoadley's 'Battle Of The Sounds', a hugely influential national band competition. (Other contenders include The Zoot, whose members include future US superstar Rick Springfield, as well as guitarist and budding songwriter Beeb Birtles, who'd find fame in Little River Band.)

The real Bon Scott, rocker, is beginning to emerge, having now lost the Amish beard and started singing with balls and heart. 'We did it for Adelaide,' a clearly stunned Scott says from the stage, when the winner is announced. Fraternity's prize is return passage to Los Angeles, a $300 recording session in Melbourne, and $2,000 prize money.

August 14 1971 The Velvet Underground are profiled in Go-Set. 'We're not anarchists or anything like that,' they tell a reporter, 'but we know what we like and the kids like it, too.'

'Their average age is twenty years,' the article reveals, 'and, not surprisingly, they play mainly at suburban dances and halls, where the kids want to hear the kind of music The Velvet Underground specialises in: "thumpy rock".

'They make no claims that their music is art, just good old rock'n'roll … of the type that the Stones used to play in 1965.'

The band dismiss their early attempt to record Jefferson Airplane's 'Somebody To Love' as 'so much crap'. In the band photo, Malcolm is the only one seated, and he stares straight down the barrel of the camera. Clearly, he's a man on a mission.

September 18 1971 Fraternity, featuring a very serious looking Bon Scott, make the cover of *Go-Set*, billed as 'The Next Big Band'. 'Fraternity are far more than a musical group,' writes Vince Lovegrove (yet again). 'They are a long-range plan.'

There's talk of creating an entire utopian community in the hills near Adelaide where they live. 'By 1972, they hope to have seven houses built on the property,' Lovegrove notes. 'Everyone has their own ideas, and everyone has the right to agree or disagree with anyone else.' Bon, however, is permitted little creative freedom in the band; if he does write any songs, they're neither performed nor recorded.

January 24 1972 Bon Scott marries Irene Thornton. They'd been introduced by Vince Lovegrove, while Bon was with Fraternity; Thornton was still in her teens. Their first exchange apparently unfolded this way: upon catching a glimpse of his tight jeans, Thornton said, 'What a well-packed lunch.' Scott replied, 'Yep, two hard-boiled eggs and a sausage.' In her book, *My Bon Scott*, Thornton describes the wedding as 'a big party'. However, despite their undeniable bond, the marriage will last only two years.

February 27 1972 Angus and Malcolm see Jimmy Page do his thing for the second time, this time with Led Zeppelin, at Sydney's Randwick Racecourse. Angus isn't as taken by Page's performance as he was when he saw The Yardbirds. He prefers the former's bluesier ways. 'I always liked The Yardbirds' thing, their approach, better,' he later tells a reporter. 'I was disappointed [with Led Zeppelin] because I expected more of the same.'

Angus also finds fault with Robert Plant's performance, concluding that there is too much flash and not enough rock'n'roll in the singer's approach. 'He'd sing like he was picking his nose.'

**"*Singer was a blond fella.
Bit of a poser.*"**

MALCOLM YOUNG ON SEEING LED ZEPPELIN
AT THE RANDWICK RACECOURSE

March 25 1972 The Velvet Underground perform at half time during a rugby league match between Sydney teams Manly and Penrith at suburban Brookvale Oval. Also on the bill is Ted Mulry. Not long after the Velvets begin playing, a stray football flies through the air and crashes into Malcolm's guitar, disrupting their set. An Aboriginal throwing boomerangs steps in to entertain the 13,000-strong crowd while a mercy dash is undertaken for a replacement six-string. The show eventually goes on.

'The pop group, looking a little like a team of under-nourished half backs, have been commissioned to appear at all of Manly-Warringah's home matches this season,' a reporter from local newspaper, the *Manly Daily*, sniffs. The half-time segment is sponsored by hair product company Pantene, and 'they couldn't have found a better advertisement than all these straggly mops,' the *Daily*'s budding Oscar Wilde adds, smugly referring to the band's mid-game appearance as 'little Woodstock'.

Go-Set magazine also reports on this unlikely combo of footy and rock'n'roll. 'Velvet [Underground] caused a recent sensation among the meat-pie sect when they played … at a Sydney football match.' Meanwhile, at the top of the *Go-Set* singles chart is 'American Pie' by Don McLean, with David Cassidy ('Cherish') and Melanie ('Brand New Key') in hot pursuit. The #1 album is Cat Stevens's *Teaser & The Firecat*. Soft pop rules.

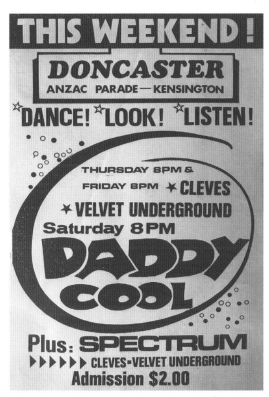

Also in 1972 ... Ted Albert visits the Youngs' home in Burwood.

'The man from the record company is coming,' William Young tells his sons. 'You better behave.'

During the visit, Albert overhears Malcolm and Angus playing together. 'Who's that?' he asks.

'That's the two boys, Malcolm and Angus,' William replies.

'If they ever want to do something,' says Albert, clearly impressed, 'send them to me.'

These prove to be fateful words. Ted Albert will go on to play a huge role in their career, just as he has with George Young.

'Ted was instrumental,' Angus recalls, many years later, 'being a very solid character. He didn't seem to be a person who'd crumble under cannon fire.'

OPPOSITE: ROBERT PLANT AND JIMMY PAGE AT THE RANDWICK RACECOURSE, FEBRUARY 27 1972. ANGUS AND MALCOLM YOUNG ARE IN THE CROWD FOR THE SHOW. ABOVE: A POSTER ADVERTISING MALCOLM'S FIRST BAND, THE VELVET UNDERGROUND.

School is not high on either Malcolm or Angus's agenda. Angus is caned on his first day of high school, purely because he is Malcolm's brother—which is enough to turn him off academia in deference to rock'n'roll.

'What's your name?' he is asked, as soon as his bum hit the seat.

'Young.'

'Come out here, son,' his teacher demands, 'I'm going to make an example of you.'

Despite his parents' concerns, Angus drops out of Ashfield Boys High as soon as he reaches the legal age of fifteen and forms Kantuckee (sometimes spelled Kantucky; both are misspellings of Angus's favourite fast-food chain) with singer Bob McGlynn, bassist John Stevens, and drummer Trevor James.

A key instigator in the band's formation is 'Uncle' Herm Kovac, Malcolm's bandmate and friend. 'I was teaching drums to a kid named Trevor James,' Kovac later recalls, 'and suggested Angus jam with him, as it would help him to play with another instrument. At that stage, Angus was into Leslie West and Mountain, so they played all of that. Velvet Underground took them as a support for gigs down at [NSW rural townships] Ulladulla and Batemans Bay.'

Besides Mountain covers, Kantuckee's setlist includes an original, 'The Kantuckee Stomp'; they also cover Cactus's 1972 album 'Ot 'N Sweaty in its entirety. Angus has long, lank hair, which almost becomes entangled with the strings of his Gibson as he plays. Printed on top of his amp, which towers over him, are the words, 'HIGH VOLTAGE'.

Kovac dismisses the long-standing rumour that George Young may have made some very basic recordings of the band. 'Except for Angus, they were pretty crappy, so I doubt George would have wasted his time on them.'

Kantukee/Kantucky gradually morph into a band called Tantrum, and they play some shows at Sydney nightclub Chequers, where AC/DC will stage their own 'coming out' in the not too far distant future. The 550-capacity Chequers was once the Sydney venue of choice for such international stars as Liza Minnelli and Shirley Bassey. Times have changed, though, and it's now more grimy than glamorous, the domain of sweaty young rock bands, hustling for a buck.

Unlike his fellow musos, Angus has no interest in booze or drugs. He does, however, have a weakness for chocolate milk. A future member of the AC/DC crew, Pat Pickett, later says of Angus's teeth, 'If there's a white one in there, he'd have a snooker set.' His other basic dietary requirements are Benson & Hedges cigarettes and spaghetti bolognese—which, when combined with the chocolate milk, makes for some nasty emissions when he plays. A bandmate describes Angus's eruptions as a 'snot cyclone'. Stage front becomes a dangerous place for unsuspecting punters—they often end up wearing the lot.

Stories will later circulate about the various day jobs Angus held down (briefly) at this time: helping out in a butcher's shop being one. He also works as a compositor with a printing business, acting on the direction of his father, William, who insists that Angus learn a trade. This doesn't last long, although Angus later claims that he works for a time printing *Ribald*, Australia's most popular hardcore porn mag. Malcolm too has developed a distaste for 'regular' employment, having quickly opted out of an apprenticeship as a fitter, much to the dismay of his parents.

Angus has now taken to introducing himself as 'Angus Young, brother of George Young from The Easybeats, also the brother of Malcolm Young'.

Meanwhile ... After their Hoadley's win, Fraternity decide to base themselves in the UK, but their rootsy take on rock—and a name change, to Fang—is way out of the step with glam, the musical flavour of the month.

'I remember London rehearsals being very gloomy, unproductive affairs,' Fraternity's John Bissett later recalls, in an interview with the *Back In Black* website. 'We had very little money, so the booze and drugs supply was severely limited. The whole mood of the band went downhill in London … the party was over. We were not up with the play, as far as sound production went.'

Although they are booked for a show supporting Status Quo, Fang's gear is not up to snuff. 'The audience was appreciative and kind,' Bissett says, 'but we could not compete with the gear we had. We had too many members to get a clear sound definition of individual instruments and we lacked good original material. We all tried to write new and better songs but to no avail. Things were briefly better in Germany. We focussed more on rock for the German audiences and went over quite well. Bon introduced a song or two in German, much to the delight of the audience.'

While they are in the UK, Fang support a Newcastle band named Geordie, whose lead singer is one Brian Johnson. Scott pays close attention when he sees Johnson wading into crowds with the band's guitarist riding on his shoulders. Johnson's quite the showman.

> **"***I did used to drink a lot of milk, yes. I don't know why, really … my body just seemed to say I had to drink that milk. And I used to have gallons of the stuff. The only one that had a problem with it was my dentist.***"**
>
> ANGUS TO *CLASSIC ROCK*, 2016

FOLLOWING PAGE: A VERY YOUNG ANGUS IN ONE OF THE SCHOOL UNIFORMS CREATED FOR HIM BY HIS SISTER MARGARET. ANGUS WOULD LATER LIKEN THE UNIFORM TO A CAPE THAT ENABLES HIM TO BECOME A DIFFERENT PERSON ONSTAGE.

Harry Vanda and George Young set up base at the Albert Productions studio in Sydney; Malcom Young brings together the first AC/DC line-up; Margaret Young inspires some key band decisions; AC/DC make their live debut and see in the new year at Sydney venue Chequers.

1973

Early 1973 Production duo Harry Vanda and George Young return from the UK and begin work on their first project, as part of a handshake deal with Ted Albert. Albert has given them carte blanche use of the Albert Productions studio, which is located on the fifth floor of Boomerang House—one of many Sydney buildings owned by the Albert family. He hopes the results will be pop/rock gold.

Both Vanda and Young resettle their families in Sydney. Harry has now married his fiancée, Robyn Thomas, while George is married to Sandra, and they have a daughter named Yvette.

The name of the first Vanda & Young project is The Marcus Hook Roll Band—one of many future guises, and essentially a front to allow them to have some fun in the studio. The roots of the project took seed while they were still in London, when engineer Wally Allen invited them into Abbey Road to record a few tracks.

One of the songs to come out of the project is 'Natural Man'. Executives at Capitol Records in the USA are keen on the song and want to hear more—Allen even scores a free trip to Australia out of the deal. But there's more to the project than a sniff of US label interest, as Harry and George decide to involve Malcolm and Angus with the sessions. It's the first time either of them has been inside a professional studio, and it's a pragmatic move by Harry and George—clearly, they figure, it will be very useful to show Angus and Malcolm how a studio operates. It proves to be an invaluable crash course.

'We thought it was hilarious, it had just been a joke to us,' George Young later tells *Bomp* magazine about The Marcus Hook Roll Band. 'We had Harry, myself and my kid brothers, Malcolm and Angus. We all got rotten, except for Angus, who was too young, and we spent a month in there boozing it up every night. That was the first thing Malcolm and Angus did before AC/DC. We didn't take it very seriously, so we thought we'd include them, to give them an idea of what recording was all about.'

The finished album, *Tales Of Old Grand-Daddy*, is significant, though, because it contains sketches of some songs that will feature on early AC/DC recordings. 'Quick Reaction' is clearly related to 'T.N.T.', while you can hear something of 'Live Wire' in 'Natural Man'. 'Goodbye Jane', meanwhile, proves what savvy songwriters Vanda & Young have become. The entire album is strong, in fact, and much more than a boozy joke, with punchy rock songs (typified by 'Red Revolution'), catchy hooks ('People And The Power'), and some quirky humour ('Shot In The Head', a not-so-sly dig at the pitfalls of the biz of music). Angus's playing, while lacking the firestorms he will soon unleash with AC/DC, is rock solid. Ditto Malcolm on rhythm guitar.

In the album credits, Angus and Malcolm are listed among the band's 'main personnel', as is their brother Alex, who's been playing with the UK band Grapefruit (also produced by Vanda & Young), who are signed to The Beatles' Apple label. With George co-producing, it's a rare instance of four Youngs working on the same project.

Malcolm, however, while all the better for the time spent in the studio, isn't thrilled by the constant overdubbing of parts—he gets the sense that the type of music he wants to play is best captured live and raw. That, to him, is real rock'n'roll.

Meanwhile ... Bon Scott has returned to Adelaide after Fraternity's failed attempt to make it big in the UK. He takes a day job at the Wallaroo fertiliser plant, quite literally shovelling shit for a living. Scott begins to sing for an outfit known as The Mount Lofty Rangers, who include some other former members of Fraternity. During this time, he cuts a song called 'Round And Round And Round', which won't officially surface until March 2015, when it's packaged with footage of Scott riding his motorbike. At one point in the film, he even comes off his bike—a worrying omen for what lies ahead for the rocker-in-waiting.

February 27 Malcolm Young witnesses The Rolling Stones' outdoor concert at Randwick Racecourse. The Stones enter in a horse-drawn carriage and depart in a blaze of fireworks that light up the Sydney sky. It is impossible not to be impressed by the spectacle—and the music. The show begins with 'Brown Sugar' and finishes, fifteen songs later, with 'Jumpin' Jack Flash' and 'Street Fighting Man'—songs packing the same kind of powerhouse riffs and blooze power that Malcolm will soon deliver with AC/DC. (He will one day say that only AC/DC and the Stones, in his humble opinion, can really bring the 'swing' to rock'n'roll.)

At the Stones' Sydney press conference, Keith Richards, his teeth resembling a broken picket fence, is at his broody best as he slouches into the room, sprawls cross-legged on a couch, and sparks up the first of an endless series of ciggies.

'You look kind of different to what we expect people are expected to look,' a hapless journo asks. 'Is this the way you like to dress, Keith?'

'Maybe it's because you live down here and I live somewhere else,' Richards snipes, as Jagger falls about laughing.

The journo foolishly digs in.

'Why do you like to dress like you do?'

FOLLOWING PAGE: GEORGE YOUNG AND HARRY VANDA AT WORK IN 'THE HOUSE OF HITS', THE ALBERT PRODUCTIONS STUDIO IN SYDNEY. IT IS HERE THAT THEY PRODUCE AC/DC, JOHN PAUL YOUNG, THE ANGELS, ROSE TATTOO, AND STEVIE WRIGHT, AS WELL AS CRAFTING THEIR OWN HITS AS FLASH & THE PAN.

"Get the song right, get the music right, get the mix right. And only then, when you are happy that you have the absolute best out of the song, out of the record, out of the mix, then you release it.

You did not release records to schedules or deadlines, or because the manager or a radio station had to have it on their playlists. You released the record when the record was finished."

TED ALBERT'S SAGE ADVICE TO GEORGE YOUNG, SUBSEQUENTLY ADOPTED AS A STUDIO MANTRA BY VANDA & YOUNG

'Probably,' Keith says, his eyes turning into daggers, 'for the very same way you like to dress like you do. I think it's a personal question.

'Australia doesn't have a good reputation, as far as bands are concerned,' he adds, clearly warmed up now, 'as far as hospitality. You're known as the most inhospitable country.'

Keith might be thinking of the time when The Who were all but run out of the country in 1968 after an in-flight drama over a bottle of booze, leading to them being escorted off their flight. On the same tour, The Small Faces' Ian McLagan told an Aussie journalist to 'fuck off' after being probed about a recent pot bust. The press called The Faces 'bad tempered louts'; The Who would not return for almost forty years. And, despite being a band borne of Australia, AC/DC will one day have reason to agree with the Stones, when they too clash with the local media.

April 21 Brian Johnson and his band, Geordie, are on tour in Europe. Only a year before, he was working as a draughtsman in his home town of Newcastle. Their second single, 'All Because Of You' has been charting in the UK; it eventually reaches #6.

'It was bloody marvellous to hear the news,' Johnson says. He and his bandmates respond in the manner expected of any young, up-and-coming act: 'What else can you do but go out and have a piss up?' he asks. At a recent gig closer to home, in Dunstable, he was mobbed and dragged into the crowd—a first for him. 'It was really frightening,' he adds, 'but I guess that's what it's all about.

'Can You Do It?' is their planned next single, which they are fine-tuning while in Europe. 'It's a real peach,' promises Johnson. It will reach #13 in June, while another single, 'Electric Lady', hits #32 in August. That, though, will be their last charting single. (In 1976, Johnson will leave the band to have a dash at a solo career.)

Mid-1973 With both The Velvet Underground and Tantrum done and dusted, Malcolm suggests that Angus joins him in a group—making it very clear that this will be *Malcolm's* band; his vision. Direction-wise, Malcolm has grown tired of the smooth sounds coming out of the USA from such acts as Crosby, Stills & Nash, James Taylor, and the Eagles; to him, it's all too mellow, too downbeat, *too dull*. He wants to form a band to play the music that appeals to him: gut-level rock, played with heart and soul and balls.

Malcolm makes the band's intentions clear from the start. 'We just wanted to be a good rock'n'roll band,' he recalled in 2000. 'That's it, that's all we can do. That's what we do best. Trends come and go … but we won't ever change.'

Angus agrees wholeheartedly. 'I think the 60s was a great time for music, especially for rock'n'roll,' he later tells a reporter from VH-1. 'It was the era of The Beatles, of the Stones, and then later on The Who and Zeppelin. But at one point in the 70s, it just kind of became … *mellow*.'

This is not a stellar year for Australian-made rock, either, so Malcolm has plenty to rebel against. The biggest artist of 1973 is singer-songwriter Brian Cadd, a sort of Antipodean Harry Nilsson. The Top 50 for the year comprises 'Tie A Yellow Ribbon Round The Old Oak Tree' by Tony Orlando & Dawn, Shirley Bassey's 'Never Never Never', Carly Simon's 'You're So Vain', local singer Col Joye's 'Heaven Is My Woman's Love', and Elton John's 'Crocodile Rock'.

Even at the very beginning, the Youngs' father, William, has a warning for his sons: 'It'll last a week.' Given the volatile nature of their relationship, he's convinced that, like many siblings, one is likely to kill the other if (more likely when) things get heated. At home, even though they share a bedroom, the brothers have designated areas in the house for their individual guitar practice: Angus hangs a *Playboy* poster on his door as a message to Malcolm to stay out. But there is also a certain pragmatism at work: both have discovered they aren't cut out for 'regular' work, and a rock'n'roll group is a far more exciting way to make a living—of sorts.

Angus needs little convincing. 'Beats working,' he figures.

Late 1973 By now, a line-up has started to take shape. Angus is on lead guitar; Malcolm is on rhythm; Colin Burgess, formerly of successful local act The Masters Apprentices, plays drums; and Angus's friend Larry Van Kriedt, a nineteen-year-old expat American, is on bass. (He and Angus bond over Gibson guitars; Van Kriedt impresses Angus because he actually owns a Gibson catalogue.) The tall, extroverted Dave Evans is out front, having met Malcolm during his time with The Velvet Underground; he sang in an outfit named Pony, which featured the members of VU.

The as-yet-unnamed band rehearse in a space in inner-city Newtown, and undertake their first photo shoot, with *Go-Set* photographer Philip Morris, outside Sydney's Her Majesty's Theatre. They're an odd-looking bunch. Angus is already wearing a school uniform; Malcolm is working through a glam-rock phase, sporting knee-high boots and a hint of satin; the others wear, variously, an Afro, an Indian cheesecloth shirt,

"When Malcolm put the band together, it was obvious what was missing at the time: another great rock band. So it was basically a reaction to that, because the music at that point had just turned into that soft, melodic kind of period, and that seemed to be all over the world."

ANGUS YOUNG TO VH-1, 2000

and candy stripes. This is not the sweaty, denim-and-T-shirt street style that will become synonymous with AC/DC. They actually look like they've been taking fashion tips from local stars Sherbet, currently dominating the Australian charts with their sticky-sweet pop confections.

Angus, on refection some years later, makes clear that this was an interim line-up, describing this 1973 vintage as 'me, Malcolm, [and] a bass player and drummer that we hired because they had a PA system, and I don't know who we had singing. We're still trying to find out.'

Clearly, Evans isn't much liked by the Youngs. 'We had this guy singing,' Angus says in another interview, 'but he was more into pop: he wanted to be like Rod Stewart.' (Angus also dismissed Evans as a 'Gary Glitter freak', as did Malcolm, who said, 'He sort of played up this Gary Glitter bisexual thing.')

On occasion, the Youngs lock into lengthy instrumental boogies in an attempt to keep Evans away from the microphone. 'The band would go down better without him,' Angus insists.

A couple of AC/DC trademarks are quickly set in place—and both come courtesy of Margaret Young, a big booster of the fledgling band. The first is Angus's school uniform. When he first started playing at home, Margaret thought it was sweet to see her brother sitting on his bed in his school uniform, thrashing away on a guitar that was almost as big as him.

'Now that you're out of school,' Margaret suggests, when the question arises, 'why don't you keep wearing the uniform? After all, it still fits.'

There is a suggestion that Angus will, over time, 'graduate' to jeans and a T-shirt—more typical stage clobber. But the school uniform stays—Angus figures he'll get more use out of it now than when he attended school—and Margaret starts stitching up new versions on a regular basis. He flip-flops between colours: there is a white outfit, plus another in canary yellow, and there's also a fetching sky-blue number. But he finds the darker hues are better for hiding the stains of spilled beer (not his) and sweat (definitely his).

Malcolm's thing for satin and knee-high boots, however, is not built to last. He'll soon graduate to denim and blue singlets—working man's clothes. His favourite clothes store is Gowings in Sydney, which specialises in affordable clobber for the regular bloke in the street.

At first, Angus has the strange idea that if he wears the outfit and keeps moving on

ONE OF THE EARLIEST INCARNATIONS OF AC/DC. LEFT TO RIGHT: ROB BAILEY, ANGUS AND MALCOLM YOUNG, DAVE EVANS, AND PETER CLACK.

stage, nobody will notice him, or at least recognise him. He is nervous about performing, and prefers to let his guitar do the talking. But, after stepping out a few times in his uniform, he realises that it frees him up—he can play a character, this crazy schoolboy shooting out sparks on his Gibson.

Angus's quest for anonymity will, over time, become the band's focal point.

'Wearing something like that helps me become something else,' he later notes. 'Normally, I'm pretty quiet, I keep to myself, but when I get the school suit on it gives me the advantage of being someone else. It's a bit like going to a fancy dress ball.'

There is also the matter of a band name.

November 3 While glam-rockers Gary Glitter, Slade, and Alice Cooper dominate the local charts, Malcolm Young sees his latest hero, Marc Bolan, play with T. Rex at Sydney's Hordern Pavilion. Though never the kind of guy to get wrapped up in hero worship, Malcolm does have a poster of Bolan on his bedroom wall at home in Burwood. 'A small poster, admittedly,' his friend Herm Kovac clarifies.

December The band play their debut show, billed for the time being as The Younger Brothers—or perhaps, The Young Brothers, no one is quite sure—at Sydney suburban venue the Last Picture Show, a venue run by Denis Laughlin, a fellow Scot, who helps the band book their earliest gigs. But it's a temporary name, and it isn't long before Margaret Young offers a suggestion that no one can better.

While sewing one of Angus's uniforms, she glances at a sticker on her trusty Singer machine. 'AC/DC,' it reads.

Angus and Malcolm agree that it's a good band name, but one incident early on almost leads to a rethink, when a cab driver asks them what their group is called.

'AC/DC,' Malcolm replies.

After a pause, the cabbie glances in the rear-view mirror. 'You know what that means, don't you?'

'No—*what*?' asks Malcolm.

'It means gay, mate.'

Malcolm is shocked. 'You looking for trouble, pal?'

The cabbie insists that he is serious; AC/DC is code for bisexuality.

With no other viable options, however, the name remains, although there'll be more confusion ahead.

'It's a funny situation,' Malcolm later tells *Entertainment USA*, 'because our sister gave us this name, from the sewing machine, [and] we thought it was great. All of a sudden, we found this agent in Sydney [Michael Chugg], and a week later we got calls from all the different cities in Australia, wanting us to come down and play. We thought, this is great, so I packed in my day gig. We got down and played to all these transvestites, because of the name of the band.'

This isn't quite what Malcolm and the others had in mind.

December 31 AC/DC ring in the new year with a gig at Sydney's Chequers, as part of a run of dates at the once-classy inner-city venue. They play several hour-long sets each night, recycling songs as the evening drags on and the clientele gets very loose. Their set includes such covers as the Stones' 'Jumpin' Jack Flash' and 'Honky Tonk Women', Little Richard's 'Tutti Frutti', and several Chuck Berry standards, along with a lengthy jam on 'Baby, Please Don't Go'. Singer Dave Evans sports nut-crunching tights and knee-high platform boots, wearing what could pass for a 'mansiere' under his candy-coloured jacket, his belly exposed.

Angus opts for his green school uniform and white sneakers, with the word 'left' scrawled on both shoes, for reasons only he understands. He also wears his Ashfield Boys High tie and satchel.

Go-Set photographer Philip Morris is invited to the gig by roadie Ray Arnold, who is helping the fledgling band secure gigs. Arnold also supplies some grade-A pot—another big draw for Morris. Angus is not impressed, though—he refers to drug users as 'hippie cunts'.

Straight away, Morris senses that the band pack some real rock'n'roll firepower—and that they are great subjects for a photographer. 'When it came to getting great live shots,' he recalls, 'nobody beat AC/DC. It was all about the energy.'

Much to the delight of Angus and Malcolm, there is a strong teen female contingent in this and other audiences during their few nights at Chequers, and much of the focus is on the Youngs—the rest of the band are way too old. The girls gather as a group at stage left, where Angus holds court.

In spite of the temporary line-up, Angus is still impressed by what is ostensibly AC/DC's debut gig. 'We had to get up and blast away … from the word go,' he later

> **"My sister Margaret used to think it was very cute that I'd come home from school and be in my little room playing guitar. I guess she thought it was cute to see a little man with a big guitar."**
>
> ANGUS YOUNG TO *60 MINUTES AUSTRALIA*, 1996

AC/DC MAKE THEIR DEBUT AT SYDNEY
VENUE CHEQUERS ON NEW YEAR'S
EVE 1973. 'IT WENT GREAT,' ANGUS
LATER RECALLS. 'EVERYONE THOUGHT
WE WERE A PACK OF LOONIES.'

tells a reporter. 'It went great. Everyone thought we were a pack of loonies—you know, who's been feeding them kids bananas?'

Dave Evans, though not long for the band, has equally strong memories of their Chequers debut. 'It was New Year's Eve, we got that gig and we killed it, we absolutely killed it because everyone was drunk, but anyway. It was a great start to the band to be in the top nightspot absolutely chock-full of people going crazy on New Year's Eve. We couldn't have had a better start.'

The venue's booker is sufficiently impressed to have the band return for more gigs in the new year.

Likely setlist: 'The Old Bay Road' / 'Midnight Rock' / 'Wishing Well' / 'School Days' / 'Nadine' / 'No Particular Place To Go' / 'I Want You (She's So Heavy)' / 'Get Back' / 'Lucille' / 'I Hear You Knockin'' / 'Jumpin' Jack Flash' / 'Honky Tonk Women'.

AC/DC release their debut single, 'Can I Sit Next To You, Girl'; Bon Scott replaces Dave Evans as the band's singer; they record their debut album, High Voltage, *with Vanda and Young, and tour Australia as the opening act for Lou Reed.*

1974

January What is clearly still an interim AC/DC line-up enter Sydney's Albert Productions studio and record 'Can I Sit Next To You, Girl', their debut single, with Vanda & Young producing. Malcolm and Angus share songwriting credits. (George Young plays bass on the track, while Colin Burgess is the drummer.)

Angus is struck by his big brother's ability to improvise in the studio. 'Everything seemed to be in his head,' he recalls in *Blood & Thunder*. 'He'll say, Play us what you've got, and then he'll say, Let's try this. Just try this, try that. He seemed to be creating things in his head.'

George has a policy in the studio: if the song they're considering can be played on the piano, it can be recorded. It proves to be a great sonic Litmus test.

The band cut a few other songs at these first sessions, including another Young–Young composition, 'Rockin' In The Parlour', which will become the B-side of 'Can I Sit Next To You, Girl', as well as 'Rock'n'roll Singer' and 'Sunset Strip', aka 'Soul Stripper'—early cuts that will later be re-recorded with Bon Scott for the *T.N.T.* and *High Voltage* albums. Originals from this time that are played live but never released include 'The Old Bay Road', 'Midnight Rock', and 'Fell In Love'.

Meanwhile, the band hold down a residency of sorts at Chequers, playing there seven times during January and February, while another very early gig takes place at a school dance at Baulkham Hills High in Sydney's northern suburbs. The exact date is unknown. Many years later, one punter in attendance recalls, 'I thought the lead guitarist was taking the mickey, wearing a school uniform at a school dance. Mind you, I reckoned they were pretty good. Very loud but good.'

Angus has by now acquired a couple of nicknames: 'Little Albie', due to his resemblance to TV's Albert Steptoe; and 'The Banker', because of his tight-fistedness. He has also introduced a new onstage move, the 'dying bug', in which he drops to the floor mid-solo and writhes around like an insect given a hefty blast of bug spray. This new move has come about completely by accident—a stroke of dumb luck, and a bit of clumsiness, resulting in a routine that will remain in his repertoire for the life of the band.

February–March The band gig in and around Sydney, rocking the front bar of the Hampton Court Hotel in the inner city several times during February and late March,

> **"I tripped over a lead [and] fell on me knees. I thought people thought I was a fuckin' idiot, so I started bobbin' around on the ground."**
>
> ANGUS TO SYDNEY RADIO STATION 2JJ ON THE ORIGINS OF HIS 'DYING BUG' MOVE, 1975

playing two, sometimes three, sets a night. They also play the Curl Curl Youth Club on the city's northern beaches, and take a rare trip out of Sydney to Gosford, on the NSW Central Coast, for a school dance on March 10. They also play Newcastle, a little further north, in March.

School dances and town halls are fast becoming useful places for the fledgling band to learn their craft. Rehearsals typically take place at Casa de Young in Burwood, using acoustic guitars and a practice drum kit, so as not to faze the neighbours.

April 5 Stevie Wright, the former Easybeats vocalist, releases the album *Hard Road*, produced by Vanda & Young. The hard-driving, guitar-heavy sound is definitely a template for AC/DC; Malcolm plays rhythm on some of the tracks. The title song, while written by Vanda & Young, tells the story of Wright's personal odyssey (much as Bon Scott will relate his on AC/DC's 'It's A Long Way To The Top').

'It's a hard, long road that I travel,' Wright shouts, 'I got my radio / Living on rock'n'roll.'

On the week of *Hard Road*'s release, the *Go-Set* album chart is an interesting mix of heavy rock (*Sabbath Bloody Sabbath* and Slade's *Old, New, Borrowed, And Blue*), prog (Yes, ELP, and Pink Floyd all feature) and the more trad pop of Paul McCartney & Wings (*Band On The Run*), Neil Diamond (*Hot August Night*), and Elton John (*Goodbye Yellow Brick Road*).

Hard Road is released in Australia by Albert Music and in the USA by Atco—the same labels that will release AC/DC's music. It reaches #2 on the *Go-Set* chart.

April 19–20 AC/DC return to Chequers in the dingy inner city for a two-night stand; they'll play further gigs here on May 18, 27, and 31, and no less than six more during June. Local band Mississippi occasionally play Chequers, too, and will soon morph into the Little River Band, becoming huge in America and blazing a live trail across the States that will be followed by such bands as AC/DC.

AC/DC's line-up undergoes various changes around this time. Angus's guitar buddy, Larry Van Kriedt, is in and then out of the band (among other things, he has a baby son to care for). After sitting in with an act called Jasper, Malcolm invites their bassist (Neil Smith) and drummer (Noel Taylor) into the fold. It helps that they own gear and a van, but they don't last long either, however; their replacements are drummer Peter Clack and bassist Rob Bailey.

MALCOLM YOUNG AND HARRY VANDA (WITH JOHN PAUL YOUNG, FAR RIGHT) BACKSTAGE AT THE SYDNEY OPERA HOUSE, PREPARING TO BACK STEVIE WRIGHT, JUNE 9 1974.

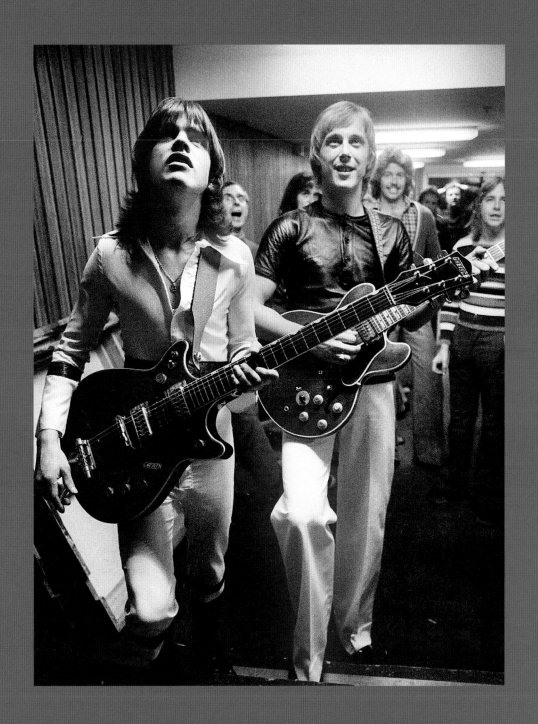

51

AC/DC's repertoire, while still covers-heavy—Beatles and Stones songs and classic 50s rockers provide the bulk of their material—is fast expanding to meet the demands of gigging as much as five nights a week, sometimes every night, and usually two sets per gig.

Setlist: 'School Days' / 'Honky Tonk Women' / 'Get Back' / 'Jumpin' Jack Flash' / 'No Particular Place To Go' / 'I Want You (She's So Heavy)' / 'The Old Bay Road' / 'Midnight Rock' / 'Show Business' / 'Rock'n'roll Singer' / 'Soul Stripper' / 'Rockin' In The Parlour' / 'Can I Sit Next To You, Girl' / 'Baby, Please Don't Go' / 'Nadine' / 'Heartbreak Hotel' / 'That's All Right Mama' / 'Tutti Frutti' / 'No Particular Place To Go' / 'Lucille' / 'All Right Now'.

May 3 After rehearsing with The Mount Lofty Rangers at the Old Lion Hotel in North Adelaide, a drunken Bon Scott crashes his Suzuki GT550 motorbike. He spends three days in a coma and eighteen days in hospital. While he gradually recovers, the ubiquitous Vince Lovegrove gives him a job helping out at Jovan, a booking agency he runs. It is there that Scott first hears about AC/DC, 'a young, dinky little glam band from Sydney,' as Lovegrove later puts it.

According to Lovegrove, it's around this time that George Young calls him, asking to recommend a new singer for the band. He suggests Bon. When Lovegrove mentions the band to Scott, however, the prospective frontman replies, 'They're too young to know what rock'n'roll is about. I'm a serious musician.' That attitude will soon change.

> **❝Bon was staying at my home, after recuperating from a motorbike accident—painting the office, general work. George Young told me they were looking for a singer. I suggested Bon.❞**
>
> VINCE LOVEGROVE TO
> ACDCCOLLECTOR.COM

June AC/DC receive their first press notice, in *Go-Set*. The article zeroes in on the youthfulness of the band—a point of difference Malcolm is keen to emphasise. 'Most of the groups in Australia are getting on, rather than getting it on,' he says. '[They're] out of touch with the kids that go to suburban dances.'

June 9 A band comprised of Malcolm, George, and Harry Vanda back Stevie Wright at an outdoor performance at the Sydney Opera House; the crowd is estimated to number around 25,000. Dave Evans is one of the backing vocalists. AC/DC open the show, which is so popular that several thousand people are turned away at the door.

'AC/DC ... showed they're a force to be reckoned with,' the *Go-Set* reports. '[They] looked great and sounded great.'

The band's set still includes such covers as 'Heartbreak Hotel', 'Shake, Rattle, And Roll', and 'No Particular Place To Go.' In what could only be seen as the kiss of death—especially for a budding hard-rock band like AC/DC—the *Go-Set* reviewer compares singer Dave Evans to teen pinup David Cassidy.

July AC/DC's recorded debut, 'Can I Sit Next To You, Girl', is released by Alberts. A performance film clip for the song, with Malcolm wearing what look disturbingly like jockey silks, was shot a few days earlier at the Last Picture Show in Cronulla, NSW, where the band played on June 30. The song also turns up on the strictly-for-radio collection *6KY Rock Steady*.

July 7 AC/DC head out of town again for a show in Corrimal on the NSW South Coast, about one hundred kilometres south of Sydney, again opening for Stevie Wright. The cover charge for the gig, staged at the Corrimal Community Centre, is $1.

According to local Rob McKie, who booked the gig, 'The promoter approached me asking if I wanted to bring down the Stevie Wright Band and, as part of that act, a young band called AC/DC. My first response was, How much? I paid $250 for Stevie Wright and $50 for AC/DC, and I thought I'd got robbed at the time. But they were a huge hit.'

One punter, Tim Jackson, later recalls, 'The place was chockers. Angus played offstage and in the crowd, doing that dead-fly thing that he does.'

The band will subsequently return to the region for gigs at the Bulli and Woonona High schools.

August 12 Stevie Wright's epic 'Evie (Parts 1, 2 & 3)' reaches #1 in Australia and becomes possibly the first ten-minute-plus song to top a singles chart anywhere in the world. The song, written and produced by Vanda & Young, features Malcolm on rhythm guitar, and is lifted from Wright's *Hard Road* album.

Post-Easybeats, Wright descended into a spiral of heroin addiction, exacerbated by deep sleep therapy (DST) at the notorious Chelmsford Private Hospital in northern Sydney, which will eventually be denounced in a Royal Commission for its brutal treatment of patients. But George Young, in particular, has maintained his faith in the singer, having seen him in his prime with The Easybeats. 'Harry and I got to work to see if we could come up with something that would put him back on the charts,' he later says.

'Evie' does much more than that, staying on the charts for six months and becoming by far the biggest Australian single of the year—and one of the finest Oz rock songs of all time.

August 13 AC/DC are tapped to open for Lou Reed on the New Yorker's first Australian tour, which includes dates in Melbourne (August 15), Adelaide (August 17), Sydney (August 21), Brisbane (August 22), and Perth (August 31).

'AC/DC to tour with Lou Reed—concerts sold out!' a local newspaper screams.

On arrival in Sydney, Reed, like the Stones before him, has a field day with the local press.

'Why do you sing about drugs?' he's asked.

'Because,' Reed replies, adjusting his oversized shades, 'because I think the government is plotting against me.'

'Do you like taking drugs yourself?'

'I don't take any. I'm high on life.'

'How would you describe yourself?'

'Average.'

'Are you a transvestite or a homosexual?'

'Sometimes.'

August 16 During downtime from the Reed tour in Melbourne, AC/DC play their first show at the Hard Rock Café, a venue managed by Michael Browning, who until recently had managed Billy Thorpe, Australia's biggest rock star. Browning, a huge Easybeats fan, has been tipped off to the band by fellow promoter Michael Chugg. But he doesn't know what to make of them when he checks in with them before the gig.

'To my surprise,' he later writes in his memoir, *Dog Eat Dog*, 'I saw this scrawny little school kid walking around the room, with a bit of a cocky swagger; apparently he was part of the entertainment. He looked like he'd walked off the pages of *Mad* magazine.'

When AD/DC play, however, Browning is won over. 'The little fucker was going off … I couldn't take my eyes—or my ears—off Angus and Malcolm.'

Browning pays them $200 and invites them back to play the Hard Rock whenever they're next in Melbourne. He's been nurturing a dream to manage an internationally

AC/DC'S FIRST SINGLE, 'CAN I SIT NEXT TO YOU, GIRL' B/W 'ROCKIN' IN THE PARLOUR'; A LIVE BOOTLEG FROM A FESTIVAL HALL MELBOURNE SHOW ON NEW YEAR'S EVE 1974.

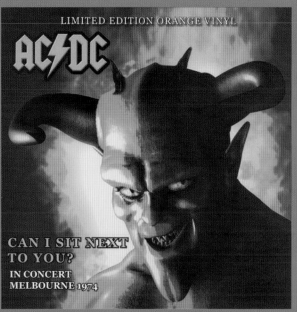

"To my surprise, I saw this scrawny little kid walking around the room . . . he looked like he'd walked off the pages of Mad *magazine."*

successful band—*an Australian band*—and he gets the sense he may have found just the act in AC/DC.

August 17 Back on the road with Lou Reed, AC/DC's Adelaide gig will become part of band folklore for reasons other than their performance. Bon Scott is looking on from the crowd when a fracas erupts.

'Hey,' someone in the mosh pit yells at Angus, 'come on down here, mate.'

'Go and get fucked,' Angus snarls, and keeps playing.

Scott instinctively braces himself for the inevitable punch-up, but is surprised when the crowd actually simmers down. Despite his size, or lack thereof, Angus has a way of flexing some muscle. The paths of Bon Scott and AC/DC will soon intersect.

According to Scott, 'There were a dozen guys in front of the stage shouting … and Angus, he walks up to the edge of the stage and screams at them, Go and get fucked. So, me, I'm looking for a microphone stand, ready for the onslaught.'

> **"*People said, Oh, AC/DC and Lou Reed—this is gonna be a big bisexual show. Every gay place in the country booked us on the name alone.*"**
>
> ANGUS TO *JUKE* MAGAZINE, 1975

August 26 'Can I Sit Next To You, Girl' enters the Oz chart for the first of ten weeks, peaking at #50. It's the first of twelve charting singles the group will achieve in Australia during the 1970s. (In total, these songs will spend an amazing 172 weeks in the Oz charts.)

This week's Australian #1 is Paper Lace's 'Billy Don't Be A Hero', with Stevie Wright's 'Evie (Parts 1, 2 & 3)' in second position. Local pop stars Sherbet are also in the Top 10 with 'Slipstream'. Angus Young is no fan—he takes to describing Sherbet as 'tea towel rockers'. He has nicknames for other local acts, too, dubbing multiracial rockers Hush 'The Blue Suede Thongs'.

August 31–September 15 AC/DC are booked to play a run of dates at Beethoven's Cabaret in Western Australia, a gay nightclub, opening for Australia's most famous transvestite, Carlotta. The promoter books them because he thinks (or, more likely, hopes) the band's name is a nod to some sort of twisted sexuality. They did open for Lou Reed, after all.

After a mammoth trip across the Nullarbor desert in their ratty tour van, five scruffy, broke, hungry rockers wander into the venue, announcing themselves as AC/DC. They are not what the promoter or the punters expect, and the gigs do not go well. Their six-week booking is cancelled after a fortnight, and in mid-September the even-broker band limp back to Adelaide—a round trip of more than five thousand miles.

September 20 After a gig at the Pooraka Hotel in Adelaide, AC/DC jam at the Adelaide home of Bruce Howe, lately of Fraternity. There, Bon Scott reacquaints himself with the members of the band, who are fast tiring of their current lead singer, Dave Evans. Malcolm, in particular, is growing weary of Evans's habit of wearing makeup on stage and blowing kisses to the crowd. 'We grew not to like it,' he later observes.

Scott agrees to get up at the jam and sing with the band. As he slugs from a bottle of bourbon on stage, Angus whispers to Malcolm, 'I'd be surprised if the guy can walk, let alone sing.' But the proof is in the singing, and Scott soon wins over the Youngs.

Talking post-gig, Scott and the Youngs learn that they share Scottish roots. Despite the age difference—Scott is seven years older than Malcolm, and has a full nine years on Angus—a bond, of sorts, forms. And Scott makes his intentions very clear. 'I can sing much better than that drongo you have at the moment,' he says, nodding toward Evans.

Irene Thornton was with Scott at the Pooraka Hotel gig, and in her memoir, *My Bon Scott*, she recalls, 'They were amazing, even back then. It was like nothing I'd ever heard, and Angus and Malcolm were just incredible to watch. It's like they were locked into each other. They were playing to the typical pissed [local] audience, but the crowd went crazy for it because the energy on stage was just electric. Angus threw himself around like a little maniac, dressed in a school uniform.'

An observation posted on the milesago.com website sums up Scott's immediate impact on the band. 'With Bon out front … [they] were reborn as a tough, uncompromising, full-tilt boogie'n'blues street outfit who could blow just about any rival off the stage … AC/DC were indisputably "mad, bad, and dangerous to know", and they revelled in the image. Most importantly, under the guidance of Vanda & Young, Angus, Malcolm, and Bon very quickly developed into a world-class rock songwriting partnership.'

With all agreed on the change, Dave Evans is out. He isn't impressed, telling the band they are 'finished' without him, according to Angus. But Angus rightfully believes that the hiring of Scott will help give the group clarity. '[Bon] moulded the character of AC/DC. Everything became more down to earth and straight-ahead. That's when we became a band.'

"_When we met Bon for the first time, it was like we'd known him forever. He almost became a brother. We just said, 'You wanna join?' That's how confident we were it was going to work._**"**

MALCOLM YOUNG TO *BEHIND THE MUSIC*, 2000

"_Music's the same all over the world. There's nothing an Australian group can't do that they're doing [overseas]. The kids want the same things. The audiences are the same._**"**

BON SCOTT TO ED NIMMERVOLL, *JUKE*, 1975

Another factor working in Scott's favour is his broad audience appeal: young women in the crowd fancy him as a bit of rough trade, while blokes see him like a tough, cool, older brother. He fast becomes a local hero.

Scott would famously make a big personal decision around this time, too—choosing the band over his wife. 'I dug the band more than I dug the chick,' he later noted. 'So, I joined the band and left her.' Despite the tough-guy pose, Scott and Thornton remain close; he frequently writes to her from the road.

With Scott on the payroll, AC/DC may have gained some clarity about their direction, but they have a more immediate problem—they're out of cash. Stranded in Adelaide—a big country town, by comparison with the more cosmopolitan Sydney and Melbourne—Malcolm puts in a call to Michael Browning at Melbourne's Hard Rock Café, asking for help.

Browning agrees to float them enough cash to return to Melbourne. 'I'd be interested in managing you,' he tells the Youngs, after another gig at the Hard Rock. A meeting is arranged in Sydney with Ted Albert and George Young. It goes well, and Browning gets the gig as AC/DC's new manager. But he hasn't quite grasped what he is taking on—and will never be fully welcomed into the inner circle of Malcolm and Angus (and George). 'I soon learned that I hadn't signed a band; I'd signed a clan,' he later writes. The Youngs refer to him simply as 'Browning'—hardly the friendliest of terms. It's all about business.

Within weeks, AC/DC have acquired a new lead singer, a new manager, and a new surrogate HQ in the Hard Rock Café. They have also chosen to relocate from Sydney to Melbourne. 'In Australia, Melbourne is the home of rock'n'roll bands like ourselves,' Angus later tells a reporter. 'Melbourne's the hub, the heart, where the biggest demand is. If you're big there, you're big all over.'

Browning puts the members of the band on a weekly wage of $60 for the next six months, with such costs as PA and gear covered by Alberts. He also offers them some sage advice: they're not to wear watches on stage—he believes rock musicians shouldn't be restrained by such mundane things as time—and they're not to use public transport.

Browning once spotted local pop duo Bobby & Laurie riding on a tram, and he was appalled: that was not how stars are supposed to travel. What kind of message were they sending to the public? AC/DC might be broke, but that doesn't mean they can't present themselves as successful. Browning knows that image is important.

October 5 With Olivia Newton-John's 'I Love You, I Honestly Love You' sitting at #1 in the Oz charts—clearly, the country could use a hot new rock band—Bon Scott, now minus the hippie beard and Jesus sandals he wore in Fraternity, makes his Sydney AC/DC debut at a gig at the Masonic Hall in the suburb of Brighton-Le-Sands.

Likely setlist: 'She's Got Balls' / 'Soul Stripper' / 'No Particular Place To Go' / 'Oh Carol' / 'It's All Over Now' / 'Jumpin' Jack Flash' / 'Rock'n'roll Singer' / 'Shake, Rattle, And Roll' / 'Love Song' / 'Front Row Fantasies' / 'Lucille' / 'Baby, Please Don't Go' / 'Honky Tonk Women' / 'Can I Sit Next To You, Girl' / 'Show Business' / 'School Days'.

October 16 Bon Scott plays his first Hard Rock Café gig with the band. 'With Bon now on board,' manager Browning later writes, 'the band had acquired a new sense of purpose as well as a sense of humour and uniqueness. Bon was one of the world's best street poets.' Scott refers to his bawdy, street-smart lyrics as 'toilet poetry'.

'It's a bit of rock'n'roll, so shake everything you got hanging, and have a good time,' Scott says, by way of introducing 'Show Business'.

During this period, the band play several gigs at the Largs Pier Hotel in Adelaide, one of many sizeable beer barns dotting the Australian suburbs—venues that form the backbone of the thriving live music circuit, and will prove the making of AC/DC. Other such rooms include the Bondi Lifesaver in Sydney, and Melbourne's Matthew Flinders and the Waltzing Matilda, which has a capacity of 1,200 and a bar that remains open until 11:30pm. AC/DC will play (and fill) these venues repeatedly over the coming months.

November The band return to Alberts with Vanda & Young to start work on their debut album, *High Voltage*. Big brother George is taken aback by new bloke Scott, with his tatts, shark-tooth earring, broken teeth, and all-round shop-worn appearance.

'He's been around the block more than a few times,' George mutters to the others. Once he hears Scott sing, however, George too senses that he is right for the band. 'He's your man, no doubt,' George tells his brothers. 'You're a rock'n'roll band now.'

Ron Carpenter, a drummer who has sat in with AC/DC at a few shows in the past, is working in the same studio with his new band, Aleph, enabling him to watch the Youngs work together from close quarters, later telling acdcollector.com: 'In the studio, George would show Angus a riff and they would both play it over and over—for many minutes. The room was concrete, with Marshalls stacked against one wall ... the lift well in King Street used to shake when they were riffing. After twenty minutes of riffing, George would signal Harry [Vanda] or go into the control room himself and record a few minutes of Angus. He'd then return to the studio and show Angus the next riff; the process would go on all day and all night.'

George plays much of the bass on the album; hired hand Tony Currenti drums on all tracks with the exception of 'Baby, Please Don't Go', a blues standard dating back to the 1930s and first popularised by Big Joe Williams, although AC/DC's version is most likely inspired by Van Morrison and Them (and, quite possibly, by the version recorded by heavy metal Brits Budgie, and/or Gary Glitter's 1972 cover). AC/DC's first drummer, Peter Clack, is credited on 'Baby, Please Don't Go', as is original bassist Rob Bailey. Scott records new vocals for the track and shares writing credits with Angus and Malcolm for all tracks on the album bar 'Baby'.

Scott also tweaks the lyrics of 'Sunset Strip', which has become 'Soul Stripper', and now features a rare guitar solo from Malcolm. As far as Angus is concerned, his older brother is an underrated lead guitarist. 'If Malcolm sits down to play a solo,' Angus later says, 'he can do it better than me.'

Scott allegedly wrote the lyrics to the oh-so-subtle 'She's Got Balls' in tribute to his former partner, Irene Thornton, while he has reworked the hitherto unreleased 'Fell In Love' as 'Love Song'. It's a very rare thing in the AC/DC canon: a ballad (mixed with a lengthy prog-rock interlude, mind you). It's not their finest five minutes.

Bizarrely, the completely unrepresentative 'Love Song' is lifted as the first single from the album, but most radio DJs will chose to flip it over and play the new, Bon Scott–sung 'Baby, Please Don't Go', which is the B-side.

High Voltage will go on to reach an Australian peak of #14, and, over time, will sell 350,000 copies domestically.

November 5 AC/DC open for touring Brits Black Sabbath at Sydney's 5,000-capacity Hordern Pavilion. Security proves to be a problem on the night; the bouncers' response to any crowd reaction is overly physical. 'These guys in their red coats, as soon as anyone stood up, it was, like, a smack round the mouth and sit down again,' Ozzy Osbourne tells a reporter from radio station 3XY. 'That's not on; they paid to see us. There's no call for any violence.'

AC/DC go on to support the English metal merchants at the Hordern on November

ANGUS YOUNG DOING HIS BEST 'DYING BUG' ON THE GRIMY FLOOR OF MELBOURNE'S HARD ROCK CAFÉ, A VENUE RUN BY THEIR MANAGER, MICHAEL BROWNING.

9, 10, and 11. By now, a few more originals have made their way into the band's set.

Likely setlist: 'She's Got Balls' / 'Soul Stripper' / 'No Particular Place To Go' / 'Carol' / 'It's All Over Now' / 'Jumpin' Jack Flash' / 'Rock'n'roll Singer' / 'Shake, Rattle, And Roll' / 'You Ain't Got A Hold On Me' / 'Love Song' / 'Front Row Fantasies' / 'Lucille' / 'Baby, Please Don't Go' / 'Honky Tonk Women' / 'Can I Sit Next To You, Girl' / 'Show Business' / 'School Days'.

November 29 AC/DC are booked to play the fourth episode of the trailblazing ABC TV show *Countdown*. They perform 'Baby, Please Don't Go'; Angus is dressed as some sort of bizarre aviation pioneer—'Aviator Angus'—with a flowing white scarf, goggles, and leather jacket, a smouldering Benson & Hedges wedged between his fingers. He's perched in the cockpit of a homemade plane, which features an Aussie flag—and, for no obvious reason, a showerhead. It's as though Biggles has morphed with Albert Steptoe. (Unfortunately, this is one of the many early *Countdown* episodes that will be erased due to in-house cost cutting at the government-run ABC, where staff are instructed to recycle the tapes.)

First broadcast on November 8, *Countdown* soon settles into a 6pm Sunday timeslot. Clearly inspired by the UK's *Top Of The Pops*, it features strong local content, and each episode closes with a Top 10 rundown. The Top 10 on the week of AC/DC's *Countdown* debut includes Olivia Newton-John's 'I Love You, I Honestly Love You', The Bee Gees' 'Mr Natural', Carl Douglas's 'Kung Fu Fighting', and Glen Campbell's 'Bonaparte's Retreat'. It's hardly a stellar week for rock'n'roll.

This is the first of about three dozen appearances AC/DC will make on the show, before a viewing audience that gradually grows to more than a million, as the show becomes a Sunday night institution for music fans. *Countdown* will prove to be the perfect vehicle for the band; the timely introduction of colour TV in early 1975 is a great boon, too. The programme has its very first star in Angus, with Scott as his partner in mirth. The band are paid $160 per appearance—money well spent by the ABC.

December 20 The Angus and Bon show returns to *Countdown* for another performance of 'Baby'. (The Top 10 now includes The Sweet's 'Peppermint Twist' and Leo Sayer's 'Long Tall Glasses.') This time, Angus transforms into Zorro, all in black—hat, cape, even socks—with a rapier held threateningly in his right hand. Jimmy Page may have played his guitar with a bow, but who ever thought it possible with a foil? (Angus will also try out a gorilla suit on *Countdown* but find it a touch too hot under the studio lights. And it's a bugger to play guitar in the suit.)

As for Bon Scott, he dons snug red bib and braces, with a shark's tooth dangling from one ear, a mile-wide grin on his face, and some highly visible presence in the trouser department. The mainly young, primarily female audience aren't quite sure whether they should be scared, amused, or excited.

Influential *Countdown* host Ian 'Molly' Meldrum is won over—he's one of many blown away during AC/DC's studio appearances by their combination of rock'n'roll muscle, humour, and theatricality. Uncharacteristically, the rambling, nervy Meldrum manages to capture his feelings about the band in one word: 'Fantastic.'

Over time, the mutual benefits grow: *Countdown* scores huge ratings, and AC/DC gain massive nationwide exposure. The band members even acquire free passport photos—leftovers from a photo shoot conducted on the *Countdown* set. (These shots will subsequently appear on their album *T.N.T.*)

Late 1974 With Browning's help, the band are now sharing a sprawling if shabby house on Lansdowne Road in St Kilda, Melbourne's red-light epicentre. There is a sunroom at the front, a family room at the rear (Bon Scott's domain), a lounge room, and a number of small bedrooms. The house is large enough for the band to set up and jam in the hallway. They'll base themselves here for the best part of a year.

Lansdowne Road fast becomes the drop-in centre for the local flotsam and jetsam: hookers, runaways, pimps, junkies, and fellow musos are all welcome. *Mojo* magazine will one day refer to Lansdowne Road as a contender for rock's 'vilest den of depravity'— quite the badge of honour.

AC/DC's crew—Tana Douglas, Australia's first female roadie, an escapee from a private girls' school in Queensland; and another crew member simply known as Ralph The Roadie—also take up residence. Soon after, Pat Pickett, a friend of Scott's from his time in Adelaide, joins the motley crew, passing himself off as the band's 'lighting director', even though they don't own any lights.

One afternoon, an angry parent storms into the house, finds Scott bedded down with his daughter, and drags the singer across the front yard and straight through a bed of rose bushes. It's during this prickly encounter that Scott loses the dental plate he had installed after his bike accident in Adelaide.

Angus relates these events to a British journalist in 1978. '[Bon] was in this big double bed we used to have in this house when the roadie knocks on the door and shouts, "Bon!" when he's busy sticking it up this young bird. Anyway … in bursts this chick's old man. He was an ex-con and built like a wall, and he drags Bon outside and beats the shit out of him with a couple of mates.'

Bon would also give his version. 'This guy comes banging on my bedroom door … loud as all hell itself, and I say to him, Fuck off, I'm having a fuck. Suddenly, the door is crashed in, and it turns out to be this girl's father, and there he finds me on top of his

> **ff*Everything was taken care of: there'd be a knock on the door at three in the morning, and a bunch of waitresses just off work would be there with bottles of booze, a bag of dope and everything else. Never a dull moment. You name it, it happened in that house. We were poor but living like kings. And we wrote a lot of songs there.*JJ**
>
> MALCOLM YOUNG TO MOJO, 2000

daughter, who I then find out was only sixteen years old. Needless to say, he beats me to a pulp. I lost two teeth in the process.'

Casa AC/DC even attracts some tabloid attention. During what is clearly a slow news week, a local newspaper sets out to record the number of young women seen passing through the doors of Lansdowne Road over a seven-day stretch. They came up with a figure of one hundred.

'One hundred and ten,' Angus corrects with a chuckle, when asked.

'There was more action happening there than ever since,' Malcolm said. 'We drank like there was no tomorrow. We woke up and drank again, and continued like that for a long time.'

'The prostitutes got to know us,' he continued. 'A lot of them would come around—all sorts of women would show up because we were young and in a band.'

The frequency of these visits will only increase as the band's star slowly starts to rise.

December 31 A chant of 'We want Angus! We want Angus!' goes up among the faithful as the band take the stage at Melbourne's Festival Hall, playing to a crowd of around 5,000 people. The show is broadcast live on radio. Other acts on the bill include Hush ('The Blue Suede Thongs'), Kush, and Jim Keays, formerly of The Masters Apprentices.

Clearly, the *Countdown* exposure has done the trick: judging by the audience's feverish response, the pintsized, snaggletoothed Angus is now the most unlikely of teen idols. A five-track recording of this set—on orange vinyl, no less—will surface in the Czech Republic in 2016, under the clumsy title *Can I Sit Next to You? In Concert Melbourne 1974*. (*Track listing*: 'She's Got Balls' / 'Soul Stripper' / 'Show Business' (with Malcolm on lead guitar) / 'Can I Sit Next To You, Girl' / 'Baby, Please Don't Go'.)

Despite the temporary line-up, there are some highlights: Angus's frenzied solo during a marathon 'Baby, Please Don't Go', and Bon Scott's growing presence on the mic. When he introduces 'Can I Sit Next To You, Girl'—a lyrical sentiment that, admittedly, doesn't quite gel with his macho swagger—he chuckles at the band's slow chart progress. '[This record] made it to number 100 in Sydney, number 200 in Perth— *and number 1,000 in Melbourne*.'

AC/DC's first full year has been spent in constant motion. They've played more than one hundred shows, cut their debut record, blown up on *Countdown*, and traversed the country. And pissed off the odd angry parent, too.

Phil Rudd and Mark Evans join the band as the classic AC/DC line-up takes shape; they brawl with Deep Purple at Sunbury, record the T.N.T. album, and shoot their legendary clip for 'It's A Long Way To The Top (If You Wanna Rock'n'roll)'; the band sign a deal with Atlantic Records in the UK.

1975

January Highly regarded twenty-one-year-old drummer Phil Rudd, recently of Buster Brown—and even more recently of his father's car yard—is recruited by the band to replace temporary drummer Russell Coleman (who'd replaced *another* stand-in, Peter Clack). Rudd, whose background is German and Irish, and whose stepfather is Lithuanian, is a big fan of the great rock drummers—Ringo Starr, Ginger Baker of Cream, Simon Kirke of Free and Bad Company. Offstage, he is known to mix it up with some colourful types—rumour has it he has one particular buddy who rarely leaves the house without slipping a pistol into the waistband of his jeans. His old band, Buster Brown, were big favourites of Melbourne's 'sharpies'—unruly gangs with shaved heads, Dr Martens, and a taste for ultra-violence.

Go-Set says of Rudd, at the time of his recruitment, that he's 'quite the swank young jackeroo. [He wears a] thick grey sheep wool Mexican cardigan despite the heat, [has] pale grey-blue eyes, regular features and [a] neatly proportioned small body fitted snugly into de rigueur crotch-tight jeans. He does, in fact, hail from the upper-middle sector of a country town.'

'Rudd's recruitment was an important advance,' notes milesago.com. 'His rock-solid, heavy-hitting style was perfect for the band, and he became the engine of AC/DC for the next ten years.'

Manager Browning backs this up in his memoir, *Dog Eat Dog*, in which he writes, 'Phil became integral to AC/DC's musical style and was over time admired worldwide by his peers for his wonderful timing and feel.' Writing in *RAM*, Anthony O'Grady notes, 'Rudd, bass player Mark Evans, and rhythm guitarist Malcolm Young are acknowledged [as] one of the most powerful rhythm sections ever bred by the uncompromising brutality of Australian pub rock.'

Early January On January 7, AC/DC play Melbourne's Station Hotel for the princely sum of $150; the following night, they're at the suburban venue the Sundowner. On the 9th, they once again play the Hard Rock Café, for a fee of $175, followed by the Matthew Flinders on the 10th, for $200. A week of dates grosses the band $1,150.

They're now residing at the Freeway Gardens Motel in North Melbourne, a little way out of town (and away from prying eyes). A frequent visitor is Dr Goldberg, aka the Rock Doctor, who does a roaring trade in penicillin. By now, the band members have gained the nickname 'the Seedies', for obvious reasons.

While residing at Freeway Gardens, Bon Scott writes a lyric about a close encounter on the road with a full-bodied woman named Rosie. Scott, apparently, has a thing for larger ladies.

Angus Young offers more detail about Scott's encounter with Rosie in a 1998 interview with *Vox* magazine, detailing how, after a gig, the singer had said he was 'going to check out a few clubs. He said he'd got about 100 yards down the street when he heard this yell: "Hey! Bon!" From what he said, there was this Rosie woman and a friend of hers. They were plying him with drinks, and Rosie said to him, This month I've slept with twenty-eight famous people, and Bon went, Oh yeah?! Anyway, in the morning he said he woke up, pinned against the wall, he opened one eye, and saw her lean over to her friend and whisper, Twenty-nine!

'There's very few people who'll go out and write a song about a big fat lady, but Bon said it was worthy.'

Malcolm Young would have a slightly different version of Rosie's roots, so to speak, describing her encounter with Bon as 'payment' for a meal she and another girl had cooked for the two of them.

January 17–20 AC/DC play several more Sydney suburban gigs this week, including the El Toro hotel in the southwest suburb of Liverpool, and the Rivoli Theatre in Hurstville.

January 23 The band return to play Melbourne's Hard Rock Café, after another show at the Station Hotel two days earlier. Due to cramped conditions in the Hard Rock's band room, the musicians and crew are forced to improvise some kind of access to the stage. They knock a hole in the wall outside the venue, big enough for the band to squeeze through, which is then sealed until the gig ends, when the procedure is reversed. Heaven help them if a fire breaks out.

In a *RAM* magazine interview, manager Browning refers to Angus as the 'band's very own Milton Drysdale'—a sly reference to the banker from TV's *Beverly Hillbillies*. Angus is the man the others go to for a pre-payday loan. 'Angus is bloody amazing with money,' adds Rudd. 'We all get the same each week, but somehow Angus always has more than any of us.' He neglects to mention that Angus is a rare teetotaller amid a group of partiers.

January 24 The band play the Matthew Flinders Hotel in the Melbourne suburb of Chadstone. Bloodhouses like the Matthew Flinders have become their life source at this early stage in their career, even though few nights pass without a brawl and/or a few arrests. The rooms are large, squeezing in a thousand or more punters, and the bars usually remain open longer than most pubs. Malcolm would later refer to these venues, and this time, as 'our school of life'. Another Hard Rock Café gig follows on the 25th.

January 26 AC/DC are slated to appear after the headliners, Deep Purple, at the second Sunbury Music Festival, 'Australia's Woodstock', at a site fifty kilometres outside of Melbourne, before an audience of about 15,000. Also on the bill are Billy Thorpe & The Aztecs (formerly managed by Browning), Daddy Cool, Buster Brown (whose lead singer is Angry Anderson, later of Rose Tattoo), and Melbourne shock-rockers Skyhooks, whose debut album, *Living In The 70's*, released three months earlier, is on its way to becoming the best-selling Australian album ever, selling upward of 200,000 copies (a record that will be smashed to bits in 1980 by *Back In Black*). AC/DC treat most other bands with disdain, but especially Skyhooks—they're currently enjoying the success and accolades that Malcolm and the band crave.

Hundreds of cardboard Anguses are distributed among the Sunbury crowd before the band's set, but when Tana Douglas, AC/DC's roadie, begins setting up their onstage gear, she is instructed by Deep Purple's crew to 'pull it'. The British band want to break down their gear before AC/DC's is set up, which would mean they'll be prevented from playing until around 2am—by which time much of the crowd will most likely have faded away.

Douglas goes backstage and tells the Youngs what's going on.

'Fuck them,' she is told, 'Go and do it again.'

When she tries once again to set up the band's equipment, an all-in brawl duly erupts in full view of the crowd. George Young, who is backstage with AC/DC, throws the first punch. Douglas knocks a Deep Purple roadie on his backside with one punch, impressing herself hugely. Manager Michael Browning draws blood when he connects with the chin of his Purple counterpart, Bruce Payne. Douglas later recalls, 'The Young brothers—in fact all of AC/DC—were neither the heftiest or tallest men on the planet. But they could be feisty bastards when they were revved up. And now they were revved up, good and proper.'

Once the violent fracas ends, AC/DC are given a choice by the promoter: play early the next morning or not at all. They duly drive back to Melbourne, making this a rare occurrence of the band blowing out a gig—but with good reason.

A belligerent Angus goes on to relate his version of events to a reporter from *RAM*

"I remember Bon saying, 'Listen Mal, there's a couple of girls, one's pretty ugly, the other's pretty cute, but she's huge — and they've offered to make us dinner.'

At the end of the night, big Rosie grabs Bon and says, 'Right, you're mine for the night,' and I ran away from the other one. I went home. Bon woke up in the morning squashed against the wall, and he tried to get away, so she grabbed him again and got more payment for the meal.

We knocked the song together in half an hour, really quick. We stuck it up against this backing track we already had."

MALCOLM YOUNG TO MOJO ON
THE ORIGINS OF 'ROSIE', 2000

magazine. Things didn't start well, he admits; he and the others learned soon after arriving that all the local bands were sharing one trailer backstage, while Deep Purple 'had everything else, all the other caravans and changing rooms, 'cause they're international, right? Then there's a brawl, and we cancelled, y'know. They wanted to put us on the next day, but we said, Up yours …

'But we cancelled them,' Angus insists. 'They didn't cancel us.'

It also emerges that Deep Purple were being paid $60,000 for the show, while AC/DC were to receive just $300.

This is a key moment for the band. It further intensifies their 'us against the world' mindset, and it also hastens their desire to get out of Australia, where they feel too many so-called 'big bands' are given the star treatment by starstruck promoters, at the expense of local acts.

In a bizarre footnote, the night after this brouhaha, Deep Purple put in a surprise jam session at Melbourne's Hard Rock Café, not knowing that it is AC/DC's HQ—or that Browning runs the venue.

January 30–31 More gigs follow, first at the Hard Rock Café, and then in the Melbourne suburb of Epping.

February AC/DC play their first show at the Croxton Park Hotel in the Melbourne suburb of Thornbury. The exact date of this show is unknown, but they will go on to play the venue eight times in total during 1975. These gigs are billed as *Rockin' At The Croc*. It's one of Melbourne's rougher pubs, which is really saying something. Also during February, they fill the Matthew Flinders Hotel (again), the Sundowner in Geelong, and, naturally, the Hard Rock Café.

February 24 The band return to Sydney for a four-night stand at Chequers, as well as a series of suburban Sydney gigs that will keep them on the road until early March. The poster for a gig (with Hush) at the Hurstville Rivoli insists 'no sharpies', but these violent gang members are out in force at the show. The sharpies' natural enemies are surfers, longhairs, and mods, although they'll willingly take on anyone up for a fight. Sharpie fashion sense, such as it is, involves extreme mullet haircuts, Dr Marten boots, and pants worn with suspenders. Angus describes them as 'yobbos … with dyed hair and big pants and big boots who'd come along to laugh at the pooftas.'

Although they do turn out in numbers at their shows, AC/DC are not the sharpies' first band of choice. That dubious honour goes to Melbourne band Lobby Loyde & The Coloured Balls. 'Coloured Balls were the greatest bunch of hippies that ever crawled,' Loyde would say of his group. 'They were really gentle guys, but on stage we let it go and spat out all the venom we had … that was our release.'

March–April AC/DC record the *T.N.T.* album at Albert Productions in Sydney. Producers Vanda & Young are hot off the success of John Paul Young's 'Yesterday's Hero', which hit #8 in Australia in March and will stay on the chart for six months, launching a twenty-plus-year association between artist and producers. Stevie Wright's 'Evie (Pts 1, 2 & 3)', another Vanda & Young production, was the biggest Australian record of 1974. Clearly, they're on a roll.

George Young plays much of the bass on the *T.N.T.* album; hired hand Tony Currenti plays the drums on 'Can I Sit Next To You, Girl'. The sessions run for two weeks in total. The first week is spent recording the band tracks, the second devoted to Angus's solos and Bon's vocals. Scott spends much of his time locked away in the studio kitchen, working on his 'toilet poetry'. The results—'It's A Long Way To The Top (If You Wanna Rock'n'roll)', 'High Voltage', 'T.N.T.' (all released as singles), 'The Jack', and 'Live Wire'—are among Scott and the band's best, and are songs that will remain in their setlist for the next forty years. Meanwhile, in a nod to one of Angus's biggest heroes, they also cover Chuck Berry's 'School Days'.

When the idea for using bagpipes in 'It's A Long Way To The Top' is floated, Scott offers his services. George Young agrees, being under the impression that Scott was a piper back in Fremantle, when in fact he was a drummer in a pipe band with his father. So the band acquires some bagpipes, which sets them (that is, Alberts) back a hefty $435. At which point they discover not that only can Scott not play them, but also that he has no idea how to assemble them. As bassist Mark Evans later notes in his memoir, *Dirty Deeds*, 'If you want a good giggle, get a bunch of Scotsmen with no previous bagpipe experience and ask them to put some bagpipes together.'

When Malcolm and Angus ask their brother whether they should try to expand their sound, as The Easybeats once did, George shakes his head. 'That's your thing,' he tells them, referring to such gut-level rockers as the title track and 'High Voltage'. 'Stick with it.' The completed album duly establishes the template for the AC/DC sound: raw and loud.

It's not all smooth sailing in the studio, though. One day, Angus and George argue; after George tells his younger brother to 'stop being such a little fuckin' prima donna', the dispute spills out into the hallway, where Angus tries in vain to land a punch. Then they get back to work.

March In a very early feature on the band, Anthony O'Grady, writing in Australian music magazine *RAM*, describes AC/DC as a 'Street Punk Band' (his caps). 'AC/DC, they play real blitzkrieger rock and roll, and you'd better not believe they won't stomp you if you make a wrong move,' he adds. The term 'punk rock' will cause some issues for AC/DC in the very near future. It's not a tag they embrace.

Meanwhile, the group are still on the search for a new bass player, so recruitment officer Scott spells out to O'Grady their requirements, both physical and musical: 'It's a pretty rare type of bloke who'll fit into our band. He has to be under five feet six. And he has to be able to play bass pretty well, too.'

March 10 *High Voltage* enters the Australian album chart. It will go on to peak at #14 and chart for a healthy thirty-nine weeks. According to Ian McFarlane, writing in the *Australian Encyclopedia Of Rock And Pop*, 'When stacked up against the melodious pop of Sherbet and the glitter/glam of Skyhooks and Hush, AC/DC's brand of hard rock was rugged, outrageous, and irrepressible. AC/DC were the bad boys … AC/DC was not doing anything original at this stage … but it was the *way* they did it that got fans excited.'

Writing in the *All Music Guide*, Stephen Thomas Erlewine notes, 'One of the perennial complaints about AC/DC is that they've never changed—and if that's true, *High Voltage* is the blueprint they've followed all their career. The album has every single one of AC/DC's archetypes … songs about rock'n'roll, slow sleazy blues, high-voltage boogie, double-entendres so obvious they qualify as single-entendres, and, of course, the monster riffs of Angus Young, so big and bold they bruise the listener upon contact … [and] Bon Scott sounded as if you could catch a disease by listening to him.'

The number one album in Australia at the time of *High Voltage*'s release is Skyhooks' *Living In The 70's*, which is in the midst of a sixteen-week run at the top of the charts. Skyhooks' next album, *Ego Is Not A Dirty Word*, will race to the #1 spot on its release in late July. Of all the local bands in AC/DC's sights, Skyhooks are the one they're most keen to beat into submission.

FOLLOWING PAGES: BON SCOTT (WITH BAGPIPES AND COKE) PRIOR TO A GIG ON SYDNEY HARBOUR; FRONT AND BACK COVER ARTWORK FOR *HIGH VOLTAGE*, RELEASED IN 1975.

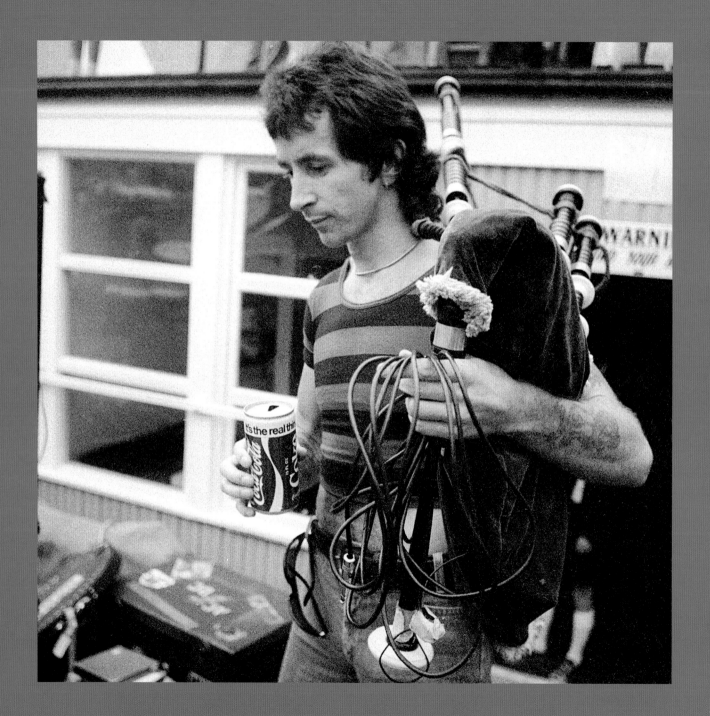

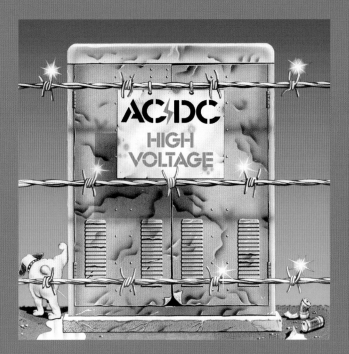

> **"Stacked up against the melodious pop of Sherbet and the glitter/glam of Skyhooks and Hush, AC/DC's brand of hard rock was rugged, outrageous, and irrepressible."**
>
> IAN MCFARLANE, *AUSTRALIAN ENCYCLOPEDIA OF ROCK AND POP*

AC/DC are currently travelling in a beaten-up Greyhound bus nicknamed 'Old Swivel Hips', due to its inability to travel in a straight line. Air conditioning and/or heating are not its best features, either. On the way to a sold-out gig at Melbourne's Festival Hall on the day of the album's release—where the headliners are pop pinups Sherbet—the bus breaks down, and the band are forced to push it to the venue. Not surprisingly, they arrive late.

March 20 New bassist Mark Evans makes his public debut with the band, at the Waltzing Matilda Hotel, a beer barn/bloodhouse in the Melbourne suburb of Springvale with a capacity of 1,200. Cover charge is $2—and (crucially) the bar stays open until 11:30pm, 90 minutes later than most pubs.

Evans had a run-through with the band a few days earlier at the much smaller and far grungier Station Hotel. The street-smart, proudly working class nineteen-year-old is currently a resident of a high-rise housing commission estate known as the 'Prahran Hilton'. He was, until recently, a public servant, and even though he's more proficient on a six-string, he's willing to strap on a bass. He's about the right size, too, at barely a few inches taller than the Youngs.

After an audition with the band and a sit-down with the Youngs, Evans met with Browning. 'This is the guy I told you about,' Malcolm Young told his manager, who looked Evans up and down—and that was it, job interview complete. He later realises that Browning was checking his height; it wouldn't work out if he were too tall.

'Michael gave me the nod and I was in,' Evans later writes of the encounter. He is put on a weekly wage of $60, just like the rest of the band. 'In essence, all I had to do was fit in with Malcolm and Phil, and they were rock solid from the get-go.'

As the Matilda Hotel gig progresses, Bon Scott turns to Evans, mid-song, and shouts, 'Going all right, Mike.' Years later, when Evans receives a selection of gold AC/DC records, he'll notice they are all inscribed 'Mike Evans.' 'Maybe he knew something I didn't,' Evans later notes.

In typical AC/DC fashion, Evans hits the road hard: gigs swiftly follow in the Melbourne suburbs of Kew (March 21) and Boronia (March 22).

Likely setlist: 'She's Got Balls' / 'Soul Stripper' / 'Rock'n'roll Singer' / 'Show Business' / 'Heartbreak Hotel' / 'Jailhouse Rock' / 'High Voltage' / 'Love Song' / 'Can I Sit Next To You, Girl' / 'Honky Tonk Women' / 'Jumpin' Jack Flash' / 'Little Lover' / 'Stick Around' / 'Baby, Please Don't Go'.

March 23 Today, what will become AC/DC's most celebrated (and downright hilarious) *Countdown* appearance begins in chaos. The entire band, bar Scott, is assembled on the ABC soundstage, ready to rock 'Baby, Please Don't Go' (again), before the obligatory gaggle of screaming teenage girls and a full crew. As producer Kris Noble glances anxiously at his watch, the band members keep looking toward the stage door, unsure exactly what is going on with their singer. No one has seen Scott since they arrived at the studio and rehearsed the song.

Then, with quite literally seconds to go before the cameras roll, Scott emerges, dressed as perhaps the ugliest schoolgirl ever to grace a stage—and certainly the hairiest. He's sporting pigtails, hoop earrings, blue eyeliner, falsies, and a skimpy tunic. The band begin playing, and Bon casually sparks up a ciggie while Angus cuts loose during his guitar solo. Scott then produces a big aqua-coloured mallet, with which he menaces Angus as 'Baby' builds to a hefty climax. It turns out that Scott has raided the ABC props room as well as the costume department. AC/DC—especially the Young brothers—are not the kind of guys to have giggling attacks, but they all struggle to keep straight faces.

When news.com.au compiles its list of the 'Ten Most Amazing AC/DC Moments' in 2014, the *Countdown* performance of 'Baby' is ranked #1: 'Australian TV audiences would never be the same, thankfully.'

The song, and the performance, clearly connects, because the band are invited back again on April 6 and 27, although on these occasions Bon retires the tunic, opting instead for fetching white bib and braces, with nothing but flesh underneath. Angus, meanwhile, turns out as Superman, cape and all. SuperAng, in fact.

Late March As is their nature, the band keep on rolling, playing gigs in the Melbourne suburbs Ringwood, Moorabbin, and Broadmeadows, before returning to the Hard Rock Café for shows on March 27 and 28. They also return to the Matthew Flinders on March 29.

March 30 The band perform the uncharacteristically schmaltzy 'Love Song'—not long for the AC/DC canon—on *Countdown*. Angus is back in his basic schoolyard blues, scabby knees on full and colourful display, while Bon sports red bib and braces, and not for the last time. It's not his best look.

Meanwhile, Michael Browning's sister Coral, who is based in London, has a copy

FOLLOWING PAGE: BON SCOTT RECORDING VOCALS AT ALBERTS IN SYDNEY. SCOTT HAS A HABIT OF LOCKING HIMSELF AWAY TO WORK ON HIS LYRICS, WHICH HE REFERS TO AS HIS 'TOILET POETRY'.

"With Bon now on board, the band had acquired a new sense of purpose as well as a sense of humour and uniqueness. Bon was one of the world's best street poets."

MICHAEL BROWNING, *DOG EAT DOG*

"It's a pretty rare type of bloke who'll fit into our band. He has to be under five feet six. And he has to be able to play . . . pretty well, too."

BON SCOTT TO *RAM*, 1975

of a video shot during a Melbourne Festival Hall gig, showing the band playing 'High Voltage'. She plays this to various UK record execs on a portable Fairchild video cassette machine, on loan from her brother—a gadget the band refers to as Browning's 'Maxwell Smart' briefcase (a nod to *Get Smart*, one of Angus's favourite TV shows).

The promo video gives Angus—this time in all white, bar his red ankle socks—loads of screen time. A fairly rudimentary lighting rig flashes the band's name, while crowd shots show fans frantically waving AC/DC banners; one reads 'AC/DC'S GOT BALLS'. Another screams 'ANGUS U SPUNK', handcrafted by the man himself the afternoon before the gig at the band's HQ, and discreetly slipped to the faithful. Those on the inside know that this high-energy, super-sweaty clip has been carefully stage-managed, but that matters little: it's the perfect promo for the band, especially when pitching AC/DC to record execs who haven't yet experienced them live.

Coral plays the video to Atlantic Records' Phil Carson, and he is sold; the sight of Angus blazing away is all he needs to see. 'Get your brother on the phone!' he tells Coral.

Within days, Browning is on a flight to London, where he meets with Carson and Dave Dee, formerly of the group Dave Dee, Dozy, Beaky, Mick & Tich, who is now the label's general manager, and who deduces that AC/DC sound like a cross between Led Zeppelin and Slade. The deal that's set in place is pure boilerplate: an advance of around £15,000 set against a royalty rate of 12 percent. 'It may not have been the most lucrative record deal ever made,' Browning later writes, 'but it was still a deal.'

Back in Oz, the band's fee per gig has now increased to $600.

Also in March ... *Countdown* stumps up the money to shoot a clip for the song 'Jailbreak', although the budget is probably little more than a few hundred dollars. The site chosen is a quarry in the Melbourne suburb of Sunshine. In keeping with the song's melodramatic theme of a prisoner making his escape 'in the name of liberty' but winding up 'with a bullet in his back', the façade of a prison and prison gates are built on the site. In what passes for a script, Bon and Angus are to race through the gates, on the lam, with Malcolm and Mark, dressed as cops, on their tail, firing away with real handguns—six-shot revolvers, fortunately loaded with blanks.

In these pre-'health and safety' times, the explosives used during the shoot are large orange-juice containers—the type typically modified into bongs. But rather than skunky bong water, they're filled with petrol and then loaded into a metal tube and fired like a cannon. Not exactly military standard, but effective enough for *Countdown*'s needs.

The band play the song while perched atop boulders; Scott almost falls off his rocky perch when the first drinks-bottle cannon explodes behind him. The cannons radiate heat and noise; the band flinch every time one detonates. Five handsome heads of hair are seared by the flames.

The grand finale, such as it is, is the moment when the prison gates are set alight and the big chase occurs. The bombs explode—'shit went everywhere,' according to Evans—and Angus, who has swapped his schoolboy blacks for convict pyjamas (popular eveningwear at the time), bursts through the flaming gates at high speed, only just avoiding being set alight himself. The look on his face is pure fear.

'Can't recall there being a safety officer on the shoot,' Evans later notes.

April 5 One of AC/DC's stranger gigs for the month is the Year 12 formal at the Ivanhoe Grammar School. As a gesture of goodwill—and probably a cost-cutting measure—they give their crew the night off and allow the students to run the lights and sound, according to Ivanhoe Old Boy Doug Golden, who'd smartly booked them before their debut album took off. 'It cost about $240 to book them to play at the dance,' he later tells Melbourne's *Herald-Sun*, 'and they held the price.'

Setlist: 'Live Wire' / 'She's Got Balls' / 'Rock'n'roll Singer' / 'Soul Stripper' / 'Show Business' / 'High Voltage' / 'Can I Sit Next To You, Girl' / 'It's A Long Way To The Top (If You Wanna Rock'n'roll)' / 'T.N.T.' / 'Baby, Please Don't Go'.

April The band's relentless gigging continues with shows in and around Melbourne, including a huge fundraiser for strife-torn Bangladesh, which is staged at the Myer Music Bowl on April 20 and broadcast on radio station 2JJ. Also on the bill are Daddy Cool, The La De Das, and Jim Keays. The 10,000-strong crowd helps raise upward of $30,000.

Distance is clearly no issue for the band: they undertake a round trip of almost 2,000 kilometres for gigs on the NSW Central Coast in Wyong on April 21, and then return for a show at the rural Victorian town of Broadmeadows on April 22.

April 25 The band take part in another big show at Melbourne's Festival Hall; also on the bill are New Zealand art-rockers Split Enz (who were roundly booed on their

" *We drove down to Lavender Bay in the band's van. The road crew had some police outfits and some spray cans. We spent about an hour doing different poses.* **"**

PHOTOGRAPHER PHILIP MORRIS

Australian debut a month earlier) and Skyhooks. Bon Scott is clearly enjoying himself; dressed in a leopard-skin outfit, he swings out over the 5,000-strong crowd on a specially installed rope, although he duly crashes into the PA and ends the show covered in bruises.

May In Sydney for another run of shows, the band, plus Browning and various members of their crew, meet with photographer Philip Morris at Lavender Bay in Sydney for a photo shoot. The resulting images will be used to promote 'Jailbreak' and the *High Voltage* album. It proves to be a very lively session.

'They arrived at my studios at about six in the afternoon and they had a slab of beer and some green ginger wine,' Morris recalls. 'We drove down to Lavender Bay in the band's van. The road crew had some police outfits and some spray cans. They sprayed the wall with "We Luv AC/DC". We spent about an hour doing different poses. Bon was drinking out of a bottle in a paper bag and arguing with the police.' (Browning and Pat Pickett dressed as police, that is.)

The band are also set to play a lunchtime show at the Hard Rock Café in May, but Bon Scott sleeps through his alarm. Those at the gig catch the very rare sight of Malcolm and Angus sharing vocal duties.

May 5 AC/DC begin a four-night residency at the notorious Sydney venue the Bondi Lifesaver, aka the Swap (as in 'wife swap'), one of the key rock spots in the harbour city. They are booked to play four forty-five-minute sets each night.

At the end of their sparsely attended first set, the venue's owner confronts the band, swearing and cursing like a maniac. The band have been playing so loudly that they've killed all the fish in the venue's aquarium—and those fish were her pride and joy. Things improve as the residency continues, with near full houses by the end of their run.

While in Sydney, the Young brothers stay at the family home in Burwood, while Scott, Evans, and Rudd share a room at the nearby Squire Inn. During downtime, when not hosting friendly fans, Scott divvies his time between reading comics—*B.C.* is a personal fave—and writing letters, which he refers to as 'dispatches from my front'.

OPPOSITE: MANAGER MICHAEL BROWNING (SECOND FROM RIGHT) AND ROADIE PAT PICKETT WITH THE BAND DURING A GUERRILLA-STYLE PHOTO SHOOT AT SYDNEY'S LAVENDER BAY.

May 8 On the day of AC/DC's final Lifesaver gig, 'Baby, Please Don't Go' enters the Oz singles chart at #38. It will spend seven weeks in the charts and peak at #19.

During the next two months, AC/DC play upward of forty shows, including a number in the Sydney suburbs of Forestville, Manly Vale, and Caringbah, before hitting the highway back to Melbourne for gigs at their happy rockin' grounds of the Matthew Flinders Hotel (May 15 and 30), the Croxton Hotel (May 20), and the Hard Rock Café (May 17 and 30).

June 4 AC/DC are featured in Oz music magazine *Juke*. In the feature, written by Ed Nimmervoll, Malcolm lays out the band's master plan. 'Music's the same all over the world,' he says, with some conviction. 'There's nothing an Australian group can't do that they're doing [overseas]. The kids want the same thing. The audiences are the same.'

Bon Scott defines George Young's role with the band. 'He's like a brother—no, a father—to the group. He doesn't tell us what to do, just shows us how to get more out of the things we start.' He also admits he got a good laugh when he first heard 'Can I Sit Next To You, Girl' on the radio in Adelaide. 'I thought, *bunch of pooftahs*. Now I'm in the group and singing the song.'

June 5 AC/DC travel to the mining town of Mount Gambier, in South Australia, on June 5, where they pack the Mount Gambier Football Club—a round trip of around 850 kilometres. 'You couldn't move in there, there was so many people,' Mount Gambier local Phillip Dunn, whose band Avenue were the support act, later tells ABC News. 'Angus was playing the guitar, and they [Angus and Bon] just went through the crowd.'

June 11 For a free show at the local park in the rural town of Bendigo, Victoria, Angus leaves his school uniform in the hangar and dresses as Zorro—an outfit he'd previously worn on *Countdown*. 'Fantastic [gig],' one fan gushes, 'even though I lost a tooth.'

June 16 The band shoot a performance video for the song 'Show Business'. Angus is in his white uniform, his cap hanging from a mic stand as he cuts loose; Scott wears a candy-coloured jacket and straw boater, and carries a cane (this is 'Show Business', after all), all of which he dispenses with as the song progresses. Down the front, a gaggle of 'sharpie chicks', distinguishable by their close-cropped hair (with long rattails) and heavy makeup, are headbanging with intent. The AC/DC sign hanging over the stage, meanwhile, is a pale imitation of the retina-wrecking number they'll utilise later on.

June 25 The band rate a mention in the current issue of *Juke*, in the 'Jazz'n'Jive' column, which features the odd story of a Japanese tourist named Izumi Tanake, who, after experiencing *High Voltage*, has decided to write a letter to the group.

'I never forget about AC/DC,' she writes. 'You are one of the greatest groups in the world. I believe you're international and I wish you come to Japan.' At least the band, not always arbiters of good taste, can't be held responsible for the title of the piece: 'AC/DC Nipped'.

July While setting up for a lunchtime gig at the North Altona Technical High School in outer Melbourne, a show organised by the students, the band undertakes an impromptu photo shoot with Graeme Webber. In a now legendary portrait of Bon Scott, Webber shoots the singer standing and smirking in a toilet stall, his fly undone and his lower stomach tattoo on full and proud display. The shoot goes so well that Scott invites Webber onto the band's bus to share a joint, even allowing Webber to snap him with a spliff dangling from his lips.

The photos Webber takes of Angus Young are just as iconic. The guitarist poses in a filthy bathroom, nursing a Coke, a ciggie in his mouth, his school satchel slung across his shoulder, a demented look on his face. 'Angus was enthusiastic,' Webber says, 'and keen to help.' The Angus images will later be used for the 1976–77 Giant Dose Of Rock'n'roll tour poster.

The gig itself is an unqualified success, according to a student named Brett, who is the band's 'chaperone' for the day. 'The teachers were mortified—and had no idea how loud they would be. The guys were fantastic and treated me so well.'

The band are constantly in motion during July, heading north for more shows at the Bondi Lifesaver (July 16 and 17), along with a series of gigs in suburban Sydney, at Ryde, Daceyville—at the local Police Boys Club, for the hefty sum of $400—and Hurstville.

August Chaos erupts during a gig at Melbourne's Manhattan Hotel, another massive suburban beer barn (the exact date of the gig is unclear). Even before their set begins,

FOLLOWING PAGES: ANGUS AND BON POSE FOR PHOTOGRAPHER GRAEME WEBBER AT THE NORTH ALTONA TECHNICAL HIGH SCHOOL, JULY 1975.

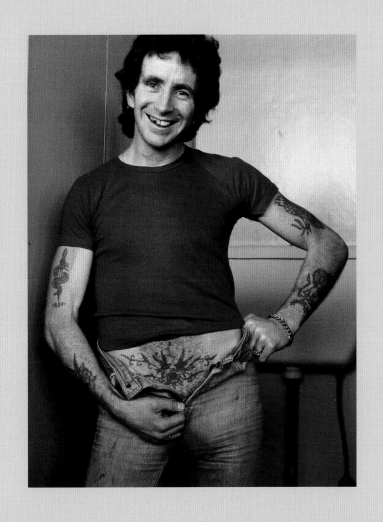

"*Bon loved the idea of working in a dunny, and was keen to show off some fresh tatts.*"

PHOTOGRAPHER GRAEME WEBBER

87

they are advised of the madness in the band room: punches are flying, as are glasses. 'You are all out of your minds if you go out there,' Ralph The Roadie warns them.

The show, of course, goes on, but when Angus scales the PA and plays on top of the speaker stacks, he is hit flush by a glass, which cuts his hand. Bleeding heavily, he leads the band offstage. The mood among the already unruly crowd turns very ugly— one unlucky punter is thrown from the top tier of the venue onto the floor below, while more glasses are hurled, and the entire room is engaged in a rolling, ongoing brawl. The police arrive on the scene, as do three ambulances, and the band are warned to remain backstage until the room is cleared—and, even then, they are instructed to wait an hour before leaving, until something resembling order is restored. One red-blooded night of rock'n'roll.

August 6 AC/DC—well, Angus, in fact—score their first *Juke* cover. The image used is the Graeme Webber shot of him grinning maniacally backstage at North Altona High. It's included in the mag as a lift-out poster—another first for Angus. He's now a pinup.

August 10–17 The band play a week of gigs in Sydney, including the Marching Girls Field at Green Valley, southwest of the city.

August 25 Today, AC/DC are due to play the first of five lunchtime shows at the most unlikely of venues, the teen clothing department of Melbourne department store Myer (the Miss Melbourne Shop). Due to their popularity on *Countdown*, they've become a big draw with underage female fans. The hastily assembled stage is barely above floor level, and easily accessible by pretty much anyone. There is no security, no barriers.

Literally thousands of screaming fans pack the store for the band's midday start— way more than the Miss Melbourne Shop can hold. 'If this lasts more than one song,' Browning tells the band backstage, 'it'll be a fucking miracle.'

As the group warily take the stage, the fans riot, charging forward like a hungry mob—'like waves of screaming banshees,' bassist Evans later writes—and the band drop their gear and scramble for safety. Bon Scott is seen racing through the lingerie department, his ever-loyal friend and roadie, Pat Pickett, at his side, as they fend off the more aggressive fans.

Evans manages to save his bass and hop an escalator straight out of the store, where he disappears into the lunchtime crowd. 'It was pandemonium,' he later writes, 'like a scene straight out of *A Hard Day's Night*. We had set off a full-on, screaming, knicker-wetting teenage riot.' When the dust finally settles, store management learns that the Miss Melbourne Shop has been looted by the craftier fans of the group, while the group's rented gear has been trashed. The remaining gigs are hastily cancelled.

August 29 The band are booked to play the Matthew Flinders Hotel in Chadstone. When Angus wades into the crowd to perform his dying-bug routine during an extended 'Baby, Please Don't Go', a punter starts kicking him while he's on the ground. Phil Rudd leaps out from behind his drum kit to defend Angus, but breaks his thumb when he punches someone in the melee. Bassist Evans, too, joins in; he's knocked out by a bouncer who doesn't realise he's part of the band.

Rudd requires surgery for his thumb and is briefly replaced in the band by Colin Burgess. From now on, the drummer is referred to as 'Left Hook Rudd'.

Afterward, Angus only half-jokingly compares the scene at gigs like these to life in the trenches during World War I. 'You pick up the guitar and just dig in.' He asks Browning if it's possible to install some kind of cage around the stage at future gigs. He's done with being a target.

During a subsequent show at the Matthew Flinders, some local coppers cook up a 'sting' to snare Angus, erroneously thinking he's underage. Some plainclothesmen stand at the back of the room, waiting for Angus and the band to begin—which is when they plan to swoop and make their arrest. But before the set starts, roadie Tana Douglas talks with the cops. One of them offers to buy her a drink, which she happily accepts. Angus is now off the hook, because the plainclothesman has just plied an underage woman—Douglas—with alcohol. It hardly matters, anyway, because Angus is both of legal age and a teetotaller.

August 31 The band return to the mining town of Mount Gambier, this time for a show at the Kings Theatre, with Colin Burgess subbing for Rudd. The theatre is filled to the brink and beyond, partly due to some clever punters who discover an unlocked back door to the venue.

September 2 A helter-skelter night for AC/DC, who play a double-header, first at the Croxton Park Hotel (another Rockin' At The Croc gig) and then at the Hard Rock Café, where shows start at midnight.

September 7 AC/DC headline a free show sponsored by radio station 2SM at Victoria Park on the fringes of Sydney's central business district—their biggest headlining show to date. The high-rating station has been very supportive of the band—a situation helped along by Alberts, which has bought airtime to promote the group.

'AC/DC is not a nice band,' the radio ad declares.

Also on the bill at Victoria Park is Stevie Wright—whose latest single, 'Black Eyed Bruiser', features Angus on guitar—and singer-songwriter Ross Ryan, who's just had a local hit with 'I Am Pegasus'—exactly the kind of touchy-feely song that encouraged the Youngs to form a loud and hairy rock band.

During their eleven-song set—which begins with 'Live Wire', works its way through

OPPOSITE: AN EARLY PROMO SHOT OF THE BAND FOR THE *HIGH VOLTAGE* ALBUM. LEFT TO RIGHT: MALCOLM YOUNG, BON SCOTT, ANGUS YOUNG, AND PHIL RUDD. ABOVE: ANGUS MEETS HIS FANS IN SYDNEY'S VICTORIA PARK, SEPTEMBER 7 1975.

91

'It's A Long Way To The Top' and 'T.N.T.', and closes with the usual 'Baby, Please Don't Go'—Angus takes full advantage of the scope of the gig by scaling a ladder and playing while perched on top of the speaker stacks. Bon Scott does likewise on the other side of the stage. Then Angus wades into the crowd, mid-solo, while manager Browning and various roadies clear a path for him through the thousands of fans in attendance.

Offstage, producer Harry Vanda looks on proudly, cradling his son Daniel, who wears one of Angus's schoolboy caps with the letter A emblazoned upon it. AC/DC is very much a family affair. 'It was fun and chaotic,' recalls photographer Philip Morris, who chased Angus up and down the ladder while photographing this era-defining gig.

September 11 'High Voltage' enters the Oz Top 40 at #26; it will peak at #13 and stay in the charts for twelve weeks. During its recording, George Young had suggested to the band that it would be a neat trick to write a song using the chords A, C, D, and C; Malcolm and Angus duly complied.

'We more of less threw them together,' Angus later recalls. 'Paid the rent.'

September 15 The band set out on a run of dates in rural Western Australia, the first at the Merredin Repertory Club. The tour poster, which features a self-portrait sketched by Angus, declares that AC/DC are 'Australia's most exciting band! High Voltage rock'n'roll appearing in concert.' The Merredin show is the most expensive on the run, with the priciest tickets costing an outrageous $4.20. (At the time of the gig, $3 would buy a tank of petrol; a pack of cigarettes was 25c, a beer about the same.) The original tour poster remains on the wall of the venue today, which is now known as the Cummins Theatre.

Those who can't afford a ticket gather in the parking lot behind the club—AC/DC play so loud that they have no trouble hearing the show.

September 16 The tour rolls into Boulder for a show at the Town Hall. Tickets are a steal at $3.20. Previous visitors to the Town Hall include the opera great Dame Nellie Melba.

September 17 The pick of Philip Morris's images from the Victoria Park gig features as a one-page pictorial in the new issue of *Juke*, under the title 'ANGUS IN ACTION!'

September 18 Angus Young verbally spars with some lubricated members of the audience at the Sandgroper Hotel in Leederville.

'Fuck, you're ugly,' one drunken punter barks in his direction.

'Have a fuckin' look at yourself,' he snaps back, and keeps on playing.

With the exception of 'Baby, Please Don't Go', the band's setlist is now all originals.

Setlist: 'Live Wire' / 'She's Got Balls' / 'Rock'n'roll Singer' / 'Soul Stripper' / 'High Voltage' / 'It's A Long Way To The Top (If You Wanna Rock'n'roll)' / 'The Jack' / 'Can I Sit Next To You, Girl' / 'T.N.T.' / 'Baby, Please Don't Go'.

September 15 Journalist Bob Granger interviews the band for a full-page feature in *RAM* ('The Lusts Of AC/DC: Band Bids For Supreme Punkdom'). Malcolm, in an admission he probably lives to regret, discusses a big night with some fans (aka 'The Midnight Knee Trembler'), revealing how two eager 'chicks' had invited him and Scott 'back to Granny's place'—an offer they readily accepted. 'So we climb over the back fence and we screw ... having relations, if you want to be polite about it, on the lounge-room floor.' Scott, meanwhile, was running around the house naked, 'turning somersaults', according to Malcolm. Then, unfortunately, Granny unexpectedly returned. 'The chick throws me off, pushes me out the window ... and throws my clothes after me. And then Bon lands beside me.'

Malcolm wishes for a lifestyle more like that of The Rolling Stones. '[They] have a plane and the stewardesses give blow jobs while they're eight miles high—and we're being thrown out of places when Granny comes home.'

September 22 The band fill the Walkabout Hotel in Geraldton, hitting the stage at 9pm and playing for what one punter will later insist is 'three hours straight'. When they first played here in 1974, an all-in brawl erupted. There are no such distractions tonight. 'Angus was blazing,' an awestruck fan reports.

September 24 The final day of WA dates includes a double-header: an all-ages, booze-free show at Bunbury's Southway Ballroom, followed by an evening gig at the Bussell Motor Hotel. Tickets for both shows are $3 a pop.

October 1 In the 'Jazz'n'Jive' section of *Juke* magazine, AC/DC's October and November tour dates are listed alongside upcoming tours by Gloria Gaynor, Neil Sedaka,

John Denver, Marty Robbins, Ray Charles, and Status Quo. 'Punk rockers throughout Australia—beware!' reads the copy. 'The AC/DC high voltage tour is underway and ready to explode in your area.'

October 1–6 In order to break up the 3,500-kilometre trip from Perth to Melbourne, the band stop in Adelaide for a week of shows.

October 7–18 With Phil Rudd back in the drummer's seat after recovering from thumb surgery, AC/DC return to more familiar territory, playing suburban Melbourne shows at the Croxton Park Hotel (October 7 and 9), Ringwood (October 12), Preston and St Albans (October 16), the Tottenham Hotel (October 17), and the Matthew Flinders Assembly Hall (October 18).

November In the midst of a particularly frenetic run of dates (which is saying something, for a band as busy as AC/DC), Scott writes to Irene Thornton, with whom he remains close. 'I reckon we'd have to be the hottest band in the country at the moment. Not bad for a twenty-nine-year-old third-time-around has-been.'

Proving that they are the sort of band for whom the term 'weddings, parties, anything' was coined, one of the stranger shows AC/DC play during November is at the Corio Village Shopping Centre in Geelong, a working-class rural centre in Victoria. Fans line the upper level of the shopping mall to catch a better glimpse of the band in action.

Geelong has become a go-to spot for the band, who end up playing there eight times during 1975. They also play shows in locations as far north as Kingaroy in Queensland—peanut-farming country—as well as the Northern Territory and rural Lismore in NSW, where they rock the City Hall. They also play the Cloudland Ballroom in Brisbane, a massive if slightly tarnished venue where The Easybeats once played. (Eighteen months later, during a royal visit, Queen Elizabeth II will attend a reception there.)

Meanwhile, when Deep Purple return to Australia for another tour, AC/DC are approached to open the shows, but memories of their Sunbury dust-up are still strong. '[Browning] told them to stick it up their arse,' Angus tells a reporter from *RAM*.

OPPOSITE: ARTWORK FOR THE BAND'S SECOND ALBUM, *T.N.T.*, RELEASED ON DECEMBER 1 1975. ABOVE: UNLIKELY PINUP STARS FOR THE AUSTRALIAN MAGAZINE *TV WEEK*.

December 1 The *T.N.T.* album is released in Australia. It will spend a total of thirty weeks on the album chart, peaking at #2—kept from the top spot by *ABBA*.

Apart from the stellar line-up of songs, many of which—'It's A Long Way To The Top', 'T.N.T.', 'Live Wire', and 'High Voltage' among them—will become AC/DC standards, there are some interesting footnotes from the album. 'Rocker' abruptly cuts out a few seconds shy of the three-minute mark, just as Angus heats up on guitar, most likely because the band had run out of tape. (On the 1986 CD reissue of the album, the song fades a few seconds earlier, but the 'uncut' version of the song appears on the 2012 iTunes release.) A similar situation occurs with 'High Voltage', which on the original album segues into a cover of Chuck Berry's 'School Days' to close the album. Later versions of the song fade slightly earlier.

T.N.T. is also the only Australian-made AC/DC album not to receive an international release. Instead, selections from the album will be combined with tracks from *High Voltage* and released (also as *High Voltage*, just to muddy the waters further) globally in 1976.

December Following *T.N.T.*'s release, AC/DC continue doing what they were born to do—play live. A tour of rural NSW, which consumes much of December, takes them to Gunnedah (December 2), country music heartland Tamworth (December 3), and onward to Wyong, Newcastle, Taree, Port Macquarie, Kempsey, Coffs Harbour (the home of the Big Banana), Grafton, Moree, and Inverell, where they fill the Town Hall on December 14. The following week, December 15–22, they play more gigs in NSW country towns, including Orange (at the Amoco Hall, the venue that hosted the final Easybeats gig), Dubbo, Goulburn, Parkes, and Cooma.

December 24 The band return to the big smoke for a Christmas Eve show at Sydney's Hordern Pavilion. The headliners are their arch rivals, Skyhooks. Trading on AC/DC's 'bad boy' notoriety, manager Browning cooks up an idea to start a fight on stage during their set, which is bound to get some headlines. Waiting in the wings are Browning and a few others, dressed as cops (in the same outfits they wore for the Lavender Bay photo shoot), ready to rush on and end the commotion by 'arresting' the band and frogmarching them off.

Unfortunately, before a punch can be thrown in jest, bassist Mark Evans gives Bon Scott a gentle shove with his foot, and Scott tumbles off the stage and into the eager audience, where he is almost eaten alive. Evans, meanwhile, jumps on Angus, and they begin wrestling on stage. Chaos ensues until finally, a barely conscious Scott is rescued from the clutches of the audience and dragged backstage, along with the rest of the band.

The madness isn't over yet, however. Margaret Young confronts Evans in the dressing room, demanding that, in the future, he keep his mitts off her little brother. If this isn't enough, an angry roadie then bursts into the dressing room, screaming blue murder about some equipment that has been damaged in the melee. The roadie then spies a cassette tape of the bagpipe solo from 'It's A Long Way To The Top', which the band have been using during gigs, and destroys it as the startled band looks on.

December 26 During a show in the rural Victorian town of Shepparton, some members of the audience antagonise Angus to the point that he and the band's crew go searching for them afterward. They track them down in a milk bar, unaware that the local police station is right next-door.

Soon after the inevitable fight begins, Angus is allegedly arrested and thrown in a cell for the night. (Another report has these events taking place across the border, in Wangaratta, on the 28th.)

December 27 Bon is clearly more at ease with the locals, having invited a few female fans back to Commodore Motel for an after-party following a show at the Convention Centre Hall in Albury. He gives them autographs, scrawled on the hotel's stationery. What else he gives them remains unknown, which is probably for the best.

December 31 The band play a late-night gig in Adelaide, South Australia—the last of more than two hundred for the year—coming on stage at 11:30pm. The power cuts out after two songs, and a 'turn on the power' chant breaks out among the crowd. Power is restored, but then a fire is lit in the middle of the mosh pit. All in all, it makes for one very lively New Year's concert.

After the gig, the band drive more than 850 kilometres overnight, en route to a New Year's Day gig in rural Inverloch, Victoria.

Likely setlist: 'Live Wire' / 'She's Got Balls' / 'Rock'n'roll Singer' / 'Soul Stripper' / 'High Voltage' / 'It's A Long Way To The Top (If You Wanna Rock'n'roll)' / 'The Jack' / 'Can I Sit Next To You, Girl' / 'T.N.T.' / 'Baby, Please Don't Go'.

As the **T.N.T.** *LP becomes an Australian hit, AC/DC relocate to London, where they struggle to make themselves heard above the din of punk rock; an unexpected death derails their first English tour, but the band blitz the Marquee and top* **Sounds'** *end-of-year poll.*

1976

January 1–5 AC/DC ring in the New Year with a gig at the football ground at Inverloch, as what is now known as the Lock Up Your Daughters Summer Vacation Tour rolls onward. During 'It's A Long Way To The Top', Scott wades into the crowd, playing the bagpipes while riding on the shoulders of a roadie—a twist on the usual practice of Angus riding Scott's brawny shoulders.

More gigs follow in the rural Victorian towns of Portland, Port Ferry, and Warnambool; the band also cross the border for a show at the football club in Mount Gambier, South Australia. By now, on the strength of their live shows, each member of the band is earning around $500 a week—good money for the mid-70s.

January 6 *T.N.T.* enters the Oz album chart, selling 11,000 copies in its first week; it will peak at #2 and chart for thirty weeks. Advance copies are sent to the media wrapped in a pair of ladies' knickers; as promotional hype goes, this was hard to resist. The first side of the album, which includes 'It's A Long Way To The Top', 'Live Wire', 'Rock'n'roll Singer', and 'The Jack', will later be described by the *All Music Guide* as 'flawless, made up of all-time classics … [while the] B-side was nearly as formidable.'

'The Jack' is a song with a colourful back-story, as Scott explains to a British reporter. 'We were living with this houseful of ladies who were all very friendly and everyone in the band had got the jack [VD]. So, we wrote this song, and the first time we did it on stage they were all in the front row with no idea what was goin' to happen. When it came to repeating *She's got the jack*, I pointed at them, one after another.'

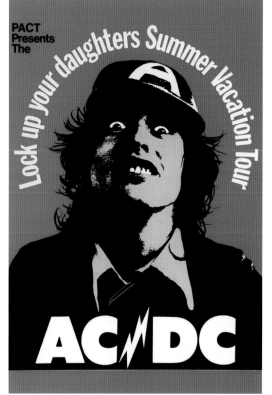

THE ICONIC LOCK UP YOUR DAUGHTERS TOUR POSTER, BASED ON GRAEME WEBBER'S SHOT OF ANGUS FROM ALTONA IN 1975.

January 8 On the same day that the band play a rapturously received show at the Technical High School in Mildura, Victoria, 'It's A Long Way To The Top' enters the Oz Top 40 at #38. It will go on to peak at #17 during an eleven-week chart run as the first of four classic AC/DC singles released during 1976 (the others being 'Jailbreak', 'T.N.T.', and 'Dirty Deeds Done Dirt Cheap').

'It's A Long Way''s rivals include ABBA's 'Mamma Mia', which is in the midst of a marathon ten-week run at the top of the Oz chart—eventually usurped, in a testimony to the commercial power of *Countdown*, by 'Jump In My Car' by Alberts labelmates The Ted Mulry Gang, members of whom had played with Malcolm in The Velvet Underground.

'It's A Long Way' will go on to achieve great longevity. In 2001, it is voted #9 on a list of the 'Best Australian Songs Of All Time' compiled by the Australasian Performing Rights Association (APRA). In 2003, it features prominently in the Jack Black film *School Of Rock*, and in 2010 it is ranked #3 in the 'Ultimate Rock 500 Countdown' conducted by Australian radio network Triple M (#1 and #2 were also AC/DC songs). In 2012, it's inducted into the National Film and Sound Archive's 'Sounds of Australia', while in 2010, the British TV network ITV uses the song during its coverage of the Tour de France (won, incidentally, by Aussie Cadel Evans). Over the years, 'Long Way' has been covered by everyone from Motörhead to Lucinda Williams, Local H. to The Dropkick Murphys, Pat Boone to Lemmy, WASP to The Wiggles. And, in 2004, Melbourne's Corporation Lane will be renamed AC/DC Lane, in honour of the band and the fact that the 'Long Way' clip was shot nearby.

January 9–23 The Lock Up Your Daughters roadshow continues to roll through Victoria, with gigs in Sunbury (the site of the band's notorious onstage brawl with Deep Purple in 1975), Cobram, Echuca (where they play an outdoors show at Victoria Park Oval), Bendigo, Apollo Bay, Ararat, Lorne, Rosebud, Wonthaggi, Sale, and Bairnsdale. The band play mainly civic and town halls during this run—gigs that can be set up quickly and don't require liquor licenses.

January 24 Back in Adelaide, AC/DC play mid-bill on a show sponsored by local radio station 5KA, the Record Breakers Concert, staged at Memorial Drive. Around 8,000 people attend the event. Also on the bill are glam rockers Hush, fresh from two Top 10 singles in 1975, as well as Alberts labelmates John Paul Young, who went one better than Hush in 1975, scoring three Top 10 singles (including the Vanda & Young classic 'Yesterday's Hero'), and The Ted Mulry Gang.

Heading the bill, much to AC/DC's collective chagrin, are Sherbet, the hottest pop act in the country, whose music Angus refers to as 'tea towel rock'. The reaction of much of the audience toward AC/DC is best summed up by twelve-year-old Sherbet fan Glynis, from Adelaide, who quickly shifts allegiances, noting, 'They blew Sherbet off the stage.'

January 27–28 The band round out a very lively month with gigs in Thornbury (another Rockin' At The Croc show) and Moorabbin in Victoria, and then Tottenham in NSW, before driving north to Sydney.

Also in January ... The band cut one of the weirder tracks in their catalogue, 'Fling Thing', which is essentially Angus riffing on the traditional Scottish song 'The Bonnie Banks O' Loch Lomond', with Bon Scott singing along, slightly off-mic (and off-key). George Young will later describe it as a 'Scottish "Amazing Grace", played in the studio for fun'. It's relegated to the flipside of the 'Jailbreak' single, which is hardly a shock. It will, however, get dusted off whenever they play Glasgow in the future.

Between January and March, amid their hectic touring schedule, the band settle in to Alberts' Sydney studio to record a new album, again with Vanda & Young. The resulting *Dirty Deeds Done Dirt Cheap* will feature such AC/DC standards as the title song, 'Problem Child' (a favourite of future lead singer Axl Rose), 'Ride On', and 'Love At First Feel'; both 'Ride On' and 'Dirty Deeds' will later feature in a list of Top 10 Bon Scott AC/DC Songs, compiled by *Ultimate Classic Rock*.

Music blogger Jason Wendleton neatly sums up the impact of the track 'Dirty Deeds' on a young listener. 'Every time I hear this song, a roaring advertisement for a dubious, back-alley problem solving service, I can see the vicious high school principal. I can see the cheating boyfriend who needs his ass kicked. The bitchy woman that needs to be put in her place. All of these people harass us throughout our lives—how often have we wished for a tough-talking wise guy to appear and magically "solve" these walking-problems by kicking some ass?' Well said.

February 4–6 The band settle in for another residency at key Sydney venue the Bondi Lifesaver, the do-drop-in for musos, journos, tastemakers, and, most crucially for the band, serious rock punters. The 250-square-metre dance floor is jam-packed each night during this run of shows.

AC/DC attract all types to their gigs: suburban rough-heads out for a spot of headbanging, teen girls who'd caught them on *Countdown*, and even skinheads, as documented by Anthony O'Grady in his *RAM* report on their Lifesaver residency.

> **"Bon could empty a whole room of women—he'd point at 'em while we were doin' 'The Jack' and 'Soul Stripper' and 'She's Got Balls', and they'd all leave or go up the back of the room, where he couldn't see 'em. But they still used to come 'round to the dressing room after we'd played."**
>
> ANGUS YOUNG TO *RAM*, 1976

February 7 The band receive one of their first mentions outside of the music press, in *TV Times*, where manager Michael Browning tells a reporter of the band's plans. 'The album is going out worldwide on the Atlantic label. … If the album and single do well overseas, we'll be free to go. If not, the boys are looking forward to a holiday.'

That holiday will prove to be a long time coming.

February 9 Reviewing *T.N.T.* for the *Canberra Times*, writer Tony Catterall doesn't quite know what to make of AC/DC. He states, 'It's not hard to reach the conclusion that AC/DC is the best punk-rock band in Australia'—a term the band would have dismissed in a heartbeat. (Malcolm will always insist that they are a 'rock'n'roll band', not punk in any way—which will become a problem later in 1976, when they reach the UK.)

Catterall seems unsure, too, as to whether the album is actually any good. 'It's really hard to know how to take *T.N.T.*,' he ponders. 'I mean, do you condemn it for its brutalising tendencies or praise it as authentic representation of a segment of society?' Weirdly, he criticises the Youngs' guitars, finding them 'too clean and pure for the overall sound'. Probably the last time *that* is said about Malcolm and Angus's playing.

Catterall's *T.N.T.* review is bracketed with coverage of *Something To Say*, the debut album by Buster Brown, the former group of AC/DC drummer Phil Rudd. Catterall rates them more highly than AC/DC, but has a problem working out exactly who—or what— Buster Brown is. '[He's] a young punk trying to better himself, trying to rise socially,' the reviewer guesses.

Meanwhile, Melbourne radio station 3XY surveys listeners who regularly request AC/DC songs and discovers that most fans of the band are working-class kids aged between thirteen and nineteen. (Kids from more upscale neighbourhoods request ABBA and John Denver, apparently.)

February 23 The soon-to-be-legendary video for 'It's A Long Way To The Top' is filmed, the production of it again funded by *Countdown*. The setup is for the band, and a few members of the Rats Of Tobruk Pipe Band, to play the song while perched on the rear of a flatbed truck rolling down Melbourne's Swanston Street during morning peak hour. (Today, the mere idea of such a concept is unthinkable; the mountain of bureaucracy would be too overwhelming, let alone the traffic.)

The clip's director is Paul Drane, *Countdown*'s studio director. Michael Browning, the band's manager, stands to the rear of the truck; and, for reasons that to this day he still

"There's a skinhead front of the stage in a denim shirt with sleeves ripped off, tatts down his arms, whose howling, dervish dance grants him wary space. Halfway through the set, Bon Scott's microphone packs up. He throws it onto the stage and grabs one of the harmony mikes. And then, get this. The guy picks up the discarded mic, holds it high, and strokes it devotedly. Then he kisses it and reverently passes it back to Scott."

ANTHONY O'GRADY DESCRIBES THE SCENE
AT THE BONDI LIFESAVER, *RAM*, 1976

can't explain, carrying a briefcase. It was Bon Scott who recruited the pipers. He took a few lessons before the shoot with piper Kevin Conlon, but made it clear that, as he'll only be miming in the video, he only needs to look as though he is playing. Scott then invited Conlon and two other pipers, Alan Butterworth and Les Kenfield, to take part in the shoot (which costs a staggering $200, all up).

As the truck rolls down Swanston Street (for the first of three circuits), a curious crowd of onlookers comes together, and a very supportive fan stealthily hands a joint to Bon Scott, just off camera. Bassist Evans points out the Royal Women's Hospital as they drive past. 'I was born there,' he informs his bandmates. They shrug; displaying enthusiasm toward anything but the band isn't in their nature—especially in the case of the Youngs.

More footage is shot of the band playing at Federation Square in the city, which will be used for a different version of the video. A third edit (nowhere near as exciting as the original) has the band playing on a soundstage. Not surprisingly, this version has never been formally released.

The song features Bon Scott's first great rock'n'roll lyric, a series of reflections about life on the road, plucked directly from his own experiences: 'Gettin' robbed / gettin' stoned / getting' beat up / broken bones.' Clinton Walker, in his definitive biography of Scott, Highway To Hell, sees this as something like an epitaph: 'It's as if Bon acknowledges he's living on borrowed time, and luckily at that. But even then, or perhaps for that very reason, the song remains celebratory.'

'It's A Long Way' may have been the first Australian rock anthem to feature the bagpipes, but it won't be the last. Psychedelic rock band The Church will use bagpipes to great effect on their 1988 hit 'Under The Milky Way', while blow-dried pop singer John Farnham would do likewise for his international hit 'You're The Voice'. (Farnham, an unlikely AC/DC fan, often performs 'It's A Long Way' live, even now.)

February 25–29 The band cross Bass Strait for shows in the Tasmanian towns of Burnie, Devonport, Launceston, Queenstown, and the capital, Hobart, playing mainly town halls and civic centres. Locals are amazed at the size of the band's amps; no one had seen such monstrous beasts before.

One Devonport fan, named Lillian, is fifteen years old at the time of the band's show at the Town Hall. 'It was very high energy,' she later recalls. 'It was extremely loud.' Another, Michael Burr, reported that his 'ears were ringing for what seemed like weeks afterward. I love(d) that band.'

March 1 A reception is held in Melbourne for the band (and Vanda & Young), where they are presented with gold records for *High Voltage* and *T.N.T.* The mothers of Phil Rudd and Mark Evans are in the house; Evans's ma describes the night as 'very nice', despite the spectacle of a young woman leaping from a cake clutching one of the group's gold records, and a belly dancer who loses her bra while gyrating around the dance floor.

Bon gives a juicy, expletive-laden acceptance speech, while Angus keeps it simple.

'I'd just like to thank me,' he says, grinning widely.

The band are now focused on their departure for the UK, which is set for early April.

March 5 AC/DC play a show as part of Melbourne's annual Moomba festival, at the Myer Music Bowl, in front of 5,000 fans. (The previous year's 'King Of Moomba' was none other than Rolf Harris.) The gig runs over, and officials from Moomba tell them that an encore is out of the question—and that, if they try to go back on stage, the power will be cut. But the audience refuses to leave; the power is duly cut, and the stage goes black. A chant begins—'We want the power!'—and the Moomba officials, realising they are outnumbered, finally give the band the OK to play one more song.

Even this isn't enough for the crowd, who stand and cheer for another ten minutes, hoping for a second encore, and venting their frustration by throwing anything handy onto or in the direction of the stage. Eventually, the band return to take a bow, and the crowd finally, reluctantly, head off into the night, whisked away by security and local coppers. The media reaction is, as ever, wildly understated. 'AC/DC CREATES ANOTHER ROCK CONCERT RIOT,' roars *TV Week*.

A ticket stub for *Moomba Rock 76*, as the gig was billed, was recently listed on eBay for $1,500.

March 3–14 More gigging ensues, with shows in various rural Victorian towns, including St Albans, Goulburn, and, on March 7, Castlemaine, where they play from the back of a truck, 'It's A Long Way To The Top' style, at the local showground. Bon arrives bearing a couple of female fans and a bottle of Stones Green Ginger wine, a local rotgut. His bagpipes fail him during 'Long Way', but locals still refer to the gig as the biggest thing ever to hit Castlemaine.

The St Albans gig is held in a school hall. Ken Griffiths, a student of the school, later describes it as a 'life-changing moment'. 'St Albans was pretty tough in those days and when Bon Scott came out with the bagpipes, we had never seen anything like it,' he tells the *Herald-Sun* in 2016. 'In a few minutes, he had the audience eating out of his hands.'

A local named John Conte brings a film camera to the gig, and the band give him consent to shoot part of the show from side stage. He shoots some forty-five minutes of footage, which he later sells to a US collector for $6,000—rights included. 'I could have bought a house with what it was actually worth,' he later laughs, having done some more research. (Some of his footage will be used in the 2007 DVD release *Plug Me In*.)

On March 8, AC/DC take part in a much larger-scale show at the Showgrounds in Korumburra. Also on the bill are Hush, Ariel, and the Little River Band (whose American endeavours are being monitored closely by Michael Browning, who is keen to break AC/DC in the States), as well as Billy Thorpe, The Ted Mulry Gang, and Jim Keays.

AC/DC play in the early evening. Around 20,000 fans cough up $5 to witness the event, billed as *Mother Rock 76*. Angus plays with his shorts not quite buttoned up properly, which causes them to fall down—accidentally, of course—frequently during their set.

From Korumburra, they cross the border into New South Wales for suburban shows at Ryde and Hurstville, and, on March 13, at the Warwick Farm racecourse, where they headline a bill also featuring retro-rockers Ol' 55, Finch, and The Richard Clapton Band. Scott's voice is not in good shape, which he tries to put right by gargling a mix of claret and honey. Heavy showers hamper the gig, which is attended by around 900 fans. Because the band started late, their gig ends in early evening darkness.

Next stop is the Hurstville Civic Centre in southwest Sydney, which, though full, is oddly subdued. 'Thanks a lot for nearly fuckin' nothing,' snarls a liquored-up Scott as he leaves the stage at the end of their set. He then heads straight to the toilet and throws up.

With Scott indisposed, Anthony O'Grady captures the backstage action for *RAM*: 'Angus is wandering around the top floor dressing room of the Hurstville Civic, holding court, waiting for his stage clothes to become less sweat soaked and perspiration sticky so he can take them off. … Offstage, Angus generally beams a glazed, good-humoured expression, backed up by a daredevil glint suggesting he'll give anything crazy a go, at least once. So when Big bro George Young tells the dressing room crowd about this great new trick he's devised for Angus—diving from a forty-foot tower into a glass of strawberry milk while not missing a single note of his guitar break … well, Angus's eyes really light up. … Better save it up for a big gig, he says. Yer probably couldn't do it twice a night 'til yer got useta it.'

When Angus's clothes dry, and Scott recovers, they cross town for yet another show at the Bondi Lifesaver. No fish are killed.

HUMAN LIVEWIRE ANGUS UNLEASHES ANOTHER GUITAR BLITZKRIEG AT A RADIO-SPONSORED SHOW ON A PONTOON ON SYDNEY HARBOUR, MARCH 27 1976. FANS JUMP IN THE HARBOUR AND SWIM OUT TO THE BAND, SHARKS BE DAMNED.

Likely setlist: 'Live Wire' / 'She's Got Balls' / 'School Days' / 'It's A Long Way To The Top (If You Wanna Rock'n'roll)' / 'High Voltage' / 'The Jack' / 'Can I Sit Next To You, Girl' / 'T.N.T.' / 'Baby, Please Don't Go'.

March 18 The single 'T.N.T.' enters the Oz Top 40 at #37; it will peak at #15 and chart for eleven weeks. C.W. McCall's trucker's anthem 'Convoy' is the #1 bestseller in the country on the week of 'T.N.T.''s release, but will be bumped soon after by Queen's epic, era-defining 'Bohemian Rhapsody'.

March 19 AC/DC are booked to open a UK tour in early April with Paul Kossoff's new band, Back Street Crawler—their first dates in England. (Earlier reports suggesting that they're to tour with The Heavy Metal Kids prove false.) But the drug addicted Kossoff dies from a mid-Atlantic pulmonary embolism on a flight from New York to London. He's twenty-five years old. Back in Oz, Bon Scott takes the news very badly. 'That cunt Kossoff fucked up our first tour,' he tells a reporter from *RAM*. 'Wait'll Angus gets hold of him.'

March 27 Prior to their departure for the UK, the band pack the Bondi Lifesaver yet again; Angus stands on the bar to play a solo, his pants around his ankles. Backstage, Angus demonstrates why he rarely smiles in photo shoots. He opens his mouth, clicks his tongue, and a tooth pops right out of its socket.

Phil Rudd explains to *RAM*'s Anthony O'Grady how this came about. 'One day he went to the freezer, got out a bar of chocolate, peeled off the wrapper and went *ka-chomp*. And he looked down, and there was half his tooth sticking out of the chocolate … it must have been like biting down on an iron bar.' Angus's peculiar diet—chocolate milk, spaghetti bolognese, chocolate, toasted cheese sandwiches, B&H ciggies—is staggering to Rudd. 'Half the time we don't know how Angus keeps on living.'

Bon Scott, meanwhile, turns his attention to the 'other three'—Evans, Malcolm, and Rudd—who he insists fares the best with women. 'They do the least moving about on stage, and they still pull more chicks than Angus or me. Bloody unfair it is. Being a singer ain't what it used to be—not in this band, anyway.'

Earlier in the day, the band played on a barge afloat on Sydney Harbour, beneath the Harbour Bridge, as part of a free show sponsored by local radio station 2SM. Below them on the bill are Billy Thorpe, The Ted Mulry Gang, John Paul Young, Finch, and Dark Tan. Bon arrived for the show in wraparound shades and sporting a mullet haircut, nursing a carton of beer and a set of bagpipes, grinning from ear to ear. Throughout the afternoon, eager fans jump in the drink and swim to the pontoon, where they dangle from the edge of the stage, soggy and starstruck.

Meanwhile, Bon records a radio jingle for 2SM. The lyrics are a landmark in local music: 'Roll over to our place and rock / Rock over to our place and roll / Roll over to our place, the one and only rock place / Where music's good for your soul / 2SM's the place to rock / 2SM's the place to roll / Roll over to our place, the one and only rock place / Rockin' down at 2SM.'

The band are now living in temporary digs at Sydney's Sebel Townhouse, except for Malcolm and Angus, who are staying with family at Burwood. Manager Browning, meanwhile, heads to the airport, to fly to the UK ahead of the others. He has a very clear plan for the band: to get them in front of audiences. 'There are some bands in England who don't sell a lot of records but are incredibly popular in concert,' he tells a reporter. 'Other bands get their records on radio and have hits but can't fill a concert hall on tour.' AC/DC, he figures, can achieve both.

In an interview with RAM, Browning makes it clear that AC/DC are an Aussie band and always will be. 'We don't want to give the impression we're glad to get out of Australia to try and make it elsewhere … AC/DC are an Australian band and, as far as we can see, want to stay based here.'

> **He's developed, has Angus. A year ago he was a raver who wore a schoolboy's satchel while playing guitar, just for the dare of it. Now he is the spunky guitarist in a schoolboy's satchel whose stage antics make the St Vitus Dance look tame.**
>
> ANTHONY O'GRADY, RAM, 1976

April 1 The band are interviewed by Countdown's Molly Meldrum at Sydney Airport, as they prepare to board a Garuda 707 for London. The trip will take thirty-six hours—a journey so lengthy that the less temperate members of the band will have to deal with two hangovers en route.

Before their sit-down interview with Meldrum, they record a series of promos for the show, proving that when it comes to self-promotion, they're a hell of a great rock band.

'Hi there, this is the boys here,' says Malcolm, trying hard not to look at the cue card just out of shot, 'and we're just reminding you that you're tuned to Countdown, Australia's top rock show.'

Angus also gives it a shot, pulling the most earnest face he can muster while trying to maintain eye contact with the camera. 'Hi, this is Angus from AC/DC, reminding you that you're on the top rock show in Australia, *Countdown*.' His eyes then turn to his right, hoping for a thumbs-up from the producer, which is duly given.

Bon is asked to project into the near future and speak as if he's already in the UK. 'Hello, this is Bon from AC/DC here,' he lisps grandly, all the while nursing a beer, 'and although we're overseas at the moment, dining with the queen, we haven't forgotten about you *Countdown* fans.'

Then the pre-trip interview begins.

Meldrum: 'Here we are at Mascot Airport to say farewell to AC/DC. What do you think you owe your success to?'

Bon, in a rare serious moment: 'It's nothing to do with us at all. Our success is due to the taste of the public.'

Angus, sporting a pudding bowl haircut that would have done Friar Tuck proud, drags on a ciggie and laughs.

Meldrum: 'So, what's going to be released in the UK?'

Malcolm: 'It's a combination of *High Voltage* and the *T.N.T.* album together, as one album called *High Voltage*.'

The talk turns to bagpipes, and the idea to use them on 'Long Way To The Top'; Bon grins and says he always knew how to 'blow and finger'. Angus keeps puffing away, looking like a guy who'd much rather be on a stage. He only speaks when Molly asks that old go-to journo question about his influences (rock'n'roll), and then about how it feels to be 'taking on the Poms'.

'We are confident,' Angus says, 'but not overconfident.'

Angus takes another puff on his B&H and wishes the discussion over. Then, Alberts labelmate Ted Mulry gatecrashes the interview, and an impromptu sing-along of 'It's A Long Way' ensues. Ted is hoisted high by Mark, Bon, and Angus, like a sporting hero—and then they're off.

STILL FINDING THEIR WAY IN THE UK, THE BAND STRIKE A DEFIANT POSE AT SHEPPERTON STUDIOS. LEFT TO RIGHT: MALCOLM YOUNG, MARK EVANS, BON SCOTT, ANGUS YOUNG, AND PHIL RUDD.

April 4 Today, the #1 single in the UK is Brotherhood Of Man's 'Save Your Kisses For Me', closely followed by ABBA's 'Fernando' and Billy Ocean's 'Love Really Hurts Without You'. Yet just the day before, the Sex Pistols packed the Nashville Rooms in London. Somewhere around this time, frontman Johnny Rotten informs *Sounds*: 'I hate hippies and what they stand for. I hate long hair. I hate pub bands. I want people to see us and start something, or else I'm just wasting my time.' AC/DC, clearly, are entering a musical minefield.

Soon after arriving in London, Bon Scott is having a quiet drink at a pub in Finchley that he used to frequent when he was in the UK with Fraternity. Within minutes of finding his favourite barstool, Scott is hit with a beer mug. He returns to the band's digs with a dislocated jaw and missing several teeth, swearing blind (when he can swear) that he's been the victim of collateral damage. 'It wasn't even my fight,' he insists.

The band's coffers are lightened some $2,000 to pay for Bon's new set of chompers. It's hardly the best way to begin their UK assault.

> **"We've always been a rock'n'roll band, that's always what we've played. That's what we always want to keep playing: rock'n'roll."**
>
> ANGUS YOUNG TO MOLLY MELDRUM, APRIL 1976

April 23 Having been stuck twiddling their thumbs for several weeks in the wake of the death of Paul Kossoff and the cancelled Back Street Crawler tour, and with Scott's new dentures now in place, the band finally make their UK debut, at a nondescript Hammersmith pub called the Red Cow, not far from their digs at 49 Inverness Terrace, Bayswater. They are booked to play two sets, for a fee of £35. A sign outside the pub reads, 'AC/DC—from Australia!' Ian Dury & The Blockheads played there recently; likewise pub-rockers Bees Make Honey.

Recalling the night for *Classic Rock*, Malcolm Dome, who was at the gig, sets the scene: 'The Red Cow was an unpretentious West London boozer-cum-venue, with a reputation for supporting young bands. The action took place at the back of the pub, in a sweatbox of a room with an official capacity of 250 and toilets that were in a constant state of disarray due to a stream of people clambering in through the windows to avoid paying to get in.

On arrival at the Red Cow, the band are greeted by the sight of a near-empty room—Patti Smith is the big draw across town—and the publican's two growling, hellhound Dobermans, who snap at them as they set up. Yet, from the opener 'Live Wire' onward, they play as though the crowd numbers thirty *thousand*, not thirty. Angus even drops to the floor and performs a stellar dying-bug routine during 'Baby, Please Don't Go'.

During a break between sets, the few punters left in the room disappear, leaving the group wondering if they'll be playing to themselves for the rest of the night. In fact, those who saw the first set have gone out to hit the phones and tell their friends to get down to the Red Cow—quickly. By the start of the second set, the room is bursting with bodies—among them Silver Smith, a woman with whom Bon Scott had an affair in 1971. They go home together that night.

Now, with way more onlookers sardined into the room, Angus decides to bust out all his best moves. At one stage, mid-solo, he dashes out of the door of the pub and down Hammersmith Road, a roadie close behind him, while the rest of the band play on.

When this now-legendary gig ends, AC/DC's UK booking agent, Richard Griffiths, who runs Headline Artists, walks over to the band, shaking his head in wonder.

'That,' he gasps, 'was the loudest, meanest thing I've ever heard in my life.'

Not long after, bassist Evans meets a fellow Aussie at the Red Cow.

'Did you know AC/DC play around here?' the drinker asks the bemused bassist. 'We're doing some gigs—my name's Mark Evans.'

'That's quite a coincidence,' Evans replies. '*My* name is Mark Evans, and I play bass in AC/DC.'

The surrogate Evans explains that the line works a treat with the 'chicks'.

'You just did it to the wrong guy, mate,' the real Mark Evans replies.

The band travel to Edinburgh to play the Sighthill Campus, a show organised by the Napier College Student Union. Usually, the student's union can only afford to pay bands fifteen quid, but after hearing their Australian recordings, they agree to up the fee to £50 for AC/DC. Ticket prices are duly increased, from 50p to 75p. One hundred and fifty punters catch the show.

April 26 AC/DC play a free gig at the Nashville Rooms in London, billed as an 'Antipodean Punk Extravaganza', pulling in around sixty fans. Three weeks earlier, the venue hosted the Sex Pistols, along with such other acts of the moment as The Stranglers and The 101ers, fronted by Joe Strummer—the very bands with whom AC/DC insist they have no connection.

A group named Captain Video open for AC/DC at the Nashville. Their manager, Bryan Taylor, is standing behind the mixing desk when Malcolm Young strikes his first power chord in anger and the band pile-drive their way into 'Live Wire'. 'From then on,' he later writes of the experience, 'I was on another planet. This was raw energy: loud, proud, vibrant.'

Caroline Coon reviews the Nashville Rooms show for *Melody Maker*. Unlike other writers of the time, she resists the inclination to slag off the Aussie rockers—she does make references to 'outback rednecks' and 'macho-chunder bar proppers', but insists neither tag fits AC/DC—before locating the band's secret weapon: their schoolboy guitarist.

'In essence,' she writes, 'AC/DC are nothing new. The legs-astride, uncompromisingly male stance of Malcolm Young (rhythm guitar), Phillip Rudd (drums), and Mark Evans (bass), their faded denims and sweat-soaked T-shirts, are a familiar sight in the rock'n'roll arena. … What, though, makes them a band to be seen and heard, are the extraordinary, virtuoso antics of the lead guitarist, sixteen-year-old [sic] Angus Young. The rest of the band are fine foils for him as he gives a not-seen-since-Quasimodo-did-a-dive-and-Richard-Neville-left-the-Old-Bailey performance of a doubled-up school kid in the throes of an ecstatic mutation with his guitar. (He wears the appropriate flannel drag and satchel).'

April 30 The international version of the *High Voltage* album is released on Atco. The album comprises songs from both the original *High Voltage* and *T.N.T.* The track listing is: 'It's A Long Way To The Top (If You Wanna Rock'n'roll)' / 'Rock'n'roll Singer' / 'The Jack' / 'Live Wire' / 'T.N.T.' / 'Can I Sit Next To You, Girl' / 'Little Lover' / 'She's Got Balls' / 'High Voltage'.

Interestingly, Angus is the only band member to appear on the cover of this edition of the album, caught mid-solo as a lightning bolt hits him. It's clear who Atlantic believe to be the star of the band. (The European edition uses an abstract, colour-drenched image of Bon and Angus, which only goes to show that pink is definitely not their colour.)

NME doesn't bother to review the record, while *Melody Maker* dismisses it as 'the same old boogie'. *Sounds'* Geoff Barton, however, gives *High Voltage* a big thumbs-up, calling it a 'tonic in the midst of the all-too-serious, poker-faced groups of today. If there ever was a good time band, this is it. … Angus Young's guitar holds it all together with quick bursts and reeling riffs which, together with his inexhaustible onstage energy, would seem to suggest that he's hooked on quite a strong stimulant. Probably orange Smarties.'

Not surprisingly, it is *Sounds*—and especially the writer Phil Sutcliffe—that fast become AC/DC's cheerleaders, even if, as Sutcliffe admits, the band's male chauvinism is a bit hard to swallow. 'They stand for everything I disagree with about our chauvinist view of the woman's role,' he writes, 'and yet they're so totally honest, open and funny about it I got carried away with liking them.'

High Voltage is panned by US *Rolling Stone* upon its release in North America. 'Those concerned with the future of hard rock may take solace in knowing that with the release of the first US album by these Australian gross-out champions, the genre has unquestionably hit its all-time low,' writes Billy Altman. 'Things can only get better (at least I hope so).

'Stupidity bothers me,' he huffs in conclusion. 'Calculated stupidity offends me.'

High Voltage reaches a 'peak' of #146 on the *Billboard* 200 chart. Over time,

THE BAND'S DEBUT INTERNATIONAL RELEASE, *HIGH VOLTAGE*, IS A MIXTURE OF TRACKS FROM THEIR FIRST TWO AUSTRALIAN ALBUMS. IT CONTAINS THE CLASSICS 'T.N.T.', 'HIGH VOLTAGE', AND 'IT'S A LONG WAY TO THE TOP (IF YOU WANNA ROCK'N'ROLL)'.

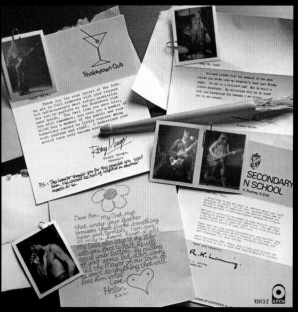

" *At the time, the British music scene was in a state of flux. Pub rock was thriving, though punk was beginning to assert itself … High Voltage and T.N.T. were only available on import in the UK, and any buzz was confined to the country's more clued-up rock fans. The band may have been stars back home in Oz, but there was work to be done overseas.* **"**

MALCOLM DOME, *CLASSIC ROCK*

though, it will go on to sell more than three million copies. Fast-forward seven years, and by the time of the 1983 *Rolling Stone Record Guide*, the mag's opinion of *High Voltage* has changed dramatically, with writer David Fricke sensing the magic amid the smuttiness. 'What the critics don't know, the heavy-metal kids understand,' he writes. 'Led by the tenacious axe-wielding Scots-born Young brothers Angus and Malcolm, AC/DC are nothing more or less than rock'n'roll party thunder, 110-decibel escapism fired up by panzer division riffs 'n' rhythms, Angus's mad-dog stare romps in sweaty schoolboy uniform, and the lecherous growl of … singer Bon Scott.'

May 'It's A Long Way To The Top' is released as AC/DC's debut UK single, but it doesn't chart (nor does the *High Voltage* album). However, 'Long Way' is the 'Hit Pick Of The Week' at Radio Luxembourg, and influential BBC DJ John Peel also plays the song.

In *Record Mirror & Disc* magazine, James Hamilton writes of the single, 'These Aussie youngsters boogie Stones/Elton John style … with bagpipe noises yet!' Over at *Melody Maker*, Caroline Coon compares them to KISS, which would have irked members of AC/DC, who had no time for the American cartoon rockers, having seen them play in London and laughed their way through the gig. The band's collective response is, 'This is the opposition?'

Countdown sources a London-based crew and a reporter named Doug Crawford to speak with the band. Angus and Bon quickly take charge of the interview, which is conducted on the move in Covent Garden. Bon wears a pair of dangerously tight shorts and a big smile, a banana tucked suggestively into his waistband.

'How's the trip been going?' Crawford asks.

'When the people come to see us,' Bon explains, between mouthfuls, 'we give them the show we give the Australian people, you know?'

'Are you rich?' the interviewer asks. 'Are you making the bread?'

'We just bought Big Ben,' Angus deadpans, his hands on his hips, barely suppressing a smirk.

The conversation shifts to songwriting: how do they find the time to write? What inspires them?

Hotel rooms are handy places to work on new material, Angus explains. And as for inspiration, well, he has that covered too. Australian marsupials are a big motivator, apparently.

Which ones?

'Kangaroos.'

Talk turns to the legends—the Stones and The Beatles.

'We're better,' Angus scoffs.

'Who needs them?' adds Bon, equally unimpressed. 'They're last year's model.'

By now, Bon has left the band's Inverness Terrace HQ and moved in with Silver Smith, a woman with a wild streak and access to the planet's biggest rock stars. The rest of the band slyly refer to them as 'Rod and Britt'—a nod to current power couple Rod Stewart and Britt Ekland. The apartment they share is mockingly referred to as a 'hippie haven'—hippies being the enemy in the eyes of Angus, in particular, who hasn't changed his opinion of dope smokers as 'hippie cunts'. Bon is currently working his way through a bottle of Scotch a day, so it's not all weed and incense.

While on a trip to Paris with Smith, Bon strikes up a friendship with Bernard Bonvoisin, from the French band Trust. When Scott and Smith return to London, manager Browning receives a call; Scott is in hospital, recovering from what is likely an overdose.

May 8 NME runs its first coverage of the band, and it typifies the current resistance to such a scruffy lot as AC/DC—surely, no band in London in 1976 with a functioning radar would be seen with tattoos and denim and long hair. 'In the middle of the great British Punk Rock Explosion,' writer Phil McNeill sniffs, 'a quintet of similarly ruthless Aussies has just swaggered like a cat among London's surly, self-consciously paranoid pigeons … and with a sense of what sells rather than what's cool, they could well clean up.'

Angus still has the local press convinced he's only sixteen—and, to his credit, McNeill recognises how essential the human livewire is to the band's success. 'They would never have blown up the storm they generated without … Angus Young. … Angus Young slobbering and doing a Jagger duckwalk in short pants is a surprisingly durable laugh.'

The article's title—'I Wallaby Your Man'—is absolutely cringe-worthy. The band photo that runs with the piece is even worse; it's captioned 'More chunder from Down Under'.

A week later, *Sounds'* Giovanni Dodomo mixes a strong whiff of condescension—his opening paragraph shoehorns in nods to Edna Everage, Barry McKenzie, Fosters, 'Abbos', and kangaroos—with a measured appreciation for Angus. 'They have the added appeal of a genuinely outré lead guitarist in Angus Young … [he] could very well find himself an alcove in the guitar-player's Hall of Fame.' Yet Dodomo's read on Bon Scott—'competent but undistinguished'—is very wide of the mark.

May 11–12 The band play their first two shows at influential London venue the Marquee, which through the years has hosted residencies by The Rolling Stones, The Yardbirds, Led Zeppelin, Jimi Hendrix, and Pink Floyd. The gig is set in place by their booker, Richard Griffiths. Angus shocks punters by leaping from one table to the next while playing, scattering drinks and ashtrays (and onlookers) in all directions. Their setlist, by now, is firmly set in place, with the constants being 'Live Wire' (their standard opener), 'High Voltage', 'Baby, Please Don't Go', 'T.N.T.', 'Can I Sit Next To You, Girl', and 'It's A Long Way To The Top'. The show on the 11th, where AC/DC open for the Kossoff-less Back Street Crawler, is a charity gig in aid of the Free Clinic. The cover charge is £1.

May 14–23 More gigs take place, at Dingwalls and the Fulham Greyhound in London, as well as Glasgow University; they also make a return appearance to the Red Cow, the site of their UK debut. They are so well received in Scotland that during subsequent visits they're treated like homecoming kings (it helps, of course, that there are three Scots in the band).

May 25 All of the band, bar Angus, see The Rolling Stones play the third of six gigs at Earls Court in London. Angus instead opts to stay behind at the band's new digs at 23 Lonsdale Road in Barnes and work on what his bandmates call 'the longest guitar solo in rock history'. In his downtime, bassist Evans buys a white Fender Precision bass, 1966 model, from Macari's Music on Charing Cross Road, paying £120. (He will later be offered—and refuse—$25,000 US for the instrument.)

Sounds writer Geoff Barton visits the band at their Barnes HQ for a cover story to run on June 12. 'The first thing that strikes you about the band is their smallness—they're all around five feet four inches; the second is their fresh-faced and bright-eyed appearances. On closer inspection, however, you find that, although the skin is smooth enough, it looks a good deal older than it should: the eyes are glazed more than shiny. On the road wear and tear, without a doubt.' Angus has Barton, too, bamboozled; the writer is convinced he's only sixteen. 'It must be said,' Barton notes, 'he looks even younger.'

The writer looks on as Coral Browning, Michael Browning's sister, collects Angus's two uniforms from the drycleaners. 'Thank God,' Coral sighs. 'I was afraid that the shop would refuse to handle them—they were absolutely filthy. Angus sweats a lot, you see, and we have to clean them regularly. It's unheard-of for him to wear the same suit two nights running. And, on top of that, when Angus gets carried away on stage—you know

THE BON AND ANGUS SHOW ON FULL DISPLAY AT THE NASHVILLE ROOMS, MAY 27 1976. BY NOW, THE BAND HAVE BEGUN TO FIND AN AUDIENCE IN THE UK AMONG THE SAME KINDS OF ROWDY KIDS WHO HAVE CHAMPIONED THE GROUP BACK IN AUSTRALIA.

how it is—his nose begins to run. Ugh! There are always some horrible streaks of snot down the fronts of his jackets.'

All-night card games are a regular event at Lonsdale Road—interminable affairs that give Angus the chance to remind the pot smokers what he thinks of their habit. 'You know why they call it dope, don't you?' he asks his glassy-eyed bandmates.

Michael Browning, meanwhile, has set in place a deal for the band with legendary amp-maker Jim Marshall, who supplies the band with gear. Marshalls were the amps of choice for Jeff Beck and Jimi Hendrix, two guitarists that the Youngs respect hugely. After they test out their gear one lunchtime at their new digs on Lonsdale Road, several angry neighbours slip notes under their door, demanding they keep the noise down.

May 27 The band play a free show at the Nashville Rooms in London.

May 28 AC/DC open for the remnants of Paul Kossoff's Back Street Crawler. One witness to their not-so-well-received set at Surrey University is the co-founder of their label, Atlantic Records, Ahmet Ertegun. (Back Street Crawler are also signed to Atlantic.) A suave, sophisticated 'music man' with an amazing track record, having worked with such greats as Ray Charles, Aretha Franklin, and Led Zeppelin, Ertegun is someone that AC/DC need very much to have on their team. Fortunately for the band, he only sees the latter part of the gig, so he isn't aware that they've just played before a subdued audience that, in bassist Evans's estimation, is more suited 'to a library, maybe even a morgue'. As such, when Ertegun greets Scott and Evans at the bar, he gushes, 'You boys brained them out there.'

May 29–30 AC/DC play another gig with Back Street Crawler, at Barbarella's in Birmingham. The show will later be bootlegged as *Barbarella's Got Balls*, and rightly so—they're on fire. 'This one you should know by now,' Scott says, as he leads the band into 'She's Got Balls'. 'It's all about your mother. She makes my heart race,' he growls, clearly in a poetic mood, 'every time she sits on my face.'

During 'The Jack', Scott, very much a man of the people, surveys the crowd. 'All the guys here tonight who have had the jack before, sing the chorus with me,' he requests. 'How many guys here have had the jack before?' After counting perhaps three blokes willing to admit to the cursed clap, he reconsiders. 'OK, how about all the guys here who *haven't* had the jack before, you sing? There's more of you.'

Dr Scott then lists all the variations of VD he can think of: 'Syphilis. Gonorrhoea. Crabs. Thrush. Oh, the dirty little whore!'

Tracklisting: 'Live Wire' / 'Rock'n'roll Singer' / 'Jailbreak' / 'She's Got Balls' / 'The Jack' / 'Rocker' / 'High Voltage' / 'Baby, Please Don't Go'.

May 30 Once again sharing a bill with Back Street Crawler, the band rock the Victoria Palace in London.

June 2 Backstage at a sparsely attended gig at the Retford Porterhouse, *Sounds'* Geoff Barton asks Angus why he doesn't drink, when the others clearly enjoy a tipple. 'If I drank, I'd be off,' Angus explains. 'The other members of the band have to drink to come up to my level.'

Barton asks him if AC/DC are the biggest Australian band of the moment.

'I'd say we are,' Angus replies.

The band, as usual, open with 'Live Wire', which inspires this from Barton, who is watching Angus intently: 'First, his upper lip curls up like a roller blind and you half-smile. Then he stoops, peering out at the audience from beneath the peak of his school cap and you snigger. Then he begins to strut about the stage and you giggle. By the time the number has built up sufficiently and his frail arm comes down on his guitar strings with a loud "daaauuummm!" you should be chortling with delight.'

Having shed most of his clothes during 'Baby, Please Don't Go,' Angus takes a lap of the venue, playing all the while, a roadie trailing in his wake. Then, upon returning to the stage, he leaps onto Scott's shoulders, and they're off again.

'Back on stage again, Angus hasn't finished yet,' Barton writes. 'He begins rushing up and down like a lightning streak—as the music gathers speed, so it acts as a series of electrical stimuli to the young lad. Ultimately, he falls to the floor and there, still holding his instrument, turns a full circle, crab-like, on his back in the grime, twitches violently, and then hits the final note of the evening with such force you expect the stage to cave in and see the whole band disappear in a cloud of dust.'

At the end of a long drive back to Barnes—it's around 4am when they return—Angus and Scott discuss what would be the ideal end to the night.

'A huge, comfortable, squashy waterbed,' suggests Scott, 'a woman lying right beside you …'

'And a big pair of tits in your face,' says Angus, neatly ending Scott's fantasy.

June 3 AC/DC record an in-studio session for John Peel, for broadcast on June 21, comprising 'Live Wire', 'High Voltage', 'Can I Sit Next To You, Girl', and 'Little Lover'. A slightly more restrained than usual take of 'Live Wire' is a highlight; the band are in top form, Evans's rocksteady bass prominent in the mix. It's the only Peel session the band ever records, but he'll remain a solid supporter of AC/DC.

June 4 AC/DC play again at London's legendary Marquee, a sauna-like room that is fast becoming a favourite of theirs. They'll rock the Marquee eight more times in 1976, before graduating to larger London venues.

Over the next few days, more dates follow, at the Fulham Greyhound, the Greyhound in Croydon, and the Guildhall in Portsmouth.

June 11 The twenty-date UK leg of the Lock Up Your Daughters tour begins at Glasgow City Hall—the first of nine shows AC/DC will play in the city during Bon Scott's tenure with the band. *Sounds* magazine sponsors the tour, along with the promoter Rockworld. The tour poster, which uses the Graeme Webber shot of a demented Angus in the dunny at Mentone in 1975, promises 'a right summer school-time frolic'. (Original tickets for this tour—starting at a cheap 50p, thanks to a voucher found inside *Sounds*—today fetch upward of $1,000 on eBay.)

Prior to AC/DC's set, a KISS concert film is screened. Drummer Rudd is no fan; to him, they're 'like a cartoon band'.

Zealous Glasgow city officials turn on the house lights at 10pm, announcing over the PA that the show is over, but the curtains part to reveal the band belting out 'It's A Long Way To The Top', Angus perched on top of a plinth. The response down the front is so feverish that fans tear up seats in the first two rows. The *Sounds* review of the gig captures the madness. 'The audience … nearly demolished the staid City Hall.' Back in Oz, *RAM* describes it as a 'riot', adding, 'The group are attracting a young, volatile working-class audience.'

A week later, *Sounds* runs a photo of the bill from Glasgow City Council for damages to the venue's seats, curtains and doors. A council representative writes to the band's label, Atlantic, stating, in part, 'We have been advised that the audience in attendance at the recent concert … were for the most of the performance entirely out of control and were actually standing up on the seats.' (A photo of Angus clutching this letter like a proud parent will soon be used as promo for the band.)

ANGUS STANDS TALL AT THE MARQUEE, JULY 10 1976. THE VENUE BECOMES A SECOND HOME FOR AC/DC; THEY BREAK HOUSE RECORDS AND FIND AN ADVOCATE IN THE OWNER, JACK BARRIE.

While in Glasgow, the non-Scots in the band—Rudd and Evans—are left wondering how many relatives their bandmates actually have in the city: every second local claims to be related to Angus, Malcolm, and/or Bon. The Young brothers briefly drop into a heavily accented brogue, clearly inspired by their surrounds. Fans refer to Angus as 'the wee man'. Scott and Rudd, meanwhile, rent a car and drive around Loch Lomond.

An ongoing part of the Lock Up Your Daughters tour is the 'dress like a schoolboy' competition; most crowds include an interesting assortment of hairy-legged, spotty-faced, mature-aged schoolboys.

The band's setlist for the tour typically features 'Live Wire', 'She's Got Balls', 'It's A Long Way To The Top', 'Can I Sit Next To You, Girl', 'The Jack', 'High Voltage', 'T.N.T.', and 'Baby, Please Don't Go', with occasional performances of 'Rocker', 'Dirty Deeds Done Dirt Cheap', and 'School Days'.

> **"There are three or four top bands back home … but each tends to cater for a certain audience. We're the only band that's able to cover the whole spectrum. This is what we wanted right from the start. We want to appeal to everyone and get rich quick. I've got this plan to buy Tasmania, you see."**
> ANGUS YOUNG TO *SOUNDS*, JUNE 1976

June 12 *Sounds* publishes a letter from Jane Hunt of Lowestoft in Suffolk, as the opening to a cover story of the band. 'Whilst scanning your pages over the past few weeks,' she writes, 'I have come across pictures of a rather delectable-looking creature who goes under the name of Angus Young and who is apparently the lead guitarist with an Aussie-rock outfit called AC/DC.

'As an ardent fan of punk-rock (and schoolboys), I reckon it to be quite possible that I should appreciate their music and wondered if you could get me any further info on this young man (sorry!) and his side-kicks.

'Surely you're not going to leave me drooling over the photos and not tell me more about Mr. Young and Co?'

Angus alone appears on the *Sounds* cover—another first. Grinning madly, he gives the camera a fearful stare. 'Would you give a job to this school leaver?' the cover line asks.

That night, AC/DC fill the Leith Theatre in Edinburgh. Bon is in an especially playful mood, even taking a cheeky swipe at the Sex Pistols, introducing 'Can I Sit Next To You, Girl' as '"Can I Shit Next To You, Girl", as John Lydon would say.' He also riffs on the lyrics of 'The Jack', snickering the line—'I curdled her cream'—like a seasoned comic, before leading the crowd into a hearty 'she's got the jack' chant. He then surveys the audience to once again see exactly who has had the curse. 'Put your hands up. And keep your hands up if you've still got it.' When some in the Leith Theatre admit to the condition, Scott laughs, 'You dirty bastards!'

June 14 While playing the Top Rank Suite in Sheffield, Bon hoists Angus onto his shoulders, and they do the obligatory lap of the venue, but when they return to the stage, Angus collapses, clearly exhausted. Over the coming days, further shows follow at St George's Hall in Bradford, the Civic Hall in Bedworth, and the Liverpool Stadium.

June 20 The band fill the Palace Lido at Douglas. Angus sports his green schoolboy's outfit, but by the end of the gig he's down to nothing more than a pair of Union Jack boxers and a cheeky grin.

Journalist Phil Sutcliffe conducts an on-the-road interview with the band that will run in *Sounds* on July 24, under the poetic title 'More Songs About Humping And Booze'. Angus and Bon talk about life with no fixed address. 'None of us have had our own places to live for the past two years,' says Scott. 'I rented a flat here, but I was only there for six weeks. All we've got is our parents' homes in Australia.'

Angus also speaks about the ways in which he's reformed Scott. 'You should have seen the man when I first met him,' Angus chuckles. 'He couldn't speak English. It was all "fuck, cunt, piss, shit". I introduced him to a new side of life. Sent 'im home with a dictionary.'

'He taught me how to say, "please fuck",' Scott confirms. 'And "thank you" afterward.'

June 23 Tonight's gig is at Mumbles in Swansea and is not a tour highlight. According to Evans, about 'five people turned up'. Over the next few nights, AC/DC play the Festival Hall in Corby and the Civic Hall in Guildford.

June 27 AC/DC rock the bejesus out of the Mayfair Suite in Birmingham. One convert would later write of this show, 'I was thirteen and knew nothing of the band … it was an incredibly rocking event. Absolutely fucking awesome.'

June 28 'Jailbreak' is released as the band's new single in Australia, reaching the Top 10 and charting for nineteen weeks. (At the time, ABBA's 'Fernando' is entrenched at the top of the Oz singles chart, sitting tight there for a remarkable fourteen weeks.) The release of 'Jailbreak' coincides with the announcement that AC/DC have now sold a million dollars' worth of records in Australia.

The fastest knees in the West

AC/DC, outrageous Aussie punk-rock combo, this week start their rampage across Britain under the SOUNDS banner. Are we doing the right thing? Are schoolboys the future of rock and roll? GEOFF BARTON reports . . .

> **"** *It's Angus's knees, you see. The more he shows them, bruises and all, the better we go over.* **"**

BON SCOTT TO GEOFF BARTON,
SOUNDS, JUNE 1976

June 30 The *Sounds* tour reaches the Top Rank Suite in Southampton, where Angus does his obligatory lap of the venue astride Scott's shoulders. The tour keeps on rolling over the first few days of July, with shows at the Woodville Halls in Gravesend, the Top Rank Suite in Plymouth, and Johnson Hall in Yeovil.

July 4 AC/DC play in Brighton—the second-to-last show of the *Sounds* tour. On the same night, The Clash open for the Sex Pistols at the Black Swan in Sheffield. A reporter asks Angus Young whether he relates to punk bands—does he feel any empathy with them? His reply is blunt. 'None.'

When Bon is asked a similar question, he replies, 'What's a punk band?' He insists that AC/DC were making a noise in the UK 'before the Sex Pistols were even thought of'—a comment that, that while not chronologically precise, clarifies his feelings about such musical fads.

Angus also gets into this in a catch-up with *Countdown*'s Molly Meldrum. 'When we arrived [in the UK], they were already getting into this punk stuff, so for us, we were lucky in the respect that people who came and saw us, it was something different. We always steered away from someone calling us punks or whatever, we kept away from any banner. A tag's a bit shallow.'

'They're just shite,' Angus tells Sydney's 2JJ, when he's once again asked about the new punk acts. 'They can't play, they can't sing.'

Malcolm has no time at all for categorising music as 'punk' or 'not punk'. 'You can classify bands in two groups: good and bad,' he tells a reporter. 'We're the good.'

Bon displays an equally strong resistance to the term 'heavy metal' when a reporter stupidly asks him how it feels to be a 'heavy metal freak'. 'We've nothing to do with that,' he snaps back. 'We play quality rock'n'roll.'

THE RELEASE OF 'JAILBREAK' ON JUNE 28 1976 COINCIDES WITH THE NEWS THAT THE BAND HAVE SOLD ONE MILLION DOLLARS' WORTH OF RECORDS IN AUSTRALIA.

Rolling Stone magazine also points out these differences in its report on the group. 'The only thing AC/DC share with such current metal champions as Ted Nugent, Van Halen, and English upstarts Def Leppard, Judas Priest, and Saxon is the universal scorn of critics. Compared to the boorish, macho plodding of most heavy-metal heathens, the AC/DC sound is nothing more and nothing less than aggressively catchy song hooks brutalized by a revved-up boogie rhythm, Malcolm's jackhammer riffing, [and] Angus's guitar histrionics.'

Punk may have been the music mood *du jour*, but the UK charts don't reflect what's happening in the clubs and pubs of London. The current Top 5 contains The Real Thing's 'You To Me Are Everything', Candi Staton's 'Young Hearts Run Free', Demis Roussos's 'The Roussos Phenomenon', Our Kid's 'You Just Might See Me Cry', and Bryan Ferry's 'Let's Stick Together'. The Top 5 albums, meanwhile, come from Rod Stewart, ABBA, The Carpenters, John Denver, and Wings. Rock albums in the Top 30 are scarce; only Ritchie Blackmore's Rainbow, Thin Lizzy, and Blue Öyster Cult are making an impression.

July 7 The Lock Up Your Daughters tour wraps up with a full house at the Lyceum Ballroom in London, a gig hosted by John Peel. The night is soured before it begins, however, when the band's lighting director, Herc, has a serious fall while setting up for the show. He ends up in hospital, badly injured, and is eventually shipped back to Oz. The night ends with a 'schoolgirl we'd most like to … ' competition, which is won by one Jayne Haynes from Harrow, Middlesex, who also scores a night with Mark Evans (not part of the official prize).

July 8 The band play a five-song live set at the Paris Theatre in London—'Live Wire', 'It's A Long Way To The Top', 'Soul Stripper', 'Baby, Please Don't Go', and 'High Voltage'—that's recorded for the *In Concert* series on the BBC. Angus clearly has the MC bluffed by his schoolboy attire. When he introduces the band after 'Long Way', he says, 'Angus Young is only sixteen years old—a schoolboy, he's even got his school uniform on and [is] playing with a satchel on his back.' (He's just hit twenty-one.)

The BBC presses one hundred copies of the 'album' for use by its affiliates—excluding 'Baby', and with fellow Aussies Max Merritt & The Meteors on the flipside—under strict instructions that the records be returned after broadcast so they can be destroyed. Not surprisingly, a few copies find their way onto the bootleg market and become highly sought-after AC/DC collectibles.

Another bootleg, named *Remastered Beebs*, compiles fourteen choice cuts recorded for the BBC during 1976–79. *Track listing*: 'Live Wire' / 'It's A Long Way To The Top (If You Wanna Rock'n'roll)' / 'Soul Stripper' / 'High Voltage' / 'Let There Be Rock' / 'Problem Child' / 'Hell Ain't A Bad Place To Be' / 'Whole Lotta Rosie' / 'Shot Down In Flames' / 'Sin City' / 'The Jack' / 'Highway To Hell' / 'Girls Got Rhythm' / 'If You Want Blood (You've Got It)'.

July 9 Bon Scott turns thirty, and his bandmates throw him a party, but he fails to show. He later boasts to journalist Anthony O'Grady that he 'fucked my birthday in', getting down to business at ten minutes before midnight and finishing twenty-five minutes later. 'It's the first birthday I've done that.'

July 13 The band take part in Marc Bolan's *Rollin' Bolan* TV special, which is filmed at Wimbledon Theatre, playing 'Live Wire' and 'Can I Sit Next to You, Girl' Harry Vanda and George Young watch from the wings, clearly proud of their charges. Although forced to use unfamiliar gear, the band are blazing—their take on 'Live Wire' will one day emerge on YouTube, accompanied by the usual comments ('best band ever' / 'Bon Scott lives!').

By contrast, Marc Bolan is quite the sight: overweight, stumbling on high heels, his makeup running under the lights. 'I was waiting for him to go arse-up,' Mark Evans admits. 'He had the look of a guy who was rapidly nearing his use-by date.' Malcolm Young opts not to mention his obsession with T. Rex from just a few years earlier.

July 16 The band play their first gig on the continent, at Falkenberg in Sweden, followed by dates in Malmo, Stockholm, Vaxjo, and Anderstorp. The Swedish press refers to AC/DC as 'Australia's answer to Status Quo'. They've come a long way from the Waltzing Matilda and the Bondi Lifesaver, that's for sure, although the crowds—or lack thereof—probably remind them of their earliest gigs in Oz.

The Swedish promoter, Tomas Johansen, also represents ABBA; in exchange for these AC/DC dates, he is able to book an Australian tour for the Swedish pop act. ABBA will travel with an entourage of more than one hundred, flying in a 727 hired especially for the tour, and play for 160,000-plus people, shooting *ABBA: The Movie* as they traverse the country. (There's even a bomb scare at their final show in Perth—the type of high drama reserved for super-duper-stars. Proper pop madness.)

Meanwhile, AC/DC cross the Channel in an old tour bus that sometimes doubles as accommodation; they feed British coins into vending machines, which cough up croquettes and cigarettes. Angus, as is his wont, moans to manager Browning, 'What the fuck are we doing in Sweden?'

The band's first Swedish concert is at an old school dance hall. Only forty people turn up; ditto their gig in Stockholm. A punter swipes Angus's cap at the Falkenberg show, but returns it when he discovers it's too small and doesn't fit.

> **"We weren't really punks — we were just a bunch of stroppy dwarves, you know?"**
>
> PHIL RUDD ON THE PUNK ERA, AND AC/DC'S PLACE IN IT

While in Stockholm, some of the band are lounging by the hotel pool when a topless local saunters by. 'It was ten minutes before we could get up without offending public decency,' Scott tells a journalist.

The band will later admit, though, that while they did acquaint themselves with some female fans in Sweden, they were perhaps not the pick of the bunch. According to Malcolm, 'In Sweden, there are 90 percent beautiful women and 10 percent ugly—guess which ones we got?' Angus will later swear blind that drummer Rudd spent his downtime with 'this female wrestler'.

July 26 A recent AC/DC convert is Jack Barrie, the owner of the Marquee, who also helps organise the annual Reading Festival. He invites the band to stage an eight-week/eight-gig residency at the 700-capacity club—a real honour. He also writes to Atlantic, the group's label, describing AC/DC as 'the best band to appear at the Marquee since Led Zeppelin'.

Although there are barely more people in the room than on stage during the first night of the residency, positive word soon spreads about the band, and they swiftly break the attendance record. Duly inspired, Angus introduces a striptease into his stage act, usually culminating in a bared bum—the ol' 'browneye'. 'I think they thought I was some kind of male stripper at one point,' he later laughs.

He's not the only one to shed clothes during these gigs. Bon Scott tells a reporter from Melbourne's *Herald* that 'the place looked like a nudist colony by the time we finished'.

'The heat is beyond belief,' gasps *Sounds*' Phil Sutcliffe. 'The humidity is just a little lower than in the deep end at the municipal baths.' Or, in the words of Browning, 'The walls were like waterfalls of sweat.'

Posters promoting the band's Marquee shows capture Angus in his schoolboy clobber, mid-solo, mouth agape, hair flying, lost in music. As for Bon, he's now proudly describing himself as the 'flash in the middle' of the AC and DC in the band's logo.

Countdown's Molly Meldrum flies out to document the band's residency at the famous venue. 'He's the best thing I've seen since Pete Townshend,' one punter tells him, nodding toward Angus.

Back in Oz, the Marquee madness is mentioned in the *Australian Women's Weekly*, of all places. 'We came to Britain to plunder and pillage,' Angus reports, 'but so far we have only plundered. Perhaps we'll take the Tower of London,' he adds. 'We don't want Big Ben, because it keeps stopping.'

ANGUS TRIES TO SMOTHER BON WITH HIS GIBSON, ON STAGE AT THE ST ALBANS TOWN HALL ON AUGUST 7 1976, AS PART OF A LENGTHY NORTHERN SUMMER TOUR.

At some Marquee gigs, up to a thousand fans are shoehorned into the venue, while several big names turn up to check out these Aussie upstarts. Deep Purple's Ritchie Blackmore is perhaps the highest-profile of them, clearly having gotten over their dust-up back at Sunbury; he is accompanied by the loopy Screaming Lord Sutch, a Marquee local. Blackmore is keen to jam with AC/DC, but they're so drained after their gig that he's left alone on the stage, guitar in hand. An upset Blackmore allegedly tells a writer from *Melody Maker* that AC/DC are 'the zero degree of rock'n'roll'. Malcom Young has his own retort: 'We actually think he's the oldest form of low in rock'n'roll.'

Creedence Clearwater Revival's Doug Clifford and Stu Cook go as far as to contact Atlantic and offer their production services after witnessing the Angus and Bon show at the Marquee. The band politely refuse. They have Vanda & Young; who needs outsiders?

July 31 The band return to Barbarella's in Birmingham for a repeat performance.

August Bon reveals perhaps a touch too much in an interview with *RAM*, explaining that the song 'Squealer', from the soon-to-be-released *Dirty Deeds Done Dirt Cheap* LP, is about 'deflowering' a virgin. In a more reflective moment, he talks about 'Ride On', a slow blues from the album that will become something of an AC/DC classic. 'It's about a guy who gets pissed around by chicks,' he says, sounding like a man speaking from experience, 'and can't find what he wants.'

August 6 The band play the influential 76 Club in Burton-on-Trent. One audience member, clearly not yet wise to the ways of AC/DC, wonders why a kid is on stage. 'I remember thinking how novel it was to have a schoolboy mimicking playing the guitar,' Steve Bowring later writes on the 76club.org.uk. 'It was only after four tracks that I realised he was playing the bloody thing.'

August 7–12 Between dates in the Marquee residency, further gigs take place in St Albans, Plymouth, and Penzance, and at Dingwalls in London.

August 14 Performing 'Jailbreak' on the seventh episode of the Granada TV program *So It Goes*, Bon is bare-chested bar a jungle-print vest, his jeans as dangerously tight as ever, while Angus dons his basic schoolboy blues, his stick-insect legs on full display. During his blistering solo, Angus pulls the kind of demented face that only a mother could love—and who cares if he is miming? Two weeks later, on the same program, the Sex Pistols will blitz through 'Anarchy In The UK', months before its belated single release.

August 18 AC/DC play the Pavilion in Bath. Their opening act is Motörhead, who somehow manage to play even louder than Angus and co. Frontman Lemmy has recently been fired from Hawkwind for what he insists is the 'crime' of 'doing the wrong drugs'.

August 19–21 The band travel to Holland (later to become Angus's home) for two shows in Amsterdam and one in Rotterdam.

August 21 Harry Doherty's review of one of the Marquee shows runs in *Melody Maker*. His coverage typifies the sometimes-stuffy press reaction to AC/DC; it's as though they're being damned with faint praise. 'Scott could be a first-class frontman,' Doherty notes, 'instead of, as he strikes me, a poor cross between Alex Harvey and Steve Marriott. His enthusiasm did seem a trifle contrived at times.'

Doherty goes on to compare Angus Young to a 'rock'n'roll Norman Wisdom, only more retarded. Though not a great guitarist … he's a great showman.

'Where do AC/DC go from the Marquee in murky Wardour Street?' he ponders. 'Judging from the wild reaction of their audiences, they could just about slip comfortably into Status Quo's shoes once they have pulled their socks up.'

Over at the *NME*, the critical tide has begun to turn in AC/DC's favour. 'Musically, AC/DC aren't doing anything you haven't heard before, anything innovative,' writes Phil McNeill. 'But as the Bard of Richmond [Mick Jagger] wrote twelve years ago, It's the singer, not the song. They've got it, from the first volley of bass shots and menacing chording from the Youngs, Angus and Malcolm on lead and rhythm, that open "Live Wire", they're right there—driving, dirty, demented. Angus Young is a star … He has everything: technique, speed, sensational presence and the feverish energy and stamina of youth.'

Yet only *Sounds* consistently and unreservedly talks up AC/DC. Scenesters consider them simply too unfashionable in this year of punk.

August 23–24 It's so hot inside the Marquee that Angus ditches his standard school uniform altogether and plays in sneakers and jocks. Rather than their usual weekly gig, the band play on consecutive nights.

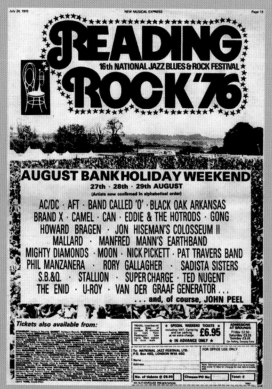

August 29 Thanks to the ongoing support of Marquee owner Jack Barrie, AC/DC have secured a mid-afternoon spot at the prestigious Reading Festival. This year's line-up includes Ted Nugent, Manfred Mann's Earth Band, Can, Eddie & The Hot Rods, Camel, Phil Manzanera, and Black Oak Arkansas. Many of AC/DC's favourite acts have played Reading, including The Rolling Stones in 1964, The Yardbirds in '65, and The Who in '66 and '69. It's a big moment for the band.

Quite an entourage accompanies the band to the site, including Michael Browning and his sister Coral, Harry Vanda and George Young, Atlantic's Phil Carson, and booking agent Richard Griffiths (who, much later, will manage One Direction). They stop en route at the Griffith family estate for lunch and a few games of croquet—hardly the typical recreational activity of a young rock band on the road.

The band members fully understand how important the Reading festival gig is. A blistering set will almost guarantee an upswing in sales for *High Voltage*, which until now has not exactly burned up the charts. Malcolm, usually the calmest man in the band pre-gig, is clearly nervous; Angus, by contrast, is always jittery before a show.

Once on stage, Bon Scott tries his best to get the crowd inspired. 'Hello there,' he yells. 'With all this rain we're having, the best thing to do about it is to cause some heat amongst ya to make it evaporate before it fucking hits ya, all right?' He gets nothing in return from the crowd but silence.

This high-profile gig is a disaster; it's AC/DC's first backward step since 'that cunt Kossoff' died earlier in the year. The general consensus is that a mid-afternoon set doesn't suit the band; they work better with a crowd fired up by booze and adrenaline. Another possibility is that the split-stage arrangement at Reading, which enables one band to set up while another plays, has restricted their ability to project to the entire audience. It's also likely that many in the crowd haven't seen the band before, and don't quite know what to expect. Whatever the reason, the response is apathetic, and the band know they've blown a big opportunity.

According to Malcolm Young, there's also some confusion offstage, regarding the influential DJ John Peel. 'Peel came up to see us there, but unfortunately one of the security blokes chucked him off when we were playing. So he wrote in the newspaper, "That's the last time I play one of these guys' fucking records." We didn't know anything about it. We didn't even have a roadie, let alone a security guy.'

Back at the band's Barnes HQ, a heated post-mortem ensues. George Young accuses bassist Evans of 'looking surly' during the set; a full-scale brawl then erupts between the

WHILE THE BAND HAVE BEGUN TO RECEIVE MORE POSITIVE PRESS COVERAGE, THEIR DEBUT AT READING ON AUGUST 29 IS A DISASTER. A PUNCH-UP ENSUES BACK AT THEIR LONDON HQ.

three Young brothers. When Evans tries to intervene, he, too, is dragged into the melee. (He and Angus had clashed after the final show of the Lock Up Your Daughters tour, during an after-party at the Russell Hotel, where Angus punched him in the face.)

September 1 The band enter Vineyard Studios with Vanda & Young, with the intention of recording an EP. They cut the songs 'Love At First Feel', 'Carry Me Home', 'Cold Hearted Man', and 'Dirty Eyes'. The EP won't ever see light of day, but 'Dirty Eyes' eventually resurfaces as 'Whole Lotta Rosie', while 'Love At First Feel' emerges in 1981, when the North American version of *Dirty Deeds Done Dirt Cheap* is finally released. 'Carry Me Home', a rocking ode to hard living, will turn up as the B-side of the Australian 'Dog Eat Dog' single, while 'Cold Hearted Man', featuring a great Bon Scott vocal, makes it to the UK, French, German, and Swedish editions of the *Powerage* album.

Meanwhile, a proposed gig at the Penthouse Club in Scarborough is cancelled because the stage is too small.

September 15 Having shifted booking agents to the much larger Cowbell Agency, which represents Rod Stewart and Roxy Music, the band have secured the support slot on a nineteen-date Euro tour with Ritchie Blackmore's Rainbow—helped, no doubt, by the £10,000 'buy-on' fee paid by their label. (Way back in the day, Rainbow's lead singer, Ronnie James Dio, played in The Electric Elves, who shared some US dates with The Easybeats.)

The opening gig is at a venue called the Fabrik in Hamburg, Germany. Prior to the gig, George Young meets the band at the dock, where they arrive by ferry. *Setlist*: 'Live Wire' / 'Rock'n'roll Singer' / 'She's Got Balls' / 'School Days' / 'Problem Child' / 'The Jack' / 'Rocker' / 'High Voltage' / 'Baby, Please Don't Go'.

Just before the tour, Bon spoke with Anthony O'Grady from *RAM*. When O'Grady asked about their plans for the tour, Scott chuckled, 'We're gonna be like Stormtroopers to the audience and like the Gestapo to the groupies.'

While in Hamburg, AC/DC play a showcase gig for *Bravo*, Germany's leading rock magazine, sharing the bill with Suzi Quatro, Scottish pop/rockers Slik—and Shaun Cassidy, of all people. Afterward, they're taken out on the town by various local journalists, label reps, and Alex Young (who's now living in Germany). Their nocturnal rambling includes a trip to the notorious Reeperbahn. The Eros Centre, a sexual supermarket deep in the heart of the city's red-light centre, is a particular highlight.

The *High Voltage* LP sold 16,000 copies on its week of release in Germany, so AC/DC's reception here is a lot warmer than it had been in Sweden in July. Malcolm has a simple explanation for this: 'They just like basic good time rock'n'roll, which is what we're about.'

September 16 The band savour another night out at the Reeperbahn after a gig in Duisburg. This time, their host is Atlantic's Earl McGrath, who will go on to become the president of Rolling Stones Records. This evening's highlight is a live sex act featuring an extremely well-hung performer. Mark Evans later describes him as having 'what appeared to be a third leg'.

While in Hamburg, the group record an Alex Young song, 'I'm A Rebel' (for which Young uses his writing pseudonym George Alexander). George Young handles the production, which is envisaged to be stage one of the band's new album. The track won't ever be released by AC/DC, although German metal outfit Accept go on to cover it in 1980.

September 18 The roadshow reaches Munich, and schnapps becomes a new favourite tipple of the band's more indulgent members—everyone bar Angus, that is. They play two sets at the PN Club, the first at 10:30pm, the second at 1:30am. Cover charge is 12.50 DM (around $5 US at the time), which grants the ticket holder two free bottles of beer. Munich will become something of a hotspot for AC/DC, who go on to play the city five times between 1976 and late 1979.

During some of the shows on this Rainbow European tour, clauses are included in the band's contract to ensure Angus doesn't bare his bum on stage. The per-gig fee of around $1,000 helps keep his pants up. The antics of Blackmore's onstage rainbow, which has a tendency to malfunction, provides the members of AC/DC with some comic relief. They also sometimes sneak backstage and extinguish the guitarist's candles, which never fails to send him into a full-blown rock-star tizzy.

September 20 The *Dirty Deeds Done Dirt Cheap* LP is released in Australia, Europe, and the UK. Australian mag *RAM*'s review cites the tracks 'Ride On' and 'Jailbreak' as 'positive signs of a NEW DIRECTION' (caps *RAM*'s).

Despite his lyrical raunchiness, Bon Scott rarely resorts to swearing—at least on record. Yet at the end of the album track 'Ain't No Fun (Waiting 'Round To Be A Millionaire)', Scott yells, not quite off mic, 'Hey Howard! How ya doing, my next-door

FOLLOWING PAGES: LEGENDARY UK ALBUM DESIGNERS HIPGNOSIS WERE CALLED UPON TO DESIGN THE COVER FOR THE INTERNATIONAL VERSION OF *DIRTY DEEDS DONE DIRT CHEAP*. IT IS NOT A FAVOURITE OF THE BAND'S.

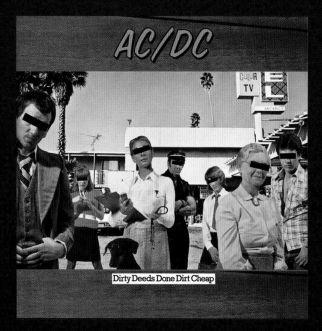

"*I don't think these two Australian kids, Angus and Malcolm, really understood it, and in fact they changed the cover later on to something that I would consider a bit more vulgar, a bit more obvious.*"

AUBREY POWELL, WHO DESIGNED THE INTERNATIONAL
ALBUM COVER, TO *ROLLING STONE*, MAY 2017

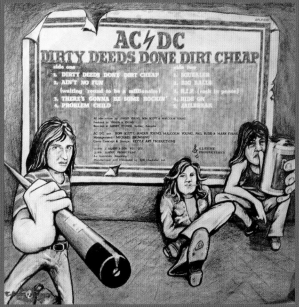

"**Dirty Deeds is AC/DC at their most lewd, simplistic, crass, gross, vulgar, unsophisticated, and tasteless. … Essentially, this album is the same old AC/DC song and dance, but I for one will never tire of it.**"

GEOFF BARTON, *SOUNDS*, NOVEMBER 1976

neighbour? Get your fuckin' jumbo jet out of my airport!' (The target of his heckle, eccentric American squillionaire Howard Hughes, is not available for comment. He died in April.)

According to Malcolm Young, Angus came up with the song title 'Dirty Deeds Done Dirt Cheap', basing it 'on a cartoon character that had the phrase as his calling card'—Dishonest John in the TV show *Beany & Cecil*, who would produce a calling card that read, 'Dirty Deeds Done Dirt Cheap. Holidays, Sundays, and Special Rates.' 'Then Bon stuck in the line *"I'm dirty, mean, mighty unclean"* from an advert for mosquito spray [Mortein] that was running on Aussie TV at the time. Yes, we were always a very topical band. We looked at what was happening in the world.'

The front cover of the Australian edition of the *Dirty Deeds* LP features a terrific cartoon drawing of the band's two central characters, Bon and Angus. The cockatoo tattoo on Scott's muscly forearm is surrounded by the album's title; he wears his pants painfully tight, his lined face is caught mid-roar. Angus, meanwhile, is in full 'Little Albie' mode, ubiquitous ciggie dangling from his lips, cap low over his eyes, giving the world a cheeky 'up yours' with his picking fingers.

Having bought the album, Oz fans can send $3 to Alberts for a copy of the *Dirty Deeds Done Dirt Cheap & Other Dino-Mite Songs* promotional songbook, which, apart from music and lyrics, includes such essentials as the 'AC/DC KWIZ', cartoons, and a dedicated space for the band members' autographs, if one is lucky enough to get close to them. (Today, this intriguing curio fetches upward of $800.)

The *Dirty Deeds* LP will not be released in the USA until March 1981, with a few tweaks from the original track list and radically different cover art. According to George Young, the band's American label 'found the lyrics too crude' and resisted releasing the album at first, but all that changed when AC/DC blew up internationally. 'It was business, pure and simple. Suddenly the album interested them.'

The international release, however, is an oddity. The band doesn't appear on the cover; instead, an abstract piece was commissioned from the highly regarded English designers Hipgnosis, who'd created striking (and very arty) covers for Pink Floyd, T. Rex, Electric Light Orchestra, and Led Zeppelin. (When the image is used as an ad for the album in the music press, a snap of Angus's mug is added, along with the caption, 'Depraved schoolboy reveals all—ring 01 499 9615.')

The end result is not a favourite of the band or their fans.

'I remember two skinny little Australian guys coming into Hipgnosis's studio,' the design collective's co-founder, Aubrey 'Po' Powell, tells *Rolling Stone* in 2017, 'and I thought, These guys aren't going to amount to a hill of beans. I really did. They were funny little guys and they started saying, We need an album cover. I was going to LA the next day, and I said, Well, why don't I shoot something in LA?'

While Powell is there, his fellow Hipgnosis founder, Storm Thorgerson, calls with an idea. He's been thinking about how magazines such as *National Enquirer* sometimes black out people's eyes to conceal their identity. What if they tried something like that?

Powell just so happens to be in the perfect place, just down the road from the Sunset Strip. 'Why don't we shoot something there and we'll get a load of characters?' he asks Thorgerson.

Powell isn't entirely sure that the Youngs grasped the final concept. 'Nevertheless, for me, it went pretty well. It sold six million albums [in North America].'

When the album finally gets a US release, *Rolling Stone*'s Greg Kot feels the noise. 'The guitars of brothers Angus and Malcolm Young bark at each other, Phil Rudd swings the beat even as he's pulverizing his kick drum, and Scott brings the raunch'n'wail. The subject matter is standard-issue rock rebellion; Scott pauses only once to briefly contemplate the consequences of his night stalking in "Ride On".'

New York critic Robert Christgau would take a typically arch approach to *Dirty Deeds*, 'grading' the album C+. 'Like Ian Hunter or Roger Chapman [from Family], though without their panache, [Scott] has fun being a dirty young man … needless to say, sexual hostility—disguised as fun, of course—is more his speed.'

Stephen Thomas Erlewine of the *All Music Guide*, however, is a true believer. 'The entire album served as a call to arms from a group that wanted nothing more than to celebrate the dirtiest, nastiest instincts humans could have, right down to the insurgent anti-authority vibe that runs throughout the record.' Five stars!

September 23–30 Still on the road in Germany, AC/DC play six more Rainbow support slots, in Hamburg, Bremen, Cologne, Dusseldorf, Nuremburg, and Munich. Along the way, Blackmore's unpredictable onstage rainbow continues to provide chuckles.

October 1–16 AC/DC and Blackmore play shows in Wiesbaden, Dortmund, and Frankfurt in Germany; Bern, Geneva, and Zurich in Switzerland; Hoensbroek in Holland; Brussels in Belgium; and various French cities, including one at the 7,000-capacity Pavillon de Paris on October 13.

IS BRITAIN READY FOR THE HUMAN KANGAROO?

Yes, it's AC/DC, hoping to make progress in leaps and bounds . . . (groan)

By ROY CARR

DEPENDING on who they were trying to impress, the best ways for any band to leave a grateful audience used to be to either viciously trash their equipment, lurch full-tilt into a rock 'n' roll medley, or disappear in clouds of dry ice.

But times change. Appetites become jaded. And with few exceptions, those well-rehearsed tactics that once transformed the front six rows of the local Odeon into a demolition area are now forgotten by the time the house lights have gone up — and the punters quietly file through the exits to the strains of "Dark Side Of The Moon."

In terms of rock brinkmanship, it seems nothing short of Hari Kari can schock a mid-70s audience — and even that might not warrant an encore!

We've seen it all before. So what else is new?

I'll tell you — the Human Kangaroo!!!

According to Angus Young, demented 17-year-old lead guitarist with AC/DC, it's a jape that he picked up from singer Bon Scott, who employed it in jolly-up apres-gig piss ups.

The Human Kangaroo?

Young Angus comes complete with instruction manual.

"What I do," he begins, masticating away weird, "is to go behind the equipment, strip off all me clothes, put me legs tightly together; me hands behind me back, and hop like mad across the stage."

Not, I assure you, a pretty sight, but it's made him the seven-stone darling of a whole new generation of thrill-seekers.

However, Angus points out in all modesty that this artistic portrayal isn't de rigeur at every gig.

"I usually do it as a special treat — I've done it at the Marquee when the audience has been really great. But in any case I make sure the kids don't go away disappointed."

Precisely how Angus Young pleases all the people all the time takes this form. Having spent the best part of an hour trashing his Gibson, stomping the stage in bright red schoolboy uniform and shaking his head as though trying to remove it from his shoulders, he strips to his briefs, mounts the highest speaker stack and, having turned his back to the crowd, dramatically lowers his underganrment below his knees to give a Full Moon.

"You've got to really entertain a crowd nowadays," maintains the fearless flasher. "Personally, I think it helps if a lead guitarist has some kind of visual gimmick."

"Truthfully," he squeaks, "I just couldn't stand there in front of the group without doing something!"

AC/DC are everything you'd expect an antipodean boogie band comprised of three ex-patriot Scotsmen and two Aussies to be. Crude, rude and exceedingly randy.

Onstage they sweat and swagger and seem to play at just one speed — flat out.

But despite the general ribald image, AC/DC are built almost entirely around the uninhibited antics of young Angus. Though as a guitarist he may be running on a quite different artistic ticket to say a Beck or a Gallagher, he has his own kind of Star Quality.

Angus makes it clear that he has no real aspirations to becoming the fastest new guitar-slinger in the west, but even so, if you cast aside his penchant for doffing his trousers, this bona fide Seventh Son builds up such a head of steam that only the very fittest can keep pace.

He equates primitivism in rock with honesty, and feels there'll always be a ready-made market for bands content to stick to basics and not get trapped by illusions of grandeur.

"I don't like to play above or below people's heads," he argues. "Basically, I just like to get up in front of a crowd and rip it up."

Tutored over the last six years by his brother Malcolm (a whizz-kid in his day) on a diet of Berry, Hendrix and Richard (Keith and Little), Angus theorises that the worst thing any rock band can do is to perform for their own amusement.

"That's why we keep it simple and make it visual. You see, there are some people who can't get off on music no matter how simple you play it. You've also got to cater for them.

"Rock is all about having fun and if you take the business part too seriously it isn't fun any more — and the audience will sense it."

Having got as far as any rock band can get in Australia, AC/DC arrived here in April with a deadline of six months in which to make or break it.

Within weeks they'd risen from a £25 a night support band to potential bill-toppers.

"I'm really not all that surprised that we happened so quickly in Britain," Angus says without any trace of egotism. "I say that because I honestly believe that we give the public what they want. If we didn't then we'd be on our way back to Australia by now."

But what if his precocious brat image eventually runs out of mileage? By the time he's grown out of his togs and teens he could be washed-up.

"Yeah," he sighs. "I might be a has been. If I am I hope I'm a rich one. But really, that's not the most important thing to me. Of course I'd like to conquer the world and go on for ever like Chuck Berry, but if I don't, if suddenly tomorrow it all ends, at least I can say I've done it.

"And," he concludes, "just so long as we don't do like so many bands do drift away from that thing that made us famous. I don't think there's much too much for us to worry about for the time being."

ANGUS YOUNG in school togs, and (inset) . . . modesty forbids. Pics: GARY MERRIN

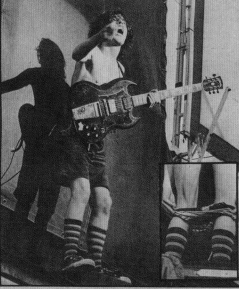

JAILHOUSE ROCK?

NEWS HAS reached us from the inside (of course) of the first ever single recorded and completed behind bars. The jail in question is at Leavenworth in Kansas and the whole project was put together by two inmates — named John Bradlin (an ex-Hollywood record producer) and Ray Williams (ex-ad agency exec) both of whom are serving sentences for drug offences.

The band consists of four other inmates who have recorded a Williams composition entitled "To Love Again". A local lawyer has set up a company called Golden Eagle Enterprises to deal with the finished product and they expect to distribute 1,000 copies as an initial outing.

□ DICK TRACY

TORIES MAKE THEIR PLAY FOR THE NF VOTE?

A GOOD friend of mine who works for one of the TV news organisations (and requested not to be named) put forward what must amount to a unique piece of media analysis. The subject was last week's Tory party conference in Brighton.

Whereas the rest of us who viewed the telly had assumed that the drum beating and flag waving was simply to turn a pound-panicked public against the Labour government, he put forward the proposition that the whole thing went subtly deeper.

His suggestion was that the real appeal of all the histrionic, red, white and blue patriotism was not, in fact, directed at the public at large. The real target of all the drama, particularly golden boy Michael Heseltine's hysterical rabble rousing that did everything short of accuse the Labour cabinet of being in the pay of Moscow, was the National Front.

According to my friend, this was a thinly veiled plea to the Front to get back in line and not make waves.

Implausible?

Not really, when you think that the National Front is currently planning to field almost 400 candidates in the next election. This could take a considerable bite out of the Tory vote, particularly in marginal industrial seats where the Alf Garnett-style traditional working-class Tory is liable to be attracted to the Front's raucous bigotry.

In a situation where majorities come in twos and threes, this could easily cost the Tories the election.

Maybe what you see isn't always what you think.

□ MICK FARREN

> If that
> Sunday joint
> is only a memory!

Sent by Mr. Warbler and Mr. Intelligens of JK Productions Ltd.

October 18 The run of dates with Blackmore's Rainbow winds up at the Congresgebouw in The Hague, in Holland, which coincides with the release of 'Dirty Deeds' as a single in Australia (where it hits #29). Despite the issues with his candles, Blackmore has invited the band to continue on to Japan with him, but they have another UK tour lined up, so they decide to pass. It's also possible that Bon Scott's pot bust with Fraternity might have prevented him from securing a Japanese visa, since the band will not tour Japan at all during Scott's tenure.

October 25 AC/DC's domestic 'rivals', Sherbet, reach the #4 spot on the UK singles chart with 'Howzat'. When asked about the achievement of his Aussie peers, Angus downplays their success. 'You have so many bands in the charts that it doesn't mean anything—look at Hot Chocolate, they've had at least six #1s [sic] and our tours sell twice as much as theirs.

'I did not even know [Sherbet] were in the country, to tell you the truth,' he adds. 'The only [Australian] group that is doing anything in England is AC/DC—the others are just nobodies, I tell you.'

October 27 A set at the Golders Green Hippodrome in London, which takes the place of a postponed gig in Great Yarmouth, is recorded for the BBC *In Concert* series, for broadcast on February 6 1978. It's the band's second appearance on the programme. Scott fills perhaps the tightest denims known to man, which might explain the slightly pained look in his eyes. Angus is a schoolboy in a big hurry; he actually *starts* the band's set with a blazing guitar solo, leading them into a furious 'Let There Be Rock'.

'This is a song that was inspired by none other than the Young boy here, Angus,' Bon says, nodding toward the guitarist, as he introduces 'Problem Child'. During 'Bad Boy Boogie', he personalises some of the lyrics, singing, *'I said stop / And they said go / I said fast / And they said slow,'* rather than the repeated *'They said'* from the studio version.

Angus is in especially fine form, dropping to his knees during 'Rosie' and blazing away. He even ditches his trademark school shirt and tie mid-set, pulling on a conventional collared top. By the time of 'T.N.T.', though, he's shirtless, as is Scott—both are drenched in sweat, putting in, working hard.

> **"You've got to really entertain a crowd nowadays. I just couldn't stand there in front of the group without doing something. … I don't like to play above or below people's heads. Basically, I just like to get up in front of a crowd and rip it up."**
>
> ANGUS YOUNG, BILLED AS THE 'HUMAN KANGAROO', TO ROY CARR, *NME*, OCTOBER 1976

DESPITE THE BAND'S GROWING POPULARITY IN THE UK, THE LOCAL PRESS OFTEN RESORTS TO CONVICT-BASHING HEADLINES SUCH AS IN THIS CLIPPING FROM THE *NME*. STILL, IT'S NOT AS BAD AS 'CHUNDER FROM DOWN UNDER'.

There's at least one Angus lookalike in the crowd, and the Beeb's cameras capture him headbanging, an ecstatic grin on his mug.

The BBC presses about one hundred copies of a mini-album taken from this set, featuring the tracks 'Let There Be Rock', 'Problem Child', 'Hell Ain't A Bad Place To Be', 'Whole Lotta Rosie', and 'Rocker'. As before, the discs are strictly for use by affiliates, but some copies (surprise, surprise) find their way onto the black market, just like the band's first *In Concert* set.

October 28–November 9 The band's UK tour takes in Swansea, Birmingham, Lancaster, Edinburgh, Glasgow, Manchester, Cardiff, Liverpool, Bristol, and Norwich. In most cases, they play either universities or town halls.

November 10 AC/DC fill the 2,500-capacity Hammersmith Odeon—their biggest London show to date. The gig almost doesn't happen, though, when Scott gets lost on the Tube. He eventually reaches the venue with just minutes to spare before show time. Prior to the gig, photos were taken of the venue's marquee, with the band's name quite literally up in lights. On closer inspection of one of these photos, latecomer Scott can clearly be seen strolling toward the dressing room, a bag casually slung over his shoulder.

A rare performance of 'Big Balls' is one of many highlights from the show, which is watched by members of such local acts as Eddie & The Hot Rods and The Damned. The gig itself is brutal, the surge at the front of the stage so intense that security staff are knocked over in the mayhem. Yet the *NME* still isn't ready to embrace the band's balls'n'all approach. According to writer Tony Stewart, who covers the gig, 'This bunch of delinquents have only an elementary musical knowledge, write pitifully trite songs, and to compensate they come on as vulgar, crass and loud.' To Stewart, clearly short of original ideas, Angus is the 'Electric Schoolboy Kangaroo', while Scott is nothing but 'muscle, mouth, and bulging trousers'.

None of this matters a jot to the faithful squeezed into the Odeon; they go berserk, from the opening salvo of 'Live Wire' to the barnstorming closer, 'Baby, Please Don't Go.'

Likely setlist: 'Live Wire' / 'She's Got Balls' / 'Problem Child' / 'Big Balls' / 'Can I Sit Next To You, Girl' / 'The Jack' / 'High Voltage' / 'T.N.T.' / 'Baby, Please Don't Go'.

November 11–15 AC/DC's final run of UK dates for the year takes the band to Guildford, Cambridge, Newcastle, and Oxford. One fan's take on the show at the Corn

Exchange in Cambridge—'blew my head off!'—sums up the musical mayhem the band are creating on stage.

November 20 Angus's bared bum makes its first appearance in the UK press, in *Sounds*. The caption reads, 'Have You Seen This Man?'

In the same issue, *Dirty Deeds Done Dirt Cheap* is given a four-star rating. 'Dirty Deeds,' writes Geoff Barton, 'is AC/DC at their most lewd, simplistic, crass, gross, vulgar, unsophisticated and tasteless. Also thoroughly enjoyable. … Essentially, this album is the same old AC/DC song and dance, but I for one will never tire of it.'

November 26 The band return to Australia for the first time since April, for yet another stint of touring and recording. The *Dirty Deeds* LP is on its way to an Australian peak of #5; it will remain on the chart for almost six months, selling, over time, more than 400,000 copies. It also keeps some interesting company on the album chart compiled by Melbourne radio station 3XY, sharing space on the listing with Rod Stewart's *A Night On The Town*, *Alice Cooper Goes To Hell*, and *Beautiful Noise* by Neil Diamond, along with records by the Bay City Rollers, ABBA, Dr Hook, and Sherbet.

At Sydney airport, after making their way past a small but loud contingent of female fans, the band members speak with local radio station 2SM. They are all nursing beers after the long flight, except for Angus, who slugs from a milkshake. He boasts of nearly being arrested at gigs in Glasgow and Liverpool, after stripping on stage. He doesn't know it yet, of course, but his bare backside is about to become a matter of some controversy. The *Dirty Deeds* album, meanwhile, is still lodged firmly in the Australian Top 10.

Press conference done, the Youngs return to their family HQ in Burwood, while the rest of the band settle into the Hyatt Kingsgate Hotel in the red-light heart of Sydney, Kings Cross. Bon Scott toasts their success (several times) with a bottle of twenty-five-year-old Chivas Regal, snapped up in duty-free.

December AC/DC have come a long way in the UK in six short months; so much so, that when *Sounds* compiles its New Order Top 20 at the end of the year, AC/DC are ranked #1, beating the Sex Pistols, The Damned, Iggy Pop (and The Stooges), Eddie & The Hot Rods, and the Ramones, among others.

'Who reigns in '76?' the mag's editorial asks. 'AC/DC.'

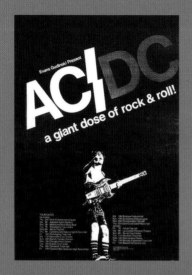

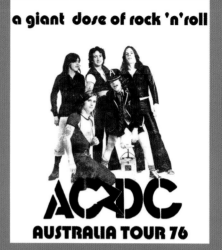

Over at the *NME*, despite the magazine's championing of punk, only one 'real' punk album—the Ramones' self-titled debut—makes the Top 10 albums of the year. Bob Dylan (*Desire*), David Bowie (*Station To Station*), and pub-rockers Dr Feelgood (*Stupidity*) snare the top three spots. AC/DC, however, fail to make this or any other *NME* end-of-year list during the 1970s.

Melody Maker, in its own 1976 wrap-up, falls somewhere in between the two, conceding that AC/DC are 'one of the most popular bands currently shooting'.

Meanwhile, the band's plans for conquering America are on hold due to US label disinterest (their album is yet to be released in North America) and potential visa problems, as a result of Scott's police record. So, while the band are back in Oz, manager Michael Browning is in New York, trying to smooth things out with Atlantic.

December 1 The band spend the afternoon sound-checking their gear at Armstrong's Studios in Melbourne, before playing a surprise gig at the Tiger Lounge in the Royal Oaks Hotel in the suburbs, the watering hole of the local Richmond Aussie Rules club. They use the kitchen as a dressing room, then jump on stage and tear through some favourite covers, including 'Roll Over, Beethoven', 'Whole Lotta Shakin' Goin' On', and 'Jailhouse Rock'.

December 5 It's back to *Countdown* for a performance of 'Dirty Deeds Done Dirt Cheap'. Hush, the glam-rockers that Angus referred to as the 'Blue Suede Thongs', are also on the show, performing 'Sunday', a minor hit. They will split up in 1977.

December 6 Melbourne's Myer Music Bowl hosts the official launch of AC/DC's Giant Dose Of Rock'n'roll tour. (The local promoters, Evans/Gudinski—both former colleagues of Michael Browning—have politely rejected the band's idea of naming the tour 'The Little Cunts Have Done It'.) Five thousand mad-for-it punters, each paying between $4.50 and $5.50, fill the outdoor amphitheatre, with cyclone fencing separating ticket-holding fans from several thousand freeloading onlookers.

'The gig was a cracker,' bassist Evans recalls. Interestingly, the audience is more female-heavy than any the band experienced in the UK, where their following is predominantly male. 'Fifteen to seventeen,' Scott explains, when asked about the age range of their female fans. 'Fuckable age.'

On the same night, elsewhere in Melbourne, tartan-clad Scots the Bay City Rollers

THE BAND AT SYDNEY AIRPORT, BACK IN AUSTRALIA FOR A TOUR THEY DID NOT WANT TO UNDERTAKE IN THE FIRST PLACE. MIDWAY THROUGH, THEY RE-CHRISTEN IT THE 'GIANT PAIN IN THE ARSE' TOUR.

play before an equally frantic audience, filling the city's Festival Hall. *Herald* journalist Debbie Sharpe catches both shows, and reports, 'For both bands, Sunday night was successful.'

December 7–11 The Giant Dose tour continues with shows in such rural centres as Shepparton in Victoria and Albury in Newcastle, and Wollongong in NSW, as well as a gig in Canberra. But controversy is starting to follow the band like a bad smell; when Angus drops trou' at these gigs, local councils threaten to ban the group from their fair towns. Some nights Bon holds a piece of cardboard to cover Angus's offending bits; some nights not. When Angus moons those in attendance at a press conference, a female reporter leaves in a huff. Trouble is brewing.

An eagle-eyed parent then spots something amiss in the Giant Dose tour program. Mark Evans is quoted as saying he'd like to 'make enough money to be able to fuck Britt Ekland'. Evans insists he didn't make the comment (it's likely Scott set him up), but it leads to complaints being made to various councils on the band's itinerary, demanding they not be allowed to play, for fear of corrupting the local youth.

'If AC/DC wants to come here again,' snorts the town clerk of Albury, reluctantly hosting AC/DC on December 8, 'they'll have to change their act.'

The tour program—which in 2012 will fetch $1,500 (US) on eBay—is duly banned from sale at the Albury show, which draws 600 fans. Angus bares his bum during the gig, and the local media goes into meltdown; an editorial in the *Border Mail* demands to know why he feels the need to expose 'his pimply white buttocks'. When the question is put to him, Angus replies, 'Because my arse is better looking than my face.'

'It's a sad commentary on his faith in the drawing power of the band's music ability,' the *Border Mail*'s editorial sniffs.

> **"Bon was a tiny bloke, but he worked the crowd so well, made a lot of eye contact. Angus was the same as you see him now. He hasn't really changed. He's got all that energy."**
> PHOTOGRAPHER TIM PETTS TO THE *BORDER MAIL*, 2010

None of this matters to the AC/DC faithful, who rarely get to see such a high-flying band in their hometown. Then-fifteen-year-old Tim Petts, who will go on to become a photography teacher, shoots the show. 'I remember all the energy coming out of Bon Scott and Angus,' he tells the *Border Mail* in 2010. 'They got you up and excited. They were the sort of band who'd just get your foot tapping and head banging.'

Some fans make their way backstage, where they are welcomed by Bon Scott. One of them, fourteen-year-old Jason James, later recalls, 'He invited us over and just sat us down and asked us if we liked the show ... then he invited us back to the after party at the Commodore Motel in Kiewa Street, where they used to stay. Malcolm was lying on the bed, Angus was somewhere else. We stayed for a while and eventually left. We couldn't sleep that night, and when we went to school the next day and showed everyone Bon's autograph, we were legends. I just get goosebumps thinking about it now.'

Another local, handpicked by the band from the crowd during the show, has a far more intimate encounter with the band, snapping photos of various Seedies in their underwear, which she shows off with some pride on her return to school.

December 9 Writer Tony Catterall of the *Canberra Times* makes up for his way-off-target review of *T.N.T.* earlier in the year when he covers the band's short, sharp, one-hour set at the Ginninderra High School hall. He describes the show—which is a steal at $5 per ticket—as a 'magnificent assault on the eardrums.

'There's a certain masochism involved in attending an AC/DC concert and not wanting to run—hands clasped over ears—from the hall as soon as the first number begins. That's not to suggest I ever felt like doing so ... AC/DC doesn't so much play loud rock and roll as mount a savage onslaught on the mind and senses ... This was what raw rock and roll is all about: getting the energy level high and keeping it there.'

RAM backs this up with a similarly effusive—if a tad pretentious—live review. 'Loud seems too tame a description for the volume they inflict on an audience. It's more a "living sound" that penetrates the flesh and bones until movement and rhythm come involuntarily and the audience is swept into the same current.'

The now-standard 'Drop 'Em Angus' banners are waved frantically by fans during the show, eager for a bit of flesh, although Angus chooses to keep his pants on, although he does briefly lose his duds while standing behind a screen. At least a dozen coppers look on, stony faced, waiting for any signs of nudity.

Many years later, one fan at the Ginninderra show neatly sums up the event: 'I can still picture Bon Scott all sweaty, with his shirt off, screaming his lungs out! We were fifteen, and they were just a pub band to us playing at our school social; if I only I knew the future I would have got his autograph or pinched his shirt off the stage!'

While in Ginninderra, the band members stay at a private house in the nearby suburb of Pearce. Any chance of a few hours of peace is shattered when local fans get the news of their whereabouts; it's like a repeat of the time in the mid-1960s when Easybeats fans besieged the Young family home at Burwood. It's a mob scene.

December 10 During the band's show at Wollongong Town Hall, a coterie of police officers keep a sharp eye on Angus, wary of the dreaded brown-eye. Tonight, his pants stay on. Meanwhile, a story runs in Melbourne's *Truth* newspaper under the headline 'Pop Hit Makes Widow's Phone Run Hot', reporting on how 'a wealthy widow was shocked and upset when she began to receive obscene telephone calls'. It turns out that she shares her number—36-24-36—with the character in the AC/DC song, and fans have been hitting the phones, calling her at all hours in need of 'dirty deeds done dirt cheap'.

This is another bad omen for the tour. Another comes when their Melbourne hotel is raided by police in search of yet another wayward daughter. Angus is told that the girl's father has formed 'a sort of posse': 'They had guns and they were after us, especially Bon.'

By now, the band has a new name for the tour: 'A Giant Pain In The Arse'.

December 11 Angus and Bon speak with Christie Eliezer from *RAM* just before a show at the Civic Theatre in Newcastle, NSW. Bon takes aim at the band's so-called punk 'rivals': 'I spent the first three weeks of our [UK] stay exploring pubs and clubs, and there was not one group doing what we do.'

He is then asked whether he thinks Angus's bum is a tad, well, overexposed. Bon admits he'd rather that than his face. 'It's preferable, as far as I'm concerned.'

Angus is usually guarded when it comes to talking himself up—the band, yes; himself, not so easily—but even he seems impressed when he relates the story of jumping into a London cab and the driver turning to him and asking, 'So where's your school uniform?'

ANGUS (ABOVE) AND BON (OPPOSITE) CUTTING LOOSE AT CITY HALL, ALBURY, DECEMBER 8 1976.

'Now there is nothing that will stop us,' Angus insists. '[Not even] the moon. We'll be there next week.'

Angus and Bon also team up for an on-air interview with Sydney station 2JJ.

'Are you the guy who goes mad on stage?' Angus is asked.

'Yeah. I'm the guy.'

Scott and the DJ egg on Angus, encouraging him to drop his duds.

'Ready, set, go,' he announces, as his pants hit the floor.

December 13–14 The band fill the Amoco Hall in the rural NSW town of Orange, where The Easybeats played their final show in 1970, and then play a show at the Civic Centre in Dubbo. The presence of at least a dozen coppers in the hall discourages Young from 'dropping 'em', despite the crowd's urging. Instead, he briefly, teasingly disrobes behind a small screen, without fully exposing himself.

Scott joins in the mayhem, tweaking the lyrics of 'Can I Sit Next To You, Girl' to '*Can I sit on your face, girl? You can sit on mine.*'

December 16 A proposed gig in Tamworth, NSW—the country-musical capital of Australia—is cancelled by a worried local council. At the same time, a crew from *A Current Affair*, a national tabloid TV program, has begun stalking the band as the Giant Dose controversies stack up. The show's host, Mike Willesee, races to Tamworth by helicopter, hoping to sniff out a story. But the band are holed up in their motel room, saying nothing, and the next day travel to Toowoomba in Queensland to play the Harristown High School Hall.

The damage has been done, however. The band, who only agreed to the tour in order to top up their bank balances, now feel as though they're being treated like criminals, when in fact they should be seen as homecoming rock'n'roll heroes.

Sydney radio station 2SM—until now a fervent supporter of the band—bans all AC/DC records. 'Members of the Australian group AC/DC must decide if they are strippers or musicians,' the station's general manager, Garvis Rutherford, states. 'Until they do, the station will not associate with them in any way.' It doesn't help that the Catholic Church owns the station. And it's telling that AC/DC haven't had a single in the Australian Top 10 all year.

When it's revealed that a teenage fan of the band has an AC/DC tattoo on her arm, Rex Jackson, the NSW Minister for Youth and Community Services, is incensed. He promises to police tattoo parlours to ensure no further desecrations take place. (A few years later, Jackson is jailed for corruption.)

December 17–22 The tour rattles along, with shows in Toowoomba, Brisbane (at the 4,000-capacity Festival Hall), Bundaberg, and Rockhampton in Queensland, as well as the NSW rural town of Murwillumbah. The Festival Hall show is later bootlegged as *Dirty Deeds Down Under*.

Bon is underwhelmed by the response of the smallish crowd at the Bundaberg Showgrounds. Perhaps his mood is dictated as much by the sight of their dressing room—a stable at the rear of the site. 'Next time we play Bundaberg,' he snarls from the stage, 'we'll play the local cemetery. We'll get more life out of people there.' He spends some of the gig sporting an oversized cowboy hat. And no shirt, of course.

December 23 The Giant Dose tour finally winds down for the year after a show on the Gold Coast in Queensland with The Saints, who've made inroads of their own in the UK with their remarkable sonic blitzkrieg, '(I'm) Stranded.' A fight breaks out between the two bands' crews; Chris Gilbey from Alberts is so taken by The Saints that he quits his job to manage them.

After the gig, AC/DC drive the fourteen hours back to Sydney. The next day, on the band's worksheet, in blazing capital letters, is this statement: 'EVERYBODY FUCKS OFF! BUT MAKE SURE THAT YOU MAKE ARRANGEMENTS TO BE BACK IN MELBOURNE BY THURSDAY 6TH JANUARY.'

Probable tour setlist: 'Dirty Deeds Done Dirt Cheap' / 'She's Got Balls' / 'Problem Child' / 'Live Wire' / 'Jailbreak' / 'The Jack' / 'Can I Sit Next To You, Girl' / 'T.N.T.' / 'High Voltage' / 'Baby, Please Don't Go' / 'Rocker'.

December 31 The band are told of another cancellation—this time a gig planned for January 12 in the Victoria town of Warrnambool—and Angus really lets loose: 'It's no good if we drive halfway across the country to stage a concert to find that someone has cancelled it because they consider us obscene. It will take only a couple more hassles from the authorities and we will leave Australia.'

The next day, a local newspaper headline screams, 'ROCK BAND THREATENS TO LEAVE COUNTRY!'

Of course, that's not going to happen—they have another album to record, for one thing—but it's clear that the constant hassles and overreactions are starting to weigh on the band. They are forced to pay bonds of as much as $5,000 to ensure that future Australian gigs still take place.

Meanwhile, Bon Scott sees in the new year at the Bondi Lifesaver, checking out notorious rockers on the rise Rose Tattoo.

After surviving the Giant Pain In The Arse tour, the band record Let There Be Rock; *Cliff Williams takes the place of departing bass player Mark Evans; and, despite label hassles, AC/DC make their American live debut and shake up New York City.*

1977

January 6 During a press conference in Hobart, a clearly wasted Bon, shades firmly in place, laughs off a journalist's suggestion that 'the Hobart city fathers are trying to put a clamp on your concert'. He shakes his head, chuckling; of course they're not. *Why would they?*

As for rumours that the Sex Pistols are using AC/DC as a model, Scott shrugs. 'Never heard of them. Don't know 'em.' It's clear he's been asked about punk and the Pistols one too many times.

'But what about punk rock?' the journalist asks. 'What's your take on that? Is it music?'

'I see us as music,' Scott replies. 'I see punk rock as nothing.'

The hapless questions keep coming.

Are AC/DC outrageous?

'No.'

Violent?

'No. We're just a straight rock group. And I've never said *fuck* on stage yet.'

And what about their biggest following in Australia?

'The police force.'

When the band reach Sydney, they play two nights at the Bondi Lifesaver, billed as the Special Surprise Mystery Band. More than 4,000 people attempt to squeeze into the venue across the two nights, way beyond its capacity.

Around this time, Michael Browning receives a call from Atlantic in the USA, indicating that the label doesn't want to pick up the option on the band, which would leave them without a deal in North America. Atlantic UK's Phil Carson—who first signed AC/DC, and who remains a true believer—talks the US label around, but only after the band agree to give up the advance commitment written into their existing contract. They are forced to sacrifice $20,000 (AU) to stay with Atlantic.

January 7–15 The band play several shows in Tasmania (Launceston on the 8th, Burnie the 9th) and Victoria (where they rock Horsham on the 11th). Some Super 8 footage is shot of AC/DC in action at the Hobart City Hall on January 7, showing Angus tearing off one solo after another while a bare-chested Scott prowls the stage. Angus, too, eventually sheds his shirt, dripping hair and sweat all over his Gibson. The big finale features Angus atop his speaker stack, soloing like a man on a mission.

Back in Victoria, they play shows at Portland and Ballarat, where the cover charge for their gig at St Pats Hall is $6.50. A rumour spreads that the band has been booked to play at schools so that Angus can continue his education, having dropped out of high school several years earlier. It's a good story, but a long way from the truth.

January 17 Frustrated by the lack of audience response during a show in the Victorian rural town of Moe, the band's crew assemble on stage after the gig has ended and collectively moon the crowd. Perhaps this is in response to a critical letter recently sent to (and published in) the *Australian Women's Weekly*, by someone using the pen name 'Rot AC/DC'.

January 30 AC/DC headline a Festival of Sydney show at the Haymarket. Filmmaker Russell Mulcahy, who will later make his name shooting Duran Duran videos and such features as *Razorback*, captures footage of much of this show, as well as other gigs on the Giant Dose tour, but the results are never formally released.

> **"*I feel sorry for people who classify as good rock music the sounds AC/DC produce. They have taken rock music to its lowest point ever … Anyone who idolizes these tattooed idiots must be lacking in the old grey matter.*"**
>
> 'ROT AC/DC', LETTER TO *AUSTRALIAN WOMEN'S WEEKLY*, JANUARY 1977

Bon tries hard to get the audience to 'fess up to having a social disease before they play 'The Jack', asking for a show of hands. He counts a few victims in the crowd. 'We've got friends here tonight,' he announces, before bellowing, 'I've just had my first case of GONORRHEA!' as if he were auditioning for *West Side Story*. Scott then leads Angus into his bluesy blitzkrieg of a solo with the clever line, 'Here's some penicillin for ya.'

'High Voltage' is a big shout-and-response number, Scott coming on like some kind of rock'n'roll preacher, shouting, 'I said HIGH!' as the band cook up a firestorm behind him. An extended 'Jailbreak' is another standout. When they leave the stage after 'Rocker', the MC winds up the crowd. 'You want some more?' he yells. 'Well, you're going to have to make a hell of a lot more noise than that!'

The audience responds accordingly, and the band return to blast 'Long Way', Scott reciting the song's litany of harsh truths about life on the road—'*Gettin' robbed / Getting' stoned / Gettin' beat up / Broken boned*'—accompanied only by the clapping of the crowd. Then the band return, and the song, and the crowd, erupt. All up, it's a killer gig.

A recording of the band's Haymarket set, as broadcast on Sydney radio station 2JJ, will become a perennial fave in the world of AC/DC bootlegs, sometimes referred to as *Can I Sit On Your Face, Girl?*

Setlist: 'Jailbreak' / 'The Jack' / 'Can I Sit Next To You, Girl' / 'High Voltage' / 'Rocker' / 'It's A Long Way To The Top (If You Wanna Rock'n'roll)'.

January–February The band return to Albert Productions in Sydney to record *Let There Be Rock*, which they cut over two weeks—standard procedure, by now, for AC/DC. Vanda & Young—and Alberts—are currently on a hot streak, having had major chart success with Ted Mulry and John Paul Young. Vanda & Young have also recently scored a richly deserved *TV Week* award for 'Best Australian Songwriters'.

Before they begin the sessions, George Young asks his brothers what type of record they want to make. They have strong ideas. 'It would be great if we could just make a lot of guitar riffs,' says Angus, 'because we're fired up after doing all this touring.'

Many years later, Malcolm picks up on this when he speaks to *Mojo* about *Let There Be Rock*. 'We used to come in from the gigs … George and Harry would have a couple of dozen [beer] cans in and a few bottles of Jack Daniels, and we'd all get in and have a party and rip it up, get the fast tracks—stuff like "Whole Lotta Rosie" and "Let There Be Rock"—done right so it was the same loose feeling like we were on stage still. The studio was just like an extension of the gig.'

While he's recording his solo on the album's title track, a Biblical ode to the rock'n'roll life, Angus's amplifier starts to give up the ghost, shooting out sparks and smoke. He hesitates, fearing a full-on studio fire, but brother George gestures frantically at him through the control room glass. 'Keep going!' he mouths, feeling the take is simply too good to shut down. 'Keep going!'

Angus's gear just makes it to the end of the song, but then craps out in what he later describes as 'a smouldering puddle of wiring and valves'. The take, fortunately, is gold.

'There was no way we were going to stop a shit-hot performance for a technical reason like amps blowing up,' George later tells *Rolling Stone*.

Angus doesn't necessarily learn from the experience. Some thirty-odd years later, when recording the *Rock Or Bust* album, a similar thing will happen. 'I thought it was a cigarette,' Angus later admits, but producer Brendan O'Brien knew otherwise. 'Ang,' he says, pointing, 'you're on fire.'

To the band, the *Let There Be Rock* sessions are one giant vent. 'Once we all found out that Atlantic had knocked us back,' bassist Evans will later write, 'the attitude was, Fuck them! Who the fuck do they think they are? So, from that point onward, it was, Fuck, we'll show them! We were seriously fucking pissed off about it. It didn't need to be discussed. We were going to go in and make that album and shove it up their arse.'

Not that they'd totally misplaced their sense of humour. Scott's lyric for 'Crabsody In Blue'—yet another ode to irritations below the waistline—is hilarious, one of his funniest yet. 'And you start to scratch,' he chuckles, 'When they start to hatch / Before you start to scream / That's when you apply the cream.'

Alberts labelmates The Angels are recording in the same fifth-floor studio as AC/DC, doing what is known as 'hot-bedding'—when one band end their session, the next set up and begin theirs. Angels drummer Graham 'Buzz' Bidstrup vividly recalls his first exposure to AC/DC in the studio. 'The lift was a bit slow,' he says, 'and, as it climbed the floors, the dull rumble of the band became more audible—until the doors finally opened and the crash of drums, guitar and bass in full fury became omnipresent. [And it] was not uncommon to see Angus climbing over his amp or spinning on the floor as a take was being recorded.'

Angus, meanwhile, loves working at Alberts. 'I would have liked to have taken the fucking walls with me and kept them,' he later admits to VH-1. 'A guitar just came to life in there. It was a little downtrodden, but it had a great vibe, this energy to it.'

Bon Scott agrees. 'Harry and George know the studio like the back of their hand,' he tells *Countdown*'s Molly Meldrum. 'It's all there. There's no need to go anywhere else. Say we went to Miami, for instance, we'd have to buy studio time, hotel it, there's just no point in it.'

Some years later, Metallica's Lars Ulrich will rank *Let There Be Rock* among his 'Top 15 Hard Rock Albums', telling *Rolling Stone*, 'This is AC/DC's heaviest record, AC/DC's densest record, AC/DC's most energetic record.' He cites the track 'Overdose' as a particular favourite. 'When the two guitars lock in, it's just the fucking heaviest thing ever.'

'Overdose' will have a similar impact on Megadeth's Dave Mustaine, who says, 'The first couple of notes just blew my mind.' He admits hearing the record was a 'defining moment in my life, when I made my mind up that I was gonna do this, no matter what.'

February 12 Alberts labelmates The Angels open for AC/DC at the Apollo Stadium in Adelaide, South Australia—the first of three shows in Adelaide.

February 14 'Love At First Feel' enters the Oz singles chart; it will peak at #63 and stay on the chart for nine weeks. It's the band's last charting single in Oz for two years, and it's hardly the hit they wanted.

February 15 The final Giant Dose concert takes place at the Perth Entertainment Centre, giving a chance for local Bon Scott to check in with his parents, Chick and Isa, with whom he remains very close.

Bassist Evans voices his discontent about the tour to *RAM*, revealing that he 'can't wait' to get back to the UK. 'They treat you properly … none of this hassling with all the hall managers shit.'

Bad blood lingers long after all the Giant Dose dramas—so much so that the band will not tour Australia again during Bon Scott's lifetime. The upside is that, while in Sydney, each band member is given a royalty cheque by Ted Albert for the sum of $3,957.29. 'On behalf of the whole company,' Albert writes, in an attached note, 'our thanks for your efforts overseas and our best wishes for the coming year.'

February 16 With the *Let There Be Rock* sessions over and the Australian tour finally done, the band return to London, where they move into two flats in Ladbroke Grove. One is shared by Malcolm and Angus, the other by the rest of the band, bar Scott, who resumes living with Silver Smith.

February 18 The band members barely have time to unpack before the *Dirty Deeds Done Dirt Cheap* UK tour resumes at Edinburgh University, beginning a twenty-six-show run that stretches through to March 20. The support act for this and many other *Dirty Deeds* gigs is Jenny Darren, who soon after this will cut a version of the song 'Heartbreaker', which will in turn become a huge hit for Pat Benatar. Trouble erupts when some members of the audience, having been squeezed in like sardines at the front, decide to sit on the monitor speakers on the lip of the stage. Fights ensue as security guards drag some of these punters away.

February 19–28 The tour rolls on through Glasgow, Blackpool, Cardiff, Derby, Malvern, Exeter, Cambridge, Reading, Edinburgh, and Bournemouth. The show in Glasgow, again for a university crowd, is reviewed by *Record Mirror*. 'Angus Young on lead guitar was amazing … he twitched, jerked and bounded across the stage non-stop, his head whipping back until it looked as though it just had to come flying off.' (And so what if reviewer Eric Wishart refers to Scott as 'Bob'? What's a typo between friends?)

After the show at the Imperial Ballroom at Blackpool on February 20, the band invite a photographer back to the Savoy Hotel. A member of the crew borrows his camera and

ANGUS YOUNG, LIVE AND SWEATY IN 1976, WEARING THE SAME CONVICT PYJAMAS THAT ALMOST CAUGHT FIRE DURING FILMING OF THE HIGH-RISK VIDEO CLIP FOR 'JAILBREAK'.

sneaks into the toilet, where he snaps a photo of Bon Scott relieving himself. The photo that has never seen light of day.

In Cardiff, some punters are disappointed when Angus decides not to drop trou'. *Melody Maker* writer Harry Doherty describes the moment when Angus wades into the crowd as 'like some scene from *Rock Around The Clock*, with fans forming a circle around him, clapping hands, tapping feet, encouraging him to batter away.'

Afterward, Angus tells Doherty why his pants stayed attached during the gig. 'I only do that when I feel like putting shit on the audience,' he says. 'Some audiences you get are really rowdy, and to shut them up, you just go, *Take that, you poof.*

'It's to keep people interested, not bored,' he adds, in an almost serious moment. 'They pay to see something.'

March 1–4 The tour continues with dates at the Locarno Ballroom in Portsmouth and the Mayfair Ballroom in Newcastle—the first of eight Mayfair gigs for the band between now and 1980.

March 5 Prior to a gig in Northampton, a van blocks the venue's entrance. Bon and Angus recruit a couple of locals to help them move the vehicle, so they can manoeuvre their van into place and set up. As a thank you, the lucky punters are welcomed backstage after the gig—they even get to share Bon Scott's booze.

Likely setlist: 'Live Wire' / 'She's Got Balls' / 'Dog Eat Dog' / 'The Jack' / 'Problem Child' / 'Jailbreak' / 'Bad Boy Boogie' / 'High Voltage' / 'Whole Lotta Rosie' / 'Baby, Please Don't Go'.

March 6–9 The tour rolls into (and then out of) Maidenhead and Plymouth, with gigs at clubs called Skindles and Fiesta.

March 10 Angus almost blows out a gig at St Andrews Hall in Norwich—a rarity for a man who lives, breathes, and craps AC/DC. He has a deadly hangover—another rarity—and can't be extracted from his room to drive to the gig until the very last minute. But eventually he plays on, shrugging off the pain he is clearly feeling.

March 11 When the tour reaches London, for a gig at the 3,000-capacity Finsbury Park Rainbow, Michael Browning invites various heavy-hitters to the show, including

US booking agent Doug Thaler and UK promoter Fred Bannister. Both will feature prominently in the band's future.

Bon, meanwhile, speaks his mind when interviewed by the *NME*; he's had enough of the fickle, trend-hungry nature of the media. He makes it clear that AC/DC are a band of the people, not darlings of the press. 'We're on the crowd's side,' he says, 'because it's a band–audience show. We're not like performing seals, we're in it together.'

March 12 The band play Leeds University, where The Who's *Live At Leeds* LP was recorded. They're surprised by the relatively small size of the venue, which has a capacity of only about 1,000. The Who's album—one of the best live rock records of all time—made the room sound as big as an arena.

March 13–20 The final week of the *Dirty Deeds* tour takes the band to Wolverhampton, St Albans, Scarborough, Manchester, Coventry, Southend, and Croydon.

AC/DC may have been making a serious impact on the live circuit, but the charts are still heavy with fluff. The UK Top 5 at the end of the *Dirty Deeds* tour features the mainstream pop of The Manhattan Transfer ('Chanson D'Amour'), ABBA ('Knowing Me, Knowing You'), and Leo Sayer ('When I Need You'). The #1 album, meanwhile, is pure nostalgia: The Shadows' *20 Golden Greats*.

March 21 *Let There Be Rock* is released, and enters the Oz album chart; it will peak at #19 and remain on the chart for twenty weeks. At the top of the chart, the Eagles' soft-rock mega-seller *Hotel California* is in the midst of a twelve-week run at #1.

Upon its release, Malcolm Young speaks with *Rock Star* magazine about the album and the power of simplicity. 'We were always big fans of early rock'n'roll, like Elvis and "Heartbreak Hotel", things like that. … If anything, for "Whole Lotta Rosie" we were looking for a feel like Little Richard, a good steamin' rock feel, and see what we could lay on top with the guitars. It evoked that, but you're just looking for the vibe, what's exciting, and that's what we were listening to. Simple to put together, but still around like a classic.'

In 2001, Q magazine will list *Let There Be Rock* among its '50 Heaviest Albums Of All Time'.

> **❝The music press is totally out of touch with what the kids actually want to listen to. These kids might be working in a shitty factory … or they might be on the dole—come the weekend, they just want to go out and have a good time, get drunk and go wild. We give them the opportunity to do that.❞**
>
> BON SCOTT TO *NME*, MARCH 1977

FOLLOWING PAGES: *LET THERE BE ROCK* IS THE BAND'S FIRST ALBUM TO MAKE A SERIOUS DENT IN THE UK CHARTS, PEAKING AT #17.

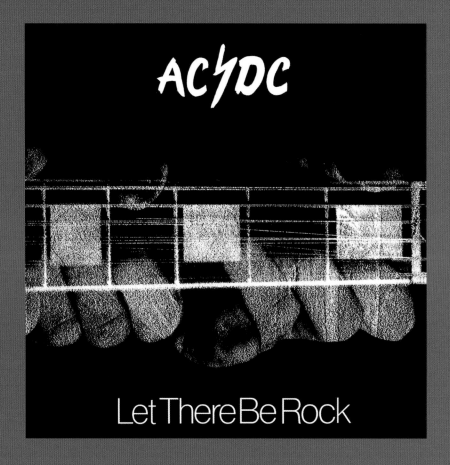

AC/DC

Let There Be Rock

> ❝ *This is AC/DC's heaviest record, AC/DC's densest record, AC/DC's most energetic record.* ❞

LARS ULRICH OF METALLICA
TO *ROLLING STONE*

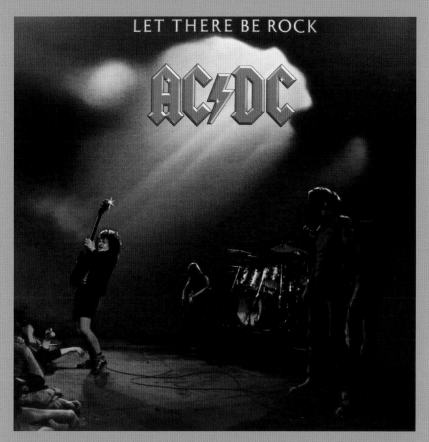

April AC/DC set out on a month-long tour of Europe with Black Sabbath, playing shows in France, Germany, Switzerland, and Scandinavia. Sabbath's Ozzy Osbourne has taken to referring to himself, with due irreverence, as the 'plumber of darkness', a nod to both his working-class roots—something the Youngs can relate to—and his reputation for evil.

April 3 A performance of 'Dog Eat Dog' is beamed to *Countdown* from London for the show's one-hundredth episode. Also appearing are Skyhooks, Little River Band, Bryan Ferry (performing 'A Hard Rain's A-Gonna Fall'), Leo Sayer (who co-hosts the show), Shaun Cassidy, Smokie, Kiki Dee, Suzi Quatro, and Elton John.

'Next on the show from London is a group that knows all about the land of Oz,' Sayer announces. 'And, believe me, England is fast learning about them. Need I say any more?'

Angus, for once, isn't dressed as a schoolboy; instead, he sports a black-and-white striped top, but with his schoolboy's cap well and truly in place—at least until he bursts into a frenzied duck walk during his red-hot solo, when it goes flying.

April 5 The band have technical hassles during their first gig in Paris, and they take out their frustration on their gear, ending their set abruptly after twenty minutes. The crowd mistake the trashing for some kind of punk statement and go nuts.

April 6–15 The tour rolls through France, Germany, Switzerland, and Denmark. During Sabbath's sets, various AC/DCs gather at the side of the stage and cheer on Geezer Butler during his interminable bass solo—their cheers reach a crescendo whenever he hits a bum note. Sabbath, to AC/DC, are just another band to muscle aside on their way to the top.

April 16 After a show in Brussels, Belgium, Geezer Butler is in the hotel bar, moaning about life on the road.

'Wait until you guys have been around ten years,' he grumbles to Malcolm Young, who is sitting nearby. 'You'll feel just like us.'

'I don't think so,' Malcolm snaps back.

With that, Butler pulls out a flick knife and starts waving it about, at which point Ozzy Osbourne walks into the bar.

'You fuckin' idiot, Butler,' he says to the bassist, 'get to bed.'

It's perhaps the first time Osbourne actually prevents chaos from occurring. He does, however, settle in and see out the night with Malcolm and others. And, despite the flare-up, the tour continues, with both bands travelling on to Amsterdam for the next night's show.

April 18 Even though the band's US touring plans remain unclear, Atlantic's Jerry Greenberg and John Kalodner have flown in to see their gig in Hamburg, Germany, at the Ernst Merck Hall. They end up with the band on the Reeperbahn, where they witness live sex acts and other assorted weirdness. At one club, a couple go at it on a table top right alongside the band and their entourage, while an eager onlooker at the next table unzips his pants as the show goes on. Some members of the AC/DC party just don't know which way to look.

'It was just like Christmas shopping,' Angus sniggers.

April 19 After a gig in Copenhagen, Denmark, Mark Evans gets into a punch-up with a drunken German tourist; Michael Browning breaks a finger in the resulting mayhem. A local Atlantic rep, their host for the night, looks on, a bit stunned by the chaos.

April 20–24 Further Black Sabbath shows follow in Stockholm, Lund, and Gothenburg in Sweden; proposed gigs in Norway and Finland are cancelled, however, so the tour ends here.

May 11 *Let There Be Rock* enters UK album chart in a week when ABBA's *Arrival* is wedged at #1. It will peak at #17 and chart for a total of five weeks.

In his review for *Sounds*, Phil Sutcliffe admits that while variety isn't the band's strongest suit—'in this forty minutes [there are] seven head-bangers and one comic slow blues'—it's hardly the point. 'That's not what you crave from them, is it?

'No surprises [here],' he continues, 'just the time honoured hard-rock message: they come along and smash your feet with ten-pound hammers, you leap in the air uttering strange cries of agony and ecstasy. Presently the element of pain fades away but you stay bouncing as if the riff was a trampoline. You sweat like a pig, you smell like a sty and you feel beautiful.'

Mick Wall, writing for teamrock.com, will later note, '*Let There Be Rock* was the [album] where AC/DC truly found their place in the scheme of things, not least on the title track, a heartfelt ode to original, no-shit rock'n'roll as evinced by the fastest, most irresistibly hair-shaking piece of high-octane noise ever committed to what was still then just poor, weak vinyl. Elsewhere, "Hell Ain't A Bad Place To Be" stood as AC/DC's own "Brown Sugar".'

And when *Rolling Stone* compiles a reader's poll of the ten best AC/DC songs, 'Let There Be Rock' checks in at #10. 'The title track to AC/DC's 1977 LP has a very simple concept,' the magazine notes. 'What would the Bible have sounded like had it been written by AC/DC?'

The album's hilarious ode to an oversized groupie, 'Whole Lotta Rosie', charts even higher, coming in at #4. 'AC/DC has never been too worried about political correctness,' *Rolling Stone* notes, stating the bleeding obvious. 'The song was one of their first to break outside of Australia, and it remains a staple of their live show to this day, complete with an inflated Rosie doll that never fails to get the crowd roaring.'

Meanwhile, the album track 'Dog Eat Dog' will become such a favourite of a young Axl Rose that when he later joins the band to play some shows in 2016, he insists they add it to their setlist.

June 3 RAM reports that Mark Evans has been sacked—sent packing back to Melbourne with a pink slip and a cheque for $2,000. *Juke* refers to his dismissal as a 'bad case of *musicalis differencius*'. Malcolm tells him that they need a bass player who can sing, but the simple truth is that he's come out second best in a clash of strong personalities, having repeatedly clashed with Angus, culminating in the one-punch fight in a London bar. They have never really connected personally, and Evans, being way lower down the AC/DC hierarchy than Angus, has to go.

'If Angus had one crucial problem with people,' Evans later writes of the experience, 'it was those who didn't share his utter commitment to the band and music; you had to be in 100 percent or you weren't worth bothering about … I believe it frustrated him when others, me included, didn't perform to his expectations.'

When a reporter from *Best* magazine asks Angus for his version of events, his response couldn't be any chillier. 'Mark left because he couldn't stand the tour anymore. He had a nervous breakdown.'

After considering Colin Pattenden from Manfred Mann's Earth Band (whose drummer, Chris Slade, will later join AC/DC), they hire twenty-seven-year-old bassist

WHEN CLIFF WILLIAMS MAKES HIS OZ DEBUT WITH THE BAND AT THE BONDI LIFESAVER, SOME STEALTH IS REQUIRED AS HE DOESN'T HAVE A WORKING VISA FOR AUSTRALIA. THE VENUE IS PACKED TO BURSTING BOTH NIGHTS.

THE BONDI LIFESAVER

56 EBLEV ST BONDI JUNCTION

THE HOTTEST, LIVEWIRE, HIGH VOLTAGE ACT IN THE WORLD

ONLY AUST. APPEARANCE
THIS **FRI 1**ST & **SAT 2**ND **JULY**

> *"We were a scandal in Australia. They love scandal there. Mums tugging their kids away from us on the street. 'Oh look—THEM!'"*

MALCOLM YOUNG TO IAN FLAVIN,
ROCK STAR, MARCH 1977

Cliff Williams, most recently of the group Bandit, who made one album for the Arista label before calling it a day. (The band's singer, Jim Diamond, scores a #1 UK hit in 1984 with 'I Should Have Known Better'.)

Williams had considered quitting music when Bandit split, but he is a fan of AC/DC. He is helped out by Browning, who wisely advises him to use a pick during his audition, for which Williams runs through 'Live Wire' and 'Problem Child' with the band. It works, and Williams gets the gig.

Also in June ... Briefly back in Australia, the group—with film crew in tow—commandeer the Kirk Gallery church in Sydney's inner-city suburb of Surry Hills to shoot a clip for 'Let There Be Rock'. Scott is dressed as a priest and Angus as a choirboy, his homemade halo bouncing madly as he plays. During the big finale, he takes a leap off the altar that's worthy of an Olympian but not really suitable for a hard-living, thirty-one-year-old rocker. He hurts his ankle and limps back to his hotel, where he's tended to by a female doctor (who he takes out that night).

The song will have a long and influential impact, appearing on four of AC/DC's six live albums, becoming a concert staple, and, much further down the line, being included on the soundtrack to the music video game *Rock Band 2*. It will also be covered by Henry Rollins (with The Hard-Ons), Foo Fighters, and LA Guns, among many others.

While in Sydney, the band return to Albert Productions to work on several new songs, but only one ('Touch Too Much') will see light of day. It's likely that work-in-progress versions of 'Up To My Neck In You' and 'Kicked In The Teeth' are cut during these sessions, and possible too that some of the tracks are to be rearranged during their next Alberts sessions, for the *Powerage* album.

July Angus puts in a very rare cameo appearance at a gig by Rose Tattoo, at the Bondi Lifesaver. Though he's not usually one for jamming with others, he makes an exception for the Tatts. Bon Scott also joins in, as they blitz their way through 'Johnny B. Goode' and 'Whole Lotta Shakin' Goin' On'. It may not be an AC/DC gig, but Angus doesn't hold back, dropping to the stage floor for a dying bug and then wading into the audience. Angus and Scott had encouraged Vanda and Young to come to the gig, too, and sure enough, Alberts signs Rose Tattoo.

A few nights later, Cliff Williams makes his live Oz debut with AC/DC at the Lifesaver, despite not having a work visa. As such, in a fairly flimsy attempt to keep the gigs secret, they're billed for two nights as 'The Seedies—the hottest livewire, high voltage act in the world'.

On the first night, during a solo, Angus treads on a beer glass, the shards piercing his flimsy tennis shoes and badly cutting his foot. 'It was a bit like a movie, you know,' he says after the gig. '[Blood] was just spurting out.'

The following night, an eager female fan jumps on stage, grabs Scott's microphone, and shoves it down her skirt. The same woman is spotted soon after, bonking a roadie in full view of the crowd, as the band plays on. According to Angus, 'It turned into a right Babylon!'

Australian reporter Ray Martin, part of the local *60 Minutes* crew, speaks backstage with Angus and the band. Speaks down to the group, truth be told.

'How many dirty deeds have you counted, son, in the last year?' he asks.

'About 450,' Angus replies, smirking.

Malcolm, apparently, isn't feeling the love, and he walks away from the interview, fuming that the reporter didn't seem at all interested in discussing their work. Another member of the TV crew catches up with him and asks, 'Would you like to storm off again, so we can get a camera to follow you?'

July 25 The *Let There Be Rock* LP is released internationally, with 'Problem Child' taking the place of Scott's Gershwin-inspired 'Crabsody In Blue', its subject matter perhaps considered a bit obscure for a non-Aussie audience. The cover of this version of the album features the lightning bolt logo designed by Gerard Huerta, which will become an AC/DC trademark.

In a review that will one day be listed among *Melody Maker*'s 'Great Moments In Rock Criticism'—a claim not to be taken literally—*Creem*'s Rick Johnson just can't understand what the fuss is about. 'These guys suck,' he writes. 'Somewhere in the granite mudpies of hard rock, there's got to be a distinction between boogie and plod, and AC/DC falls into the latter category.'

July 27 After various delays and frustrations, AC/DC finally begin their debut US tour. It isn't a bad time for them to be in America, with the recent rise of such hard-rock acts as Aerosmith, Van Halen, and the cartoon clowns of KISS. Among the usual fluff on the US Top 40 pop charts can be found guitar-driven songs like Steve Miller's 'Jet Airliner' and Foreigner's 'Feels Like The First Time', while even the dreaded Eagles have toughened up their sound considerably on 'Life In The Fast Lane', having enticed The James Gang's reprobate Joe Walsh to sign on as guitarist and hotel-room redecorator.

Much like when they first arrived in the UK, AC/DC are forced to start from the bottom, which means doing everything on a low budget. Band and crew squeeze into a rented station wagon for their six-week run, staying at various Red Roof Inns—a chain of cheapie hotels they'll visit so often over the next couple of years that it could have been renamed in their honour.

Angus, as is his nature, gets into Browning's ear about this.

'Why are you being such a tight-arse?' he asks.

Having signed with leading booking agent American Talent International, the band begin their tour at Willie Nelson's venue in Austin, Texas, the Armadillo World Headquarters, opening for the Canadian band Moxy to a rowdy crowd of around 1,500. They're paid $350 (US) for their services—and Angus gets a contact high while riding around the pot-shrouded venue on Bon Scott's shoulders. According to Browning, it's so hot inside the room that it seems as though they're playing 'under the shower'.

The promoter of this gig is Jack Orbin, who will make his name not only by enticing such acts as AC/DC, Judas Priest, and Scorpions to Texas, but also for bailing Ozzy Osbourne out of jail after he's caught pissing on the Alamo Cenotaph.

Likely setlist: 'Live Wire' / 'She's Got Balls' / 'Problem Child' / 'Jailbreak' / 'Whole Lotta Rosie' / 'Dog Eat Dog' / 'The Jack' / 'Baby, Please Don't Go'.

July 28 Tonight's gig is in San Antonio—a city that claims to be the rock'n'roll capital of the world—for which the band pocket $1,000. Further shows follow in Corpus Christi and Dallas, Texas, and in West Palm Beach, Florida.

August 6 The band play a gig in Jacksonville, Florida, where they have made some inroads thanks to the support of local promoter Sidney Drashin and WPDQ FM DJ Bill Bartlett—a big fan of Oz music who previously championed their arch rivals, Skyhooks. They gross a handsome $6,781.78 opening for REO Speedwagon at the 8,000-capacity Jacksonville Coliseum. Members of Lynyrd Skynyrd are invited to the show by Drashin, and they instantly become AC/DC converts.

August 7 The band play to a crowd of barely one hundred in Fort Lauderdale, Florida. Earlier in the afternoon, along with The Charlie Daniels Band (of 'The Devil Went Down

ANGUS AND BON BACKSTAGE AT THE PALLADIUM IN NEW YORK, AUGUST 24 1977, WITH TWO HELPFUL FANS. ANDY SHERNOFF OF THE DICTATORS, ALSO ON THE BILL THAT NIGHT, IS STUNNED. 'HOW CAN SHORT GUYS MAKE A SOUND LIKE THAT?'

To Georgia' fame), they were involved with a gig at the Hollywood Florida Sportatorium, helping to raise nearly $100,000 for a local kids' charity.

August 8 While in Miami to play at an Atlantic Records convention, the group (bar Angus) are taken shark fishing close to the Bermuda Triangle; the catch of the day (OK, the night) is hauled on board and beaten to death with a baseball bat.

The Atlantic Records gig takes place at the 4 O'Clock Club, allegedly a Mob-run venue. Tom Judge from local radio station WHSE is given the task of introducing the band—and inspiring a typically distracted industry gathering to get involved. 'I don't make speeches, let alone write them,' he admits, 'but all summer long, record companies have been supplying WHSE with bands for charitable events, and we appreciate it. … We're gonna bring a band out here who was there on August the 7th—AC/DC. Join me in a typical South Florida welcome for our friends from Australia. AC/DC!'

Bon seems in a big hurry, introducing 'Hell Ain't A Bad Place To Be' even before the band's opener, 'Live Wire', has ended. Industry gigs are neither his nor the band's natural environment; it's clear they'd much rather be playing to the great unwashed: the true believers.

'This one'll get you off your asses and on your feet,' he says, a tad hopefully, before ripping into 'Baby, Please Don't Go.' To their credit, the band play with the same ferocity as they would when fronting a crowd of thousands of genuine, ticket-buying fans, with Scott, especially, working himself into a fair lather by the end of their eight-song set.

The next day—in a promo stunt cooked up by an Atlantic staffer whose cousin just so happens to be the local mayor, Michael Colodny—the band are given the keys to the city of North Miami. Angus and Bon sport oversized sun hats at the presentation, grinning broadly. Bon also wears his favourite cut-off denim shorts, his … equipment on full and ample display. So much for civic formality. A photo of the presentation ceremony will later be used on the cover of a bootleg recording of the Atlantic Records gig, *Lauderdale Larrikins*.

August 9–21 More shows ensue in St Louis and Kansas City; Schaumburg, Illinois, where Angus clears the drinks off the bar as he struts it like a catwalk, playing a wild solo; Cleveland and Columbus, Ohio; Madison and Milwaukee, Wisconsin; Indianapolis; and back to Ohio for gigs in Dayton and Youngstown. Several of these shows see

AC/DC opening for other acts: either Foreigner, Mink DeVille, or, in a monumental mismatch, Latin rockers Santana.

August 22 A gig at the Agora Ballroom in Cleveland, Ohio, is recorded, the bootlegged results going by the oh-so-poetic title of *Burning Balls*. The MC's intro is priceless: 'For anyone who was at the ultimate experience recently at the Cleveland Convention Center, I don't think I need to introduce these guys. For the rest of you people, passed out tonight … live and in person, can we have a very big hand for Atco recording artists, AC/DC.' The band swiftly and efficiently lock into 'Live Wire', and they're away.

Track listing: 'Live Wire' / 'She's Got Balls' / 'Problem Child' / 'The Jack' / 'High Voltage' / 'Baby, Please Don't Go' / 'Rocker'.

August 24 The band play a bottom-of-the-bill set at the Palladium in New York, opening for The Dictators. Angus and Bon befriend Dictators founder Andy Shernoff, who is surprised by the sight of the band—quite literally. He later tells salon.com, 'Angus is a midget! Bon Scott was small, too. It's amazing. How can short guys make a sound like that? It's almost technically impossible.'

Afterward, the band dash downtown to play legendary hole-in-the-wall CBGB, completely unannounced—much to the surprise of a band named Marbles, who are just finishing their set. Angus's thing for wandering into the crowd takes on a whole new meaning at such a small club; he ends up in the street outside, mixing it with the bums from the nearby Palace Hotel, who seem just as surprised by the sight of the schoolboy axe-wielder as the guys from Marbles.

Mind you, the audience at CBGB is equally stunned. 'Oh, those legs!' an onlooker shrieks, as Angus takes the stage. 'Isn't Angus the name of the monster from *Lost In Space*?' another asks. Any further chat is silenced when the band tear into 'Live Wire'; the walls of the venue shake from sheer volume.

Interviewed by the *Punk* fanzine while in New York—AC/DC's label have bought advertising for them in the mag, hoping to connect with a punk audience—Bon is asked about the meaning of life.

'As good a time and as short as possible,' he replies.

'I thought there would be more rock,' Angus later tells *Guitar World*, when quizzed about the American music scene. 'But when we got here, it was a disco type thing.'

Angus is right on the money. The US Top 10 at the time features dance-pop hits from the Emotions ('Best Of My Love'), expat Aussie Andy Gibb ('I Just Want To Be Your Everything'), and Rita Coolidge ('Your Love Has Lifted Me Higher'). One of the few rockers in the Top 20 is Alice Cooper, and even he is singing a ballad ('You And Me'). The album charts are big on mellow, too, with bestselling records from Fleetwood Mac (*Rumours*), James Taylor, Peter Frampton, and Barry Manilow.

August 27 AC/DC share a curious bill, opening for albino bluesman Johnny Winter and Southern rockers .38 Special, at the 4,600-capacity Masonic Auditorium in Detroit.

Likely setlist: 'Live Wire' / She's Got Balls' / 'Problem Child' / 'Whole Lotta Rosie' / 'Dog Eat Dog' / 'The Jack' / 'Baby, Please Don't Go'.

August 29–31 AC/DC host a three-night stand at influential music biz watering hole the Whisky a Go-Go in LA, where recent headliners include she-rockers The Runaways and Van Halen. The opening night is the best attended of the three; there are barely eighty people in the room come their final gig. Regardless, Gene Simmons of KISS is sufficiently impressed to invite the band to open at some future American shows. He shares a late dinner at a Denny's diner on Sunset with Angus and Michael Browning.

The band stay at the notorious Hyatt House—aka the Riot House, where Keith Richards first experimented with the aerodynamics of TV sets and John Bonham would ride his Harley down the hallways—which is stumbling distance from the Whisky. Bon Scott and Phil Rudd also check out Disneyland, when Scott tires of the many eager groupies who kindly offer him their services. Angus, meanwhile, has an interesting take on the many women who linger at their shows in the States. 'In America, the chicks who come backstage all want to screw you,' he tells *Sounds*' Dave Lewis. In another interview, with *Rock Gossip*, he jokingly comes clean about his motivation for being in a rock'n'roll band. 'In general, girls inspire us a lot. It is an inexhaustible source. They're our major concern. We really live for the chicks.'

While in LA, thanks to Atlantic staffer Michael Klenfner, the group are introduced to Ken Schaffer, a trailblazer in the high-tech world of wireless guitars and microphones. Schaffer presents Angus with a wireless transmitter (the Schaffer-Vega Diversity System, valued at around $3,300 and currently being tested by Rick Derringer, Peter Frampton, and members of KISS) and Bon with a wireless mic. Schaffer tells Angus, 'Once you've used this, you'll never want to play with a lead again.' He is dead right.

ANGUS AND THE BAND TEAR IT UP AT THE WHISKY A GO-GO DURING A THREE-NIGHT STAND IN AUGUST 1977. IT'S DURING THIS RESIDENCY THAT THEY'RE INTRODUCED TO THE WONDERS OF WIRELESS TECHNOLOGY.

Not only will these high-tech gadgets create a whole new world of performance possibilities for the pair, they will also lighten the load on the band's roadies, who until now have been forced to follow the two like Sherpas whenever they decide to 'go rogue' and mix it with the crowd. They will also save Angus from onstage shocks, such as the time he reached for a Coke can and suddenly found 'the amp and the can and me all stuck together and shaking'.

En route to the West Coast, Bon Scott goes AWOL somewhere around Phoenix, eventually surfacing in a rowdy bar, playing pool and drinking with the locals. 'I'm playin' this big-titted black chick, and beatin' her, too, when I happen to look around and the whole bar is goin, Grrr.' He wisely opts to throw the game and save his skin— and somehow still makes that evening's gig.

September 2–3 The final US shows of this run are held at the Old Waldorf in San Francisco, with 750 people attending each night. The show will later be bootlegged as *Definitely Not The Glimmer Twins*. The band win over another true believer in Howie Klein, who covers this and other West Coast shows for *New York Rocker* magazine.

> **❝We just call ourselves a rock band. [And] if I said we were a punk band, people would say, Yeah, right. These bands are violent—they like shittin' and pissin' on carpets, smashin' up rooms and the like.❞**
>
> ANGUS YOUNG TO *NEW YORK ROCKER*, SEPTEMBER 1977

'These guys rock out,' he writes. 'Perhaps Angus Young, their Billy Gibbons-oid guitar genius, was a trifle self-indulgent, perhaps even a little [God forbid] excessive with the licks for the hard-core pinhead set, but most rock'n'rollers could relate right away to their raw, basic youthful energy. AC/DC does a show cathartic in the way a Patti Smith show is cathartic. Sure, the albums are great, but there are just some bands that ya gotta see live.'

The dreaded subject of punk rock comes up in a backstage chat between Angus and Klein, but the guitarist's response is surprising. 'Actually,' he admits, 'the punk rock thing is pretty cool in America. It's not like in England, where it's a very political thing … [here] it's just a young thing, [a] new breed type thing.' Yet Young remains adamant that AC/DC are anything but punk-rockers.

All up, the run of sixteen American dates, from July 27 to September 3, which swings from Austin to New York, grosses some $18,789 and 18 cents. Just as importantly, it snags the band new fans and influential supporters, if not major record sales.

During this first US tour, although the band have travelled mainly by rented station wagon, they have also had had the chance to fly on Southwest Airlines, and they are quite taken by the Southwest stewardesses, whose uniform features hot pants. According to Angus, 'It was very impressive to a young rock'n'roll band at the time.'

September 14–October 8 The band return to Europe, for shows in Sweden, Finland, Germany, Belgium, and Switzerland. The September 24 show in Braunschweig, Germany, is sparsely attended, yet the band still play so loudly that at least one fan's ears are still bleeding the next day.

October 9 Chaos erupts during a show at the Thier Brau Hof in Kontich, Belgium. The opening act, Mothers Of Track, have had an accident en route so haven't made it to the gig, and then a technical hitch delays AC/DC's set. They eventually take the stage at 10:45pm. Meanwhile, outside the venue, the behaviour of some boisterous fans has resulted in two units of local police swinging by. The police officers then enter the venue and, feeling threatened by the crowd, request backup. As cops surround the stage, AC/DC crewmembers encircle the band in a vain attempt to keep the gig going, but a brawl erupts involving the crew, the fans, and the law.

By 11:30pm, the show, and the tour, is over. The madness inspires the song 'Bedlam In Belgium'.

October 14 The band fill the Mayfair in Newcastle, opening with 'Let There Be Rock', an Angus guitar showcase. Within seconds, the crowd erupts, chanting 'AC/DC! AC/DC! AC/DC!' and, in the words of *Sounds*' true believer, Phil Sutcliffe, 'bask in their own hell heat while soaking in Angus's sweat and snot as if it were holy water.'

In a funny footnote, Sutcliffe says of Angus, 'The school-kid image will have to go one day, but at the moment it's still dead right.' Forty-odd years later, we're still waiting.

Setlist: 'Let There Be Rock' / 'Problem Child' / 'Hell Ain't A Bad Place To Be' / 'Whole Lotta Rosie' / 'High Voltage' / 'The Jack' / 'Bad Boy Boogie' / 'Rocker' / 'T.N.T.'

October 15–31 Further gigs follow in Malvern, Dunstable, Liverpool, Glasgow, Middlesbrough, Manchester, London, Cambridge, Southend, and Birmingham. During their October 21 show at Lancaster University, Angus plays the encore of 'T.N.T.' while perched atop the PA; below him, roadies grapple with the stacks, ensuring they don't collapse.

FOLLOWING PAGES: THE BAND ROCK ATLANTIC STUDIOS IN NEW YORK CITY, DECEMBER 7 1977. A RECORDING OF THEIR SET, RELEASED AS *AC/DC LIVE FROM THE ATLANTIC STUDIOS*, WILL BECOME A HIGHLY COLLECTABLE ARTEFACT.

"*AC/DC does a show [that's] cathartic in the way a Patti Smith show is cathartic. Sure, the albums are great, but there are just some bands that ya gotta see live.*"

HOWIE KLEIN, *NEW YORK ROCKER*

At the Middlesbrough gig, Angus's new wireless guitar has at least one punter scratching his head: ''is guitar's not plugged in,' someone yells, as Angus makes his way through the crowd.

November 1 Bon Scott speaks with *Countdown*'s Molly Meldrum in London, wearing a bulky faux-fur coat and a winning smile. He toys with the typically nervous Meldrum, suggesting he be careful with his microphone—'You shouldn't put it down there, Ian'—and talking up the rock'n'roll heartland that is Great Yarmouth, Suffolk.

'What, you've never heard of Great Yarmouth?' Bon asks, in mock incredulity.

Those dreaded words 'punk' and 'Sex Pistols' come up early in the conversation. Scott laughs it off, but he seems tired of the subject.

'We're pulling bigger crowds than they are,' he insists. 'It's not new wave and it's not punk, it's just people who like our band. We honestly thought the punk and new wave thing might spoil things a bit for us, but it hasn't at all. It was a big fad for a while … the main thing is that it gave rock a kick in the guts, you know?'

Meldrum asks where their hit single is; what's going on there?

'Singles bands over here, without already having established a road following, are going to suffer the same effect of Sherbet, who had a big hit over here and their UK tour consisted of one gig. They're a record band with no road following. We have the [live] following.

'Australia's different altogether,' he adds. 'Over here, the album is the main thing. If radio picks up a track, it helps sell the album.'

So why do they continually return to Australia to record? Meldrum asks.

'George and Harry are there, and they know the studio like the back of their hand. It's a perfect setup. It's all there. We don't need to go anywhere else.' ('Hey, St Peter', Vanda & Young's first single under the guise of Flash & The Pan, has just breached the Oz top 5. It will also reach the Top 10 in Holland and Belgium, and hit #76 in the USA.)

Scott also reveals that the band are about to tour the USA with KISS. 'I saw them in London,' he adds, slyly cocking an eyebrow. '*Quite spectacular.*'

November 3 According to some reports, Angus clobbers some 'gobbing' punks with his guitar during AC/DC's gig at rock's ground zero, Great Yarmouth. Clearly, he is not a spittoon—and he's no fan of punk rockers, either. (Further, incident-free shows follow this week in Norwich and Cambridge.)

November 16–December 21 AC/DC return to the USA for their longest run of American dates so far: twenty-two in all, beginning in upstate New York and ending in Pennsylvania. Many are mid-bill, between headliners UFO and openers The Motors. Tickets range from $3–$5, and most of the venues are mid-sized halls.

During the run, UFO's Pete Way becomes a friend and huge admirer of Bon Scott, later telling *Classic Rock*'s Geoff Barton, 'He was fantastic. Do you know who Bon reminds me of? Alex Harvey. I'm a big fan of Alex Harvey—*Faith Healer* and that. It's the same thing; Bon had the same attitude. Sensational.

'AC/DC wrote the law about playing rock'n'roll. As simple as that. And Bon was brilliant. You'd see him first thing in the morning, and he'd been with the barmaid or something, and he'd go, Had a good workout last night. He'd get out of the elevator, he'd clap his hands, and he'd say, Large Jack Daniels. Brilliant.'

November 24 Only a small crowd turns up for the band's show in Johnson City, Tennessee, due to a snowstorm. There are perhaps 1,000 fans in the 8,000-seat Freedom Hall Civic Center. Scott hangs about to mingle and drink with those who have made it after the show.

November 26 The morning after a show at the Municipal Auditorium in Charleston, West Virginia, the *Gazette* newspaper complains about the amount of smoke that hovered over the crowd throughout the gig. Soon after, smoking will be banned at the venue.

"We don't write singles—something specifically for a single. No way. We're a road/album band; singles don't mean a pinch to nobody. The BBC might pick something up, but we'd never do it intentionally."

BON SCOTT TO MOLLY MELDRUM, COUNTDOWN, NOVEMBER 1977

November 27 AC/DC headline their own show at the Capri Theater in Atlanta, Georgia. Atlanta FM station 96 Rock has been very supportive of AC/DC and helped drum up a good crowd. On stage, Bon explains to the locals that 'The Jack' is what Americans refer to as 'the clap'. During Angus's lengthy solo in 'Let There Be Rock', he prowls the aisles of the theatre, headbanging wildly, stopping briefly to catch his breath in an empty seat alongside some gobsmacked punters.

December 4 When the band come to headline the Electric Ballroom in Milwaukee, Wisconsin, the poster promoting the gig—which promises 'A Giant Dose of Rock'n'roll' —still features Mark Evans, sacked from the band several months earlier.

December 7 AC/DC play a live set at Atlantic Studios in New York; the results are made available for use by radio stations and, in 1978, released on vinyl as *AC/DC Live From The Atlantic Studios*.

Track listing: 'Live Wire' / 'Problem Child' / 'High Voltage' / 'Hell Ain't A Bad Place To Be' / 'Dog Eat Dog' / 'The Jack' / 'Whole Lotta Rosie' / 'Rocker'.

December 9 AC/DC begin a run of shows opening for KISS at the 10,000-capacity Mid South Coliseum in Memphis, Tennessee. Over the next fortnight, they will play further gigs with KISS in Indianapolis, Indiana; Louisville, Kentucky; and Landover, Maryland—all at venues with a capacity of around 20,000. Gene Simmons will later boast about giving AC/DC their start in the USA, and with good reason.

December 12 The band play the Freedom Hall in Louisville. Two reviews of the show run locally, the first in the *Courier-Journal*. 'AC/DC [rely] on a lot of athletic prancing around by its lead guitarist, who strips from a Little Lord Fauntleroy outfit down to shorts, and does a lot of falling down while continuing to perform,' notes the paper's John Finley. 'It's hard to see where groups like KISS and AC/DC can go from here.'

The second review, which runs in the *Lexington Leader*, is a doozy. 'One bit of advice,' writes Ellen Aman. 'Unless you are addicted to this sort of music, you can skip the opening act, a forty-five-minute set by something called AC/DC … AC/DC's concept of "good music" seems to be the ability to play the guitar while running. And I don't think they're any too strict about the calibre of guitar playing, either.'

Meanwhile, a fan visiting Louisville radio station WSAC is shocked to discover that the station has no intention of playing AC/DC's 'Problem Child'. A programmer happily gives away the station's copy of single.

A SELECTION OF LIVE BOOTLEGS FROM 1977. (AC/DC BOOTLEGGERS DID A LIVELY TRADE DURING THE BON SCOTT ERA AND BEYOND.)

December 15–21 The band round out the tour, and the year, with further shows in Fort Wayne, Indiana (supporting Styx); Charleston, West Virginia (opening for Aerosmith); Greensboro, North Carolina (with Cheap Trick); Landover, Maryland (KISS again); and finally Pittsburgh, Pennsylvania (Blue Öyster Cult).

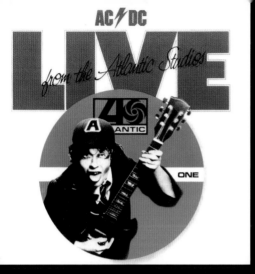

AC/DC
LIVE
from the Atlantic Studios

ATLANTIC

ONE

AC/DC

Burning Balls

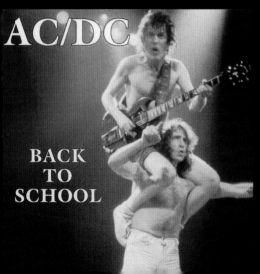

AC/DC

**BACK
TO
SCHOOL**

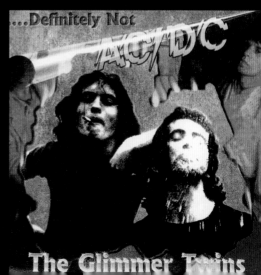

...Definitely Not

AC/DC

The Glimmer Twins

The fan-favourite LP **Powerage** *is released; the band endure union troubles at Top Of The Pops; AC/DC's American assault continues, as Alice Cooper, Van Halen, Keith Richards, and Aerosmith become true believers; and the live album* **If You Want Blood, You've Got It** *rounds out the year.*

January–February The band spend the southern summer in the Albert Productions studio with Vanda & Young, recording *Powerage*, their fifth studio record—and their first with new bassist Cliff Williams. But Williams almost doesn't get to play on the album; he has problems with the Australian Musician's Union, which needs convincing that he can do what an Australian musician cannot (an irony that wouldn't have been lost on the recently sacked Mark Evans). Eventually, after much formal correspondence, Williams is given the OK, and joins the rest of the group during January.

In an interview with *RAM*, Angus grumbles to writer Anthony O'Grady about the treatment dished out to Williams by the Aussie authorities (in the Embassy's UK office, admittedly) and the residual fallout from the Giant Dose tour controversy. 'We're not allowed to play in Australia,' he says.

'They kept our bass player out of the country,' adds Bon Scott. 'They said us having a UK bass player puts an Australian out of work. It was some Australian arsehole official in London. It was harder for us to get our English bass player and roadie into Australia than it was for all of us to get working permits for America. And that's a joke.'

Williams then relates a conversation he has with an Australian embassy official. 'The guy who handled my file told me, "I do not see why an Englishman has the job. An Australian could have gone very well." I had a lot of problems [before] I finally got to Australia.'

Scott also takes aim at the Aussie media, including, surprisingly, a long-time advocate. 'We lost a lot from people in the media not pushing us,' Scott snarls. 'If you don't show your arse to Molly Meldrum on *Countdown*, you're fucked. You just don't get on TV and your records aren't played on radio.'

'We used to think of ourselves as an Australian band,' Angus adds, 'but we're beginning to doubt that now. The fuckers won't even let us play here.'

These early 1978 album sessions run for an unusually lengthy eight weeks—a marathon by AC/DC standards. *Powerage* is engineered by Australian Mark Opitz, who will go on to work with such successful acts as The Angels, Cold Chisel, INXS, The Divinyls, and The Hoodoo Gurus.

Some tracks from the finished album—'Up To My Neck In You' and 'Kicked In The Teeth' among them—actually date back to the July 1977 sessions with Vanda & Young. Another track cut at these sessions, 'What's Next To The Moon', will only surface on the British, French, German, and Swedish versions of *Powerage*.

On his first listen to the album, Phil Carson from Atlantic in the UK, who signed

FOLLOWING PAGES: *POWERAGE* WILL BECOME THE AC/DC ALBUM OF CHOICE FOR MANY, INCLUDING KEITH RICHARDS. 'YOU CAN HEAR IT,' SAYS THE ROLLING STONES' RIFFMASTER. 'IT HAS THE SPIRIT.'

"*We don't really give a fuck about the media. We never have. We only care about the kids who come up after a show and say, 'That really rocked, that had balls' — that's what matters. So many kids would come up to us on the street and say, We heard about you being banned, that's really shithouse ... the kids cared ... we cared.*"

ANGUS YOUNG TO ANTHONY
O'GRADY, *RAM*, JANUARY 1978

the band, can't hear an obvious song for radio. After some heated discussion, the band agree to return to Alberts and record another track, 'Rock'n'roll Damnation'. It's a song that sounds more like a heavier Easybeats than traditional AC/DC, with its handclaps and overdubbed percussion—and what appear to be female backup vocals (though there's no credit to confirm this). It also lacks the traditional Angus solo. Still, 'Damnation' becomes *Powerage*'s lead single, with thirty seconds trimmed from the album version.

While in Australia, Scott seeks out the services of a tarot reader, who tells him, 'You will meet a blonde, get divorced, meet a dark-haired girl, and have a short life.' He shares the revelations with some friends in Melbourne: 'I'll be dead by 1980.'

January 26 Bon and Angus put in a non-playing cameo at the Williamstown Rock Festival in Victoria. They're flown in by chopper and interviewed by radio station 3XY.

February 1 According to a note in the *Australian Women's Weekly*, the current address for the AC/DC Fan Club is in the UK, not Australia. It's listed as 18 Watson Close, Bury St Edmonds, Suffolk, UK.

March Alberts has plans to release an AC/DC album titled *12 Of The Best*, a snapshot of their work with Vanda & Young between November 1974 and February 1977. Cassettes of the album are produced—and then destroyed, when the release plans are shelved. Just a few test pressings of the vinyl album are produced, along with a handful of album sleeves, and these items will become possibly *the* most sought-after AC/DC rarities.

Proposed track listing: 'It's A Long Way To The Top (If You Wanna Rock'n'roll)' / 'High Voltage' / 'Problem Child' / 'T.N.T.' / 'Whole Lotta Rosie' / 'Let There Be Rock' / 'Jailbreak' / 'Dirty Deeds Done Dirt Cheap' / 'The Jack' / 'Dog Eat Dog' / 'She's Got Balls' / 'Baby, Please Don't Go'.

Meanwhile, a series of possible Australian dates for March are cancelled, in the wake of Williams's visa hassles and the work required for *Powerage*.

April 27 A month-long run of UK dates to promote *Powerage* begins, days prior to its release, at the Victoria Hall in Hanley. The four-month gap between gigs is the longest live break the band have had since forming.

April 29 A proposed show in Aberdeen is cancelled because Angus is unwell—a rare occurrence of AC/DC missing a gig.

April 30 The show at the Apollo Theatre in Glasgow is recorded for a possible live album. 'Any virgins in Glasgow?' Bon enquires, as he leads the band into 'The Jack'. For their encore, the band return dressed in the Scottish football strip—a nod to the locale, and to Scott and the Youngs' heritage.

A scribe from *Record Mirror* speaks with Bon backstage. Scott again makes it clear that it's the audience, not the press, that matters to the band. 'As long as the kids like what we're doing and keep coming to see us,' he says, 'that's all we care about. They can play along with us on their imaginary guitars, have a good time and really get their rocks off.'

Setlist: 'Riff Raff' / 'Problem Child' / 'Hell Ain't A Bad Place To Be' / 'Rock'n'roll Damnation' / 'Bad Boy Boogie' / 'Dog Eat Dog' / 'The Jack' / 'High Voltage' / 'Whole Lotta Rosie' / 'Let There Be Rock' / 'Fling Thing' / 'Rocker'.

> **"*If you can provide something to look at, it makes all the difference. He'll probably be in short trousers for a while yet.*"**
>
> BON SCOTT MAKES CLEAR TO *RECORD MIRROR* THAT ANGUS'S SCHOOLBOY OUTFIT IS A KEEPER, APRIL 1978

May 2–4 At least a dozen Angus lookalikes are spotted in the audience at a gig in Coventry on May 2. The band then travel to Liverpool, for a show at the Empire.

May 5 *Powerage* is released globally—a first for an AC/DC album. (An Australian release would typically precede an overseas launch.) However, there is an extra track on the European release, 'Cold Hearted Man', as well as a slightly altered track listing and a different, heavier mix (for the initial pressings).

The album will later be remixed for the US market, for which a radio spot is also produced. It begins with the sound of an explosion, followed by a voiceover delivered with a newsreader's sense of gravitas. Samples of the album play loudly in the background. 'Nuclear energy is dead, the neutron bomb can kiss my [bleep]—AC/DC's newest blast has arrived, *Powerage*. The ultimate AC/DC album.'

A second radio ad is subsequently produced, this time exclusively for Streetside Records in St Louis, and it's slightly less portentous than the first. The message is simple: 'If it's relentless, gut-wrenching rock'n'roll you want, then overload your circuits with AC/DC and *Powerage*.'

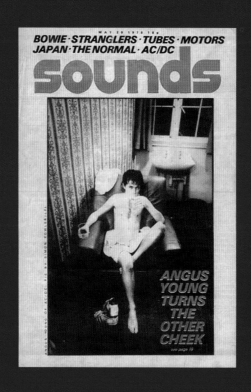

*"**Angus's frenzied schoolboy lunacy makes Chuck Berry's duckwalk look like a parapelgic's hobble, oozing sweat, snot and slime like some grotesque human sponge.**"*

DAVE LEWIS, *SOUNDS*, MAY 1978

Reviewing the album for the *Canberra Times*, Luis Feliu feels the noise. 'Ahhhhh, welcome some juicy rock'n'roll, the sweaty, loud sort and yes, from Australia's best-ever rock export. Hurrahs from the British and the Americans will soon know LRB [Little River Band] was just nonsense compared with this.

'I've accused this album of blowing some of my stereo channels silly, at least when I first got it, but it still sounds just smashing on the one channel and speaker. … *Powerage* is nothing more or nothing less than open-throttle rock'n'roll. … A damn good party rage record.'

Powerage will go on to sell one million copies in North America, but on its release reaches only #133 on the *Billboard* 200. *Rolling Stone* awards the album a paltry two-and-half stars, but the album will receive its dues over time. It is rated at #26 on *Kerrang!* magazine's '100 Greatest Heavy Metal Albums Of All-Time' list, and is later given a big thumbs-up by none other than Keith Richards, who says, 'You can hear it; it has the spirit.'

Malcolm Young, meanwhile, would cite it as among his band's most underrated albums. 'I know a lot of people respect it—a lot of real rock'n'roll AC/DC fans, the real pure rock'n'roll guys.'

May 5–24 As the UK tour continues, the band pack small halls and clubs in Liverpool, Newcastle, Manchester, Oxford, Swindon, Cambridge, West Runton, Birmingham, Derby, Keighley, Colchester, Leeds, Sheffield, Bristol, Bournemouth, Plymouth, Carlisle and Edinburgh. The average ticket price is £1.50.

May 20 *Powerage* enters the UK album chart, where it will hit a peak position of #26 during a nine-week chart run. A lone Angus appears on the cover of *Sounds*, wearing nothing more than a towel and a grin, recovering backstage somewhere after another gig. The headline? 'Angus Young Turns The Other Cheek.' Dave Lewis, who writes the cover story, feels the need to shoehorn the words 'tube', 'Fosters', 'Rolf Harris', 'outback', and 'kangaroo' into the opening sentence, stretching beyond its limits a joke that isn't funny in the first place (and, given the three Scots in the band, not very accurate).

May 26 'You've probably had them, probably still got them,' says Bon, as he introduces 'Down Payment Blues' at King Georges Hall in Blackburn.

ANGUS YOUNG, *SOUNDS* COVER STAR, MAY 20 1978. THAT SAME DAY, *POWERAGE* HITS THE UK CHART, EVENTUALLY PEAKING AT #26.

May 27 Angus is passed around, crowd surfer–style, during an extended solo for 'Let There Be Rock', while playing the Market Hall at Carlisle.

May 28 While in Edinburgh, after a show at the Odeon, Bon speaks on the local station Radio Forth, accompanied by the singer from a local band named Brodie. When he's asked why they have just decided to record a live album, Bon say it's the 'culmination' of the past four years touring, and a chance to take stock of what they've achieved and then 'start afresh': 'In the past we've had an album out in Australia, an album out in Europe, an album out in America, all at different times, you know? We've had nothing that has been out at the same time. Now we want to try and treat the world as a whole, rather that country by country.'

And where do they get their best audience response?

'Scotland,' he replies, without a moment's hesitation, before making it clear he's not sucking up. 'It's true.' (In a later interview with WDIZ's Neal Mirsky, Scott insists that Glasgow is 'the home of rock'n'roll. People say Detroit is, but to them I say, Shit!')

The DJ runs a theory by Scott, regarding the track 'Up To My Neck In You'.

'It isn't the most romantic song you've ever written, is it?'

'What?' Scott replies, feigning shock. 'That's my most ardent love song. It was written for a woman I loved very dearly. Still do.'

Talk turns to 'Rosie', as it often does, which makes Scott chuckle.

'Rosie's become quite famous because of that song,' he reveals. 'It's a woman I knew back in Australia. I tell the truth here—she was nineteen stone twelve pounds. Red curly hair. Freckles. And very, very lusty.'

Asked where he and the band are now based, Scott simply says, 'The world.'

Rosie isn't the band's only groupie of considerable girth. Another is a Melbourne local known as Ruby Lips, who, according to drummer Phil Rudd, isn't the kind of girl 'you could have taken home to meet your parents'.

May 29 During the final gig of the UK *Powerage* tour, at Caird Hall in Dundee, a stage invader rocks out alongside Angus, playing air guitar; he dives back into the crowd before security can catch him.

June 8 The band are scheduled to play 'Rock'n'roll Damnation' on *Top Of The Pops*, but they encounter a problem. A British Musician's Union rule states that for a song to be performed on the show, it has to have been recorded in the UK, which is clearly not the case with 'Damnation'. A staffer from Atlantic, along with a rep from the union, heads into Island Recording Studios with the band to 're-record' the song, even though the Atlantic rep makes sure that at the end of the session, the original recording is swapped for the 'new' version. The union rep doesn't notice, and the band is now clear to appear.

The appearance itself is notable for a couple of things: the raised eyebrows on BBC host Noel Edmonds when he says the name 'AC/DC'—and Bon's surprisingly conservative outfit. He wears a red sweater, like some sort of rock'n'roll accountant, with a watch on his left wrist. (Clearly, he'd missed Browning's 'no timepieces when performing' directive.) Angus, meanwhile, commands the stage—he's positioned down front, stage left—and tears through the song, which will become their first UK chart hit in October, reaching the Top 20 and charting for nine weeks. Apparently, it's the first Australia-produced rock song to crack the UK Top 20. In Australia, surprisingly, it barely scratches the surface of the Top 100, reaching only #83 during its eight-week run.

June 24 The band are back on the road in the USA, this time opening for shock-rocker Alice Cooper; AC/DC are billed as the Coop's 'special guest'. Their first gig is at the 13,000-capacity Scope stadium in Norfolk, Virginia. In what is clearly a choreographed move, Angus does his nightly tour of the venue while perched on the shoulders of a burly security guard, who has conveniently positioned himself at the front of the stage. Their path is cleared by two other bruisers. Even Cooper's diehard fans are impressed.

Setlist: 'Live Wire' / 'Problem Child' / 'Sin City' / 'Rock'n'roll Damnation' / 'Bad Boy Boogie' / 'High Voltage' / 'Whole Lotta Rosie' / 'Rocker'.

June 25–28 Clearly intent on blasting the Coop away, Angus and co hit the stage running at the Rupp Arena in Lexington, Kentucky, another 15,000-seater. When Bon piggybacks Angus through the crowd, Angus sprays drool and sweat in all directions, much of it coming to rest on members of the local police force, who are sticking tight to the pair. This is the first of seven visits the band will make to the Rupp Arena between 1978 and 1996.

An equally well-received show with Cooper follows at the Birmingham-Jefferson Civic Center Coliseum in Birmingham, Alabama. After a third show opening for Cooper, at the James White Civic Coliseum in Knoxville, Tennessee, the band return to Florida, where a planned concert in Orlando—a festival gig with Bob Seger, Foreigner, and

Pablo Cruise—is cancelled. AC/DC are allegedly bumped by Seger's crew, although official reports simply state, 'AC/DC was scheduled to play this festival but cancelled.'

July 2–4 The next run of shows are support slots for Aerosmith around Texas: first at the 17,000-seat Summit in Houston, then the Texas World Music Fair at the Fairgrounds in Dallas, followed by the Municipal Coliseum in Lubbock.

July 6–8 A handful of headlining gigs in Texas follow, first at the 1,700-capacity Opry House in Austin on July 6. The next night, at the Ritz Music Hall in Corpus Christi, Angus and Bon disappear at the side of the stage, Angus playing all the while, before finally emerging in the rear of the hall to the surprise of much of the crowd. They then trek down the centre aisle, slowly making their way back to the stage, high-fives (and sweat) flying in all directions.

    The July 8 gig is staged at the much larger Municipal Auditorium in San Antonio; almost 6,000 punters squeeze into the room.

July 10–21 More arena shows with Aerosmith follow, in Salt Lake City, Long Beach, Fresno, and Portland. With Aerosmith's 'Toxic Twins', Steven Tyler and Joe Perry, in bad shape, AC/DC take the opportunity to win over hordes of new fans; one convert reports that they 'absolutely blew Aerosmith off the stage'. The Fresno crowd creates some friction, however; one fan later claims that the band stormed offstage after Angus was hit with a flying cup. 'Fuck you, Fresno,' is, allegedly, his parting shot at the audience.

    They also support Ronnie Montrose in San Jose, and headline their own gig in Los Angeles at the 750-capacity Starwood, which is sold out. Cherie Currie, until recently the lead singer of she-rockers The Runaways, opens the latter show.

THE BAND'S FIRST 7-INCH TO CRACK THE UK TOP 20, 'ROCK'N'ROLL DAMNATION' IS AN AFTERTHOUGHT, RECORDED AFTER THE MAIN SESSIONS FOR *POWERAGE* ARE COMPLETED TO SATISFY LABEL DEMANDS FOR A RADIO-FRIENDLY SINGLE.

July 23 Before the band take the stage at the Oakland Coliseum, as part of the Day On The Green festival, a journalist asks Bon what the crowd should expect.

    'Blood,' he replies, and a song is born.

    AC/DC are the opening act ahead of Aerosmith, Foreigner, Pat Travers, and Van Halen, playing to upward of 50,000 people—even the bleachers at the rear of the stage are full. Although AC/DC's setlist is brief and the barrier between the stage and the audience is large, the band leave an indelible impression, captured for posterity by a film crew.

    During their set, which begins at the ungodly hour of 10:40am, Angus takes his

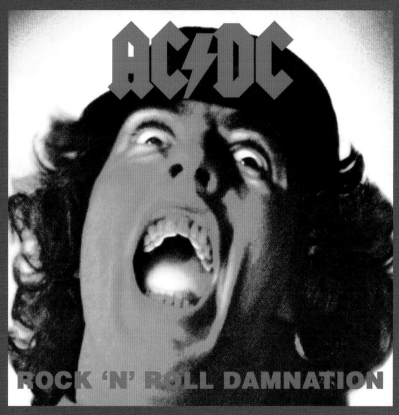

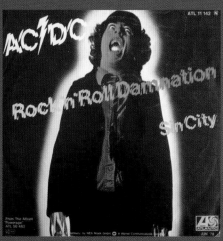

onstage antics to the people, racing through the concrete bleachers of the huge open-air stadium, weaving in and out of the stunned crowd, all the while playing his heart out, before finally returning to the stage on Bon's muscular shoulders. The crowd goes berserk—not the usual reaction for a support band relatively unknown to the masses.

Backstage, however, there have been problems. Foreigner, currently riding high on the success of their *Double Vision* album, were not keen to go on after AC/DC, and their manager, Bud Prager, almost came to blows with Michael Browning. AC/DC won out, and the show went on.

> **"AC/DC was probably one of the most powerful bands I've ever seen in my life. I was sitting in my trailer and heard this rubble-pounding noise from the stage. I went up there and saw 60,000 people bopping up and down at the same time. I remember thinking, We have to follow these motherfuckers?"**
>
> EDDIE VAN HALEN TO *GUITAR PLAYER*, JANUARY 1997

Steve Leber, who is managing Aerosmith (and, soon enough, AC/DC), is staggered by Angus's performance. 'Truth is,' he later admits, 'Angus is fucking amazing. He's of the people, for the people. One hundred percent high energy.' Eddie Van Halen catches AC/DC's set too and then walks away, shaking his head in despair.

After their set, Malcolm Young takes the wooden AC/DC sign that hangs on their dressing room door away with him as a souvenir, while Bon reclines in the backstage pool with a bottle of bourbon. It's an important gig in AC/DC's American journey—a powerful statement that they are a band to be taken seriously.

Backstage, Bon meets Sammy Hagar, already a diehard AC/DC fan. They become friends (and will later share some bills). 'I wasn't on that bill,' Hagar later recalls, 'but went to see AC/DC, of course.'

Setlist: 'Live Wire' / 'Problem Child' / 'Sin City' / 'It's A Long Way To The Top (If You Wanna Rock'n'roll)' / 'Bad Boy Boogie' / 'Rocker' / 'Whole Lotta Rosie'.

July 25–30 The seemingly never-ending road takes the band to Vancouver, Canada; then to Spokane, Washington, and Billings, Montana; and then back over the border to Winnipeg, again supporting Aerosmith, though the general consensus is that AC/DC leaves the deepest (and loudest) impression. During the show at the Winnipeg Arena, a 'We want AC/DC!' chant begins—during Aerosmith's set.

Back in the States on July 29, at the 5,000-capacity Evansville Coliseum in Indiana, they open for Molly Hatchet. Scott is suffering from some kind of injury, but he sings his heart out while seated on a stool for part of the gig. A bottle of booze helps ease his pain. He leaves it to the roadies to carry Angus through the crowd.

August 1–3 Two more Aerosmith shows follow, in Rapid City, South Dakota, and East Troy, Wisconsin.

August 5 The band's set at the huge Comiskey Park in Chicago is captured on what will become a much-sought after bootleg, simply titled *AC/DC In Chicago 1978*. This concert is entitled Summer Jam; Aerosmith headline, on a bill that includes Foreigner and Mahogany Rush. More than 60,000 fans attend; many of them interrupt their car-park partying to witness AC/DC, who open the day's proceedings.

   Track listing: 'Live Wire' / 'Problem Child' / 'Sin City' / 'Gone Shootin'' / 'Bad Boy Boogie' / 'Rocker' / 'Dog Eat Dog'.

August 8 An Atlantic Records convention gig in Nashville, Tennessee, which is broadcast live on radio, results in another of the more popular AC/DC live bootlegs, *Blues, Booze, And Tattoos*. Barry Bergman, the president of Atlantic, introduces the band at the event to what is, frankly, a lacklustre crowd.

   'Quiet, aren't ya?!' Bon bellows at the audience, most of whom are busy schmoozing and pocketing freebies. 'We'll change that.' The band then rip into 'Live Wire'.

   Track listing: 'Live Wire' / 'Problem Child' / 'Sin City' / 'Gone Shootin'' / 'Whole Lotta Rosie' / 'Rocker'.

August 9–13 AC/DC share a series of bills with Cheap Trick—in Salem, Fayetteville, Atlanta, Jacksonville, and Miami—and form another useful on-the-road bond with a band in a similar situation, career-wise, right on the fringes of the mainstream and touring relentlessly. Cheap Trick guitarist Rick Nielsen, whose onstage antics rate with Angus Young's, becomes a big fan of AC/DC; he also takes Bon Scott to his first Mexican restaurant, where Scott orders a taco and a tumbler of scotch.

   Years later, Nielsen will pay AC/DC the ultimate compliment. 'They were just great. They were the only band [with whom Cheap Trick shared a bill] that I stayed every night to watch.'

August 11 Angus and Bon speak with Vince Lovegrove, Bon's old friend and Valentines bandmate, for a program called *Australian Music To The World*. Lovegrove asks about the 'Aussie invasion' of America, it being a very hot time for such pop acts as The Bee Gees, Little River Band, and Olivia Newton-John.

Scott seems a bit confused. What invasion?

'We're the only ones that are invading anywhere,' he insists.

Angus also laughs at the idea. 'We're like Martians.'

Scott, however, can see the benefits of their relentless work regime.

'The more we work, the more we tour, we get more ideas,' he says. 'It's going to get better and better. I can't see it ever coming to an end—it's like infinity rock'n'roll.'

August 18–24 AC/DC re-acquaint themselves with Ritchie Blackmore's Rainbow, who they opened for several times on one of their first European trips in 1976. They play three gigs together, the first at Hempstead, New York, and the second in central Pennsylvania, at Wilkes-Barre. Then, at their show at the Palladium in New York on the 24th, Blackmore's rainbow misbehaves, and his band's set is cut very short. Once again, the raw energy and ferocity of AC/DC's set wins over many fans who've never heard them before—or, more crucially, never seen them live.

Back in Australia, *Juke* magazine reports on a flare-up at one of these Rainbow gigs. Angus was being heckled, and a woman alongside the heckler suggested, strongly, that he shut up and let the band play. Rather than shut his trap, the heckler punched her in the face. 'Angus saw this,' reports *Juke*, 'and dived from the stage over the four rows to king-hit the cretin.'

US magazine *Aquarian* sums up the incident succinctly: 'Blackmore didn't do anything half that interesting. AC/DC is a tough act to follow.'

August 21 A set at Boston's Paradise Theater is broadcast on WBCN. The station's Tony Berardini speaks on air with Bon, just before they play 'Dog Eat Dog', introducing him as 'Bon Tyler'. (Bonnie's long-lost brother, perhaps?)

'Say something to Boston, Bon.'

'Hi Boston,' Scott gasps, still catching his breath. 'We wish you were all here, because we're having a ball.' Anything else he has to say is drowned out by a screaming Angus solo, and the gig duly rocks and rolls to a close.

While it is probably apocryphal, one lively piece of AC/DC folklore has Angus stepping off the stage while playing this solo, leaving the venue, hailing a cab, and then emerging at WBCN's studio across the city, still playing.

Setlist: 'Live Wire' / 'Problem Child' / 'Sin City' / 'Gone Shootin'' / 'Bad Boy Boogie' / 'The Jack' / 'High Voltage' / 'Rocker' / 'Dog Eat Dog'.

ANGUS LETS LOOSE DURING A SET AT BOSTON'S PARADISE THEATER THAT'S BROADCAST LIVE ON RADIO STATION WBCN. A RUMOUR LATER SPREADS THAT ANGUS JUMPED A CAB FROM THE VENUE TO WBCN'S STUDIO AND CONTINUED TO PLAY ALL THE WAY.

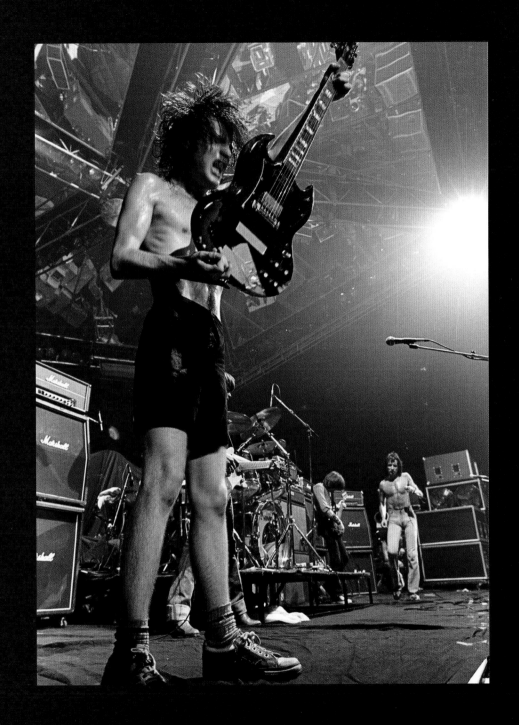

August 25–31 The band go coast to coast, first playing a show in Warwick, Rhode Island—a promo for local station W-PRO FM—and then travelling to Willimantic, Connecticut; Owing Mills, Maryland; Seattle, Washington, where they appear at the bottom of the bill headlined by Ted Nugent; and Portland, Oregon, where they double-bill once again with Cheap Trick.

The air-con packs it in early in their set at the 2,500-seat Painters Mill in Owing Mills, yet the band play on. The headliners on this occasion are bluesy Brit rockers Savoy Brown, who've already had six LPs in the US charts and scored radio airplay with the song 'Tell Mama', but again AC/DC overpower the crowd.

September 2 The band return to the Oakland Coliseum for another of promoter Bill Graham's massive Day On The Green events; the crowd is almost 60,000. Ted Nugent headlines; Blue Öyster Cult, Journey, and Cheap Trick also do their hard-rockin' thing.

Setlist: 'Live Wire' / 'Problem Child' / 'Sin City' / 'Gone Shootin'' / 'Bad Boy Boogie' / 'Whole Lotta Rosie' / 'Rocker' / 'Let There Be Rock' / 'Dog Eat Dog'.

> **"*Listen, I want to introduce to you a bunch of boys from Australia. These boys were out on the road with us, did the whole last tour with us. AC/DC.*"**
>
> AEROSMITH'S STEVEN TYLER INTRODUCES AC/DC ON *THE MIDNIGHT SPECIAL*, SEPTEMBER 1978

September 4 AC/DC and the Blue Öyster Cult fill the Red Rocks in Denver, Colorado, long before U2 make their mark at the amphitheatre.

September 6 The band play 'Sin City' on popular music TV show *The Midnight Special*, shot in Hollywood. Also on the show are K.C. & The Sunshine Band, Teddy Pendergrass, Donna Summer, and Aerosmith. Angus is his usual livewire self, alarming some of the disco-loving fans standing at the front of the stage.

September 8 AC/DC and Cheap Trick reunite for shows at the Civic Center in Wheeling, West Virginia, where close to 10,000 punters turn up, paying between five and seven bucks for a ticket. Then they play the Freedom Hall Civic Center in Johnson City, Tennessee, for a crowd of around 8,500.

September 10 AC/DC headline the Veterans Memorial Auditorium in Columbus, Ohio, where a serious crush occurs at the front of the stage and punters spill over into the (fortunately) empty orchestra pit. Scott restores order with a few well-chosen words, and then the band rip into 'Dog Eat Dog'.

September 12–16 At Milwaukee's Riverside Theater, AC/DC share a bill with UFO. The next night, while doubling up with Thin Lizzy at the Royal Oak in Michigan, an onstage ruckus occurs. The city has recently introduced a noise ordinance prohibiting any performance registering over 100 decibels—and AC/DC are clocked at 125. Attempts by city officials to silence the band during their set leads to a clash with the crew. The show, as usual, goes on. A subsequent show with Thin Lizzy, at the Palace Theatre in Cleveland on September 16, passes without incident, apart from the usual bruises to both band and audience.

September 17 The band play their own show at the Schnecksville-Lehigh County Community College—shades of their school gigs back in Australia when they first started out. Some 1,600 fans squeeze into the hall.

September 20 After an indulgent (for them) three-day break, AC/DC resume touring with Cheap Trick, playing the 6,000-seat Civic Center in Huntington, West Virginia.

September 22–24 The band aren't yet done with Thin Lizzy, either, splitting bills with them and The Dictators at the Aragon Ballroom in Chicago (a lively venue known locally as the Aragon Brawlroom), the Uptown Theatre in Kansas City, and the Music Hall Civic Center in Omaha, Nebraska.

September 27 Back on the Aerosmith tour, AC/DC front a rowdy gathering at the 17,000-capacity Buffalo Memorial Auditorium. Aerosmith are forced to stop their show a few times when audience members use them for target practice, with bottles and fireworks hurled their way. Bon and Angus do their usual lap of the venue, emerging bruised and sweaty. Once again, the Aussie upstarts steal the show (as they will do a few days later, on September 30, at the AC Centre in South Bend, Indiana).

September 28 AC/DC, along with the Blue Öyster Cult and Thin Lizzy, fill the 10,000-seat Rochester County War Memorial. 'Sin City' has been receiving some local radio airplay, so the band aren't a mystery to many in the crowd.

October 2–3 A lengthy three-month run in the USA ends with two more Aerosmith shows, at the Toledo Sports Arena in Ohio, and the Allen County War Memorial Coliseum

" *Other concert records may boast more songs, more Top 40 hits, or even more crowd-pleasing gimmicks. But very few can challenge the sheer excitement and reckless abandon captured on AC/DC's terrific concert document.* **"**

EDUARDO RIVADAVIA, *ULTIMATE CLASSIC ROCK*

in Fort Wayne, Indiana. Soon enough, the two bands will be sharing management.

October 10–11 AC/DC begin a European tour with a pair of shows in Sweden, at Folkets Park in Malmo on the 10th and Gota Lejon in Stockholm on the 11th.

October 13 On the day of the third show of the tour, the live album *If You Want Blood, You've Got It* is released in Europe. It was recorded earlier in the year, much of it at a show in Glasgow—'the magic show', according to Angus.

In a retrospective review of the record for the *All Music Guide*, Greg Prato gives some relevant context. 'AC/DC was fast becoming one of rock's top live acts by the late 70s. Few others could match the band's electrifying live performances. … While most other rock bands of the era were busy experimenting with disco or creating studio-perfected epics, AC/DC was one of the few specializing in raw and bluesy hard rock.'

Though not a massive seller on its release, the album will go on to appear at #2 on *Classic Rock* magazine's readers' poll of the '50 Greatest Live Albums Ever', just pipped by Thin Lizzy's *Live And Dangerous* (and just ahead of Cheap Trick's *Live At Budokan*). 'The title of this live album spoke volumes,' the magazine notes. 'So did the cover: Angus impaled on his own guitar, Bon beside him, eyes glazed. It was symbolic of a band that gave everything they had on stage.'

October 23 Following headlining shows in Nuremburg, Zurich, Mannheim, Dortmund, Cologne, Offenbach, Munich, and Amsterdam, the band's gig at the Vereenigning Hall in Nijmegen, Holland, is broadcast live on radio and then (of course) duly bootlegged.

Track listing: 'Live Wire' / 'Problem Child' / 'Sin City' / 'Gone Shootin'' / 'High Voltage' / 'The Jack' / 'Whole Lotta Rosie' / 'Rocker' / 'Rock'n'roll Damnation' / 'Let There Be Rock'.

October 24 French band Trust open for AC/DC at the Stade de Paris. Bon Scott and Trust's lead singer, Bernard Bonvoisin, become tight; Scott does his best to ensure Trust's onstage sound is clean and clear during their set, checking in at the desk while they play. Afterward, Scott tells Bonvoisin that he was once a drummer, but found the gig too restrictive. 'When you're a singer, you can walk to the front of the stage and see all the chicks.'

THE BULK OF AC/DC'S FIRST LIVE ALBUM, *IF YOU WANT BLOOD, YOU'VE GOT IT*, WAS RECORDED AT A CONCERT IN GLASGOW—A 'MAGIC SHOW', ACCORDING TO ANGUS.

October 26 After a show at L'Arenahall Deurne de Deinze, Bon speaks with a reporter from French magazine *Ecoute*. His response to whether his lyrics are 'written according to your voice' may have lost something in translation.

'Maybe unconsciously,' he accepts, 'but they are mostly based on the aggressiveness of the music. We find inspiration in the things of life, which we do not take too seriously.

'In Europe, words obviously don't have the same impact as in Australia, because people do not understand the exact meaning. For example, do you see what we mean by "The Jack?" The jack is a disease that you catch by fucking right and wrong …

'My mother does not like my songs. She sends me letters all the time asking me to write a love song.'

Bon is then asked to give a definitive explanation of the band's name. 'You have to solve the riddle,' the reporter pleads.

'On the one hand,' Scott replies, 'it means alternating current—direct current. Moreover, an AC/DC is a guy who alternately jumps chicks and guys. We jump only chicks, and not enough!'

October 28 *If You Want Blood, You've Got It* enters the UK album chart. It will hit a high of #13 and chart for an impressive fifty-nine weeks. Meanwhile, fellow Aussie Olivia Newton-John is on top of the UK singles chart with 'Summer Nights'.

October 30–November 14 The band that clearly have no concept of the word 'downtime' begin another UK tour with a show at the Empire in Liverpool. The next night, they play the Odeon in Edinburgh, followed, over the next fortnight, by a two-night stand at the Mayfair Ballroom in Newcastle, plus shows in Sheffield, Wolverhampton, Southampton, Coventry, Birmingham, Manchester, Stoke-on-Trent, Bristol, and Derby.

November 15–16 AC/DC close out the epic *If You Want Blood* world tour with two nights at London's 3,000-seat Hammersmith Odeon. Australian reporter Ian Cross is at the second show. 'It was a long way from the RSL club in Canberra where I'd last seen the band, about four years ago, [when] they were booed off the stage,' he reports.

Angus clones in school uniforms—Angi?—are dotted throughout the Odeon crowd, while there are sixty security guards present, struggling to maintain order at stage front. Cross describes a 'monstrous crush' as the band launches into 'Live Wire', although no one seems to have been hurt. According to Cross, despite Bon Scott's undeniable presence, this is the Angus Young show. 'He darted and bounded his way around the stage at such a frantic pace that you got exhausted just watching him … He's undoubtedly AC/DC's strongest point.' As for the ear-shattering volume, 'It didn't seem to worry the other 3,000 or so ecstatic fans packed into the Odeon. To them, AC/DC can do no wrong.'

'The schoolboy brat up on the rostrum smirks maliciously,' reports the *NME*. 'AC/DC conquered London.'

Setlist: 'Live Wire' / 'Problem Child' / 'Sin City' / 'Gone Shootin'' / 'Bad Boy Boogie' / 'Hell Ain't A Bad Place To Be' / 'High Voltage' / 'The Jack' / 'Whole Lotta Rosie' / 'Rocker' / 'Let There Be Rock'.

November 16 AC/DC rate a mention in *Rolling Stone*, where Angus is still passing himself off as nineteen (he's now twenty-three). Writing about the band's recent Palladium show, Ira Kaplan is impressed. 'There's nothing new going on musically, but AC/DC attacks the old clichés with overwhelming exuberance.' Malcolm Young reflects on the sometimes-confusing nature of audiences. 'You play shitass, the kids go wild. Play great and everybody sits there.'

Elsewhere, in a chat with another US mag, *Rock Gossip*, Angus reveals a touch too much. '[Bon gets] letters from women all over the world, about how they would like to screw him and give him head. I mean pages and pages of it. We used to read them and get off on them.'

Scott then chimes in, revealing that he once received a come-on scrawled on the back of a tampon, 'saying how this girl would like to suck me off … I thought it was great. She may have been an old biddy in disguise, but I'm always open for a little excitement.' He also once received a letter from a writer convinced he was a bad influence on Angus. 'Bon Scott, I hate you,' it read. 'You're a dirty old man and you're leading poor little Angus astray.'

November 21 *If You Want Blood, You've Got It* is released in North America. Interestingly, while the album contains choice live cuts from a Glasgow show, the cover image, of Angus and Bon, was shot at a gig at Boston's Paradise Theater by Atlantic house photographer Jim Houghton. (And, according to my extensive research, despite the image on the cover, Angus didn't impale himself at the show.)

November 27 *If You Want Blood, You've Got It* is released in Australia, where it will reach #37 on the chart, hanging about for fifteen weeks. The album will remain Malcolm Young's favourite live document of the band. 'We were young, fresh, vital, and kicking ass.'

December 14 Angus is profiled in the *Canberra Times* under the headline, 'Tiny Angus Is Cult Figure.' 'In 1978, they've emerged as one of the giants of British rock,' writes Ian Cross (again), noting that *If You Want Blood* has cracked the UK charts, 'despite continual snubbing by the music press and radio'.

BON SCOTT ON STAGE IN BOSTON, 1979. AROUND THIS TIME, HE RECEIVES A LETTER FROM SOMEONE CONVINCED HE IS A BAD INFLUENCE: 'YOU'RE A DIRTY OLD MAN AND YOU'RE LEADING POOR LITTLE ANGUS ASTRAY.'

Despite changes of producer and aborted sessions, the Highway to Hell *LP becomes a stone-cold classic; Bon Scott plays his last show in Australia; the band criss-cross America with UFO, Cheap Trick, and Journey; and Angus Young sprouts his signature devil's horns.*

1979

January Atlantic's Michael Klenfner, a huge supporter of the band, flies to Sydney for probably the most uncomfortable meeting in AC/DC's history to date—a sit-down with manager Michael Browning, reps from Albert Music, and band mentors Vanda & Young (to follow an earlier meeting between Browning, Atlantic boss Jerry Greenberg, and Klenfner in New York). The subject is the production of the band's next album, for which Atlantic is convinced that they need to change producers if they are to continue climbing the rock'n'roll ranks. In the label's view, they need a producer with a stronger feel for American FM radio.

Klenfner only has one name on his list: studio vet Eddie Kramer, who has worked with everyone from Jimi Hendrix to The Small Faces, Led Zep to Peter Frampton. It's made clear that if a change isn't made, the band will most likely be dropped by Atlantic. Soon after, Kramer flies to Sydney to meet with Alberts and Browning.

Vanda & Young respond surprisingly well to what is essentially a sacking. To them, the band comes first: always has, always will. Malcolm and Angus, however, are gutted: losing George, in particular, is like losing the sixth member of the band—and their big brother, to boot.

During an interview with Sydney radio station 2JJ, Malcolm hints pretty strongly that the band's hand has been forced. Regardless, sessions are scheduled in Miami for early in the year.

February 5 Word spreads among AC/DC insiders that the group are to play a secret gig at the Strata Motor Inn at Cremorne in Sydney's north, after a set by pop band The Ferrets. AC/DC duly appear, but in a very rare configuration: George Young plays bass, while Ray Arnott, who helped the band in its very earliest incarnation, plays drums. In his photographic memoir *It's A Long Way*, Philip Morris, who shot the gig, recalls seeing 'a hundred jaws drop at the same time' when the band took the stage around 10pm. No one beyond the band's inner circle knew about the gig in advance.'

Despite the small crowd and informal nature of the evening, and even though he's not wearing his school uniform, Angus goes through his full routine, jumping from table to table as he tears off a blistering solo and dropping to the venue's dirty floor to pull off a perfect dying bug. His grand finale is to drop trou' and moon the crowd, with Scott standing alongside him, smiling broadly.

'It's fantastic,' says Morris, 'the best surprise gig you could ever imagine attending.'

It is also the last time Bon Scott will appear on an Australian stage.

February Sessions for what will become *Highway To Hell* begin at Criteria Studios in Miami, Florida (aka the Hit Factory), the studio used by The Bee Gees for many of their huge disco hits. Derek & The Dominos recorded their classic 'Layla' there, too, while the Eagles recorded part of their West Coast classic *Hotel California* at Criteria.

Two weeks into the sessions, however, Malcolm Young calls Michael Browning, insisting that he 'get us the fuck out of this situation' with Eddie Kramer, whom the band have found to be nowhere near as collaborative as Vanda & Young. Among other things, he has allegedly urged the band to record a cover of The Spencer Davis Group's 'Gimme Some Lovin''.

'I went there,' Kramer later tells loudersound.com, 'hung out with them, tried to do some demos, and realised that there was an obvious difficulty with the singer. ... He had the most incredible voice but trying to keep him in check from his drinking was a very tough call. But I think more than anything, the band resented me being foisted onto them. It was like sticking a pin into them.'

Miami doesn't agree with the band, either. It is, Bon notes, a 'horrible place, full of rich old crocks who flock there for the winter'.

Browning agrees to extract the band from the arrangement with Kramer. In the interim, he has been speaking with Clive Calder, who manages various record producers, to try to entice his client Robert 'Mutt' Lange to produce AC/DC. Lange's biggest hit to date is The Boomtown Rats' 'Rat Trap', but despite this, Browning assures Malcolm Young—who's never heard of Lange—that it'll work, then breaks the news to Atlantic's Michael Klenfner.

Despite the label's resistance, plans are set in place for the group to work with Lange at London's Roundhouse Studios.

One good thing to come out of Miami is the bare bones of the track 'Highway To Hell'. Angus has a guitar part; Malcolm sits in on drums. The results are recorded onto a cassette that is duly broken by a staffer's child. Fortunately, Scott is able to piece the tape back together, and the song survives.

March–April The band settle in at the Roundhouse with Mutt Lange, whose perfectionism is a new sensation for the band—and a huge contrast to the 'get it while it's hot' approach of Vanda & Young. His fifteen-hour days are a big call, too, but he gradually extracts great takes from the group. Rather than throwing himself around the

> **"***Eddie Kramer was a bit of a prat. He might've sat behind the knobs for Hendrix, but he's certainly not Hendrix, I can tell you that much.***"**
>
> MALCOLM YOUNG TO *CLASSIC ROCK*, JANUARY 2001

studio, playing as if he were on stage, Angus cuts all his solos seated alongside Lange.

Lange also gives Bon Scott some advice about breathing techniques. Ian Jeffery, the band's tour manager, later relates to loudersound.com, 'I remember one day Bon coming in with his lyrics to "If You Want Blood". He starts doing it and he's struggling, you know? There's more fucking breath than voice coming out. Mutt says to him, "Listen, you've got to co-ordinate your breathing." Bon was like, "You're so fucking good, cunt, you do it!" Mutt sat in his seat and did it without standing up! That was when they all went, "What the fucking hell [are] we dealing with here?"'

Bon will later say this of Lange: 'He really injected new life into us and brought out things we didn't know we were capable of. We were really trying to be acceptable for American radio without sounding drippy like those stupid American bands. And it works, too.'

'With Mutt,' Angus tells *Guitar World* in 2011, 'the operative was more to put it into a structure and keep it neat, so he'd keep going at you until it was right. Sometimes, though, it was a useless exercise. He'd run off a few tracks with different ideas, and then he would come to you and say, "Well, what were you playing in the beginning? Let's go back to that."

'There were times where we would simply put a stop to it and say, "It's simply not us, Mutt. We've got to keep it raw and dirtier for us to get what we want on the tape." He was good in that sense. If you weren't happy with what you were hearing back, he would work with you. Mutt was never dictatorial.'

Ultimate Classic Rock will later rank *Highway To Hell* #4 on a list of Lange's Top 10 productions. 'Not just anyone could have persuaded Australia's obstinately no-fuss hard rockers to … streamline their bruising, three-chord songs. It took AC/DC's career to the next level.' (*Back In Black* is #1.)

Lange also receives due credit in the book *The 100 Best Australian Albums*: 'Lange brought polish without losing any of AC/DC's trademark grit and power. … Smartly, Lange honed in on the band's core strengths—the primal groove of the rhythm section … Angus's short, sharp blues-based lead guitar attack and Bon's high timbred "weasel on heat" rasp.' (Scott had told Lange that his voice was once compared to a 'weasel on heat', adding, 'Do you reckon you can work with that?')

During the *Highway To Hell* sessions, the band revisit 'Touch Too Much', first recorded in 1977, radically rearranging it for the new album. Bon has a fine old time throughout the record, dropping dodgy double-entendres ('Beating Around The Bush')

THE BAND—WITH GEORGE YOUNG AND RAY ARNOTT SITTING IN—PLAY A SURPRISE GIG AT SYDNEY'S STRATA MOTOR INN, FEBRUARY 5 1979. IT WILL BE BON SCOTT'S LAST APPEARANCE WITH AC/DC IN AUSTRALIA.

211

and singing about the high life ('Get It Hot', 'Shot Down In Flames') and/or pure lust ('Love Hungry Man', 'Girls Got Rhythm'). He even gives a nod to the hit TV show *Mork & Mindy* on the closer, 'Night Prowler', when he signs off with Robin Williams's signature 'Shazbot, na-nu na-nu'. These will be the last words Bon Scott ever utters on an AC/DC record.

May 8 AC/DC's latest North American sortie begins in Madison, Wisconsin, at the Dane County Veterans Memorial Coliseum, with UFO supporting. The venue is almost full to its 4,000 capacity; tickets go for $7 a pop.

> **"We're not residents of anywhere right now. Most bands live on the Virgin Islands or whatever … but we're mainly Australians. Three Australians born in Scotland. And one Polish guy. We're international."**
>
> BON SCOTT TO NEAL MIRSKY, WDIZ, MAY 1979

May 10 The band's gig at the 7,000-capacity Veterans Memorial Auditorium in Des Moines, Indiana, is billed as 'the world's loudest concert'—quite a call. UFO open yet again.

May 11 The AC/DC roadshow reaches Dubuque, Indiana, where they fill the 5,000-seat 5 Flags Arena.

May 12–15 During their sold-out show at the 3,000-capacity Orpheum Theatre in Davenport, Indiana, Bon hoists Angus onto his shoulders, and they disappear in the direction of the venue's balcony. The crowd, of course, goes crazy. The next night's show is staged at the 8,000-seat Toledo Sports Arena—another full house. The run of full houses continues at the 6,500-capacity Fairground Coliseum at Columbus, Ohio, again with UFO.

May 16 Oddly, the 7,500-seat Morris Civic Auditorium in South Bend, Indiana, is almost empty—barely 2,500 fans have turned out for the show. Regardless, as one punter testifies, the band play hard and loud. 'Our ears were bleeding and we couldn't hear for a week,' reports Mike, a fan from Warsaw, Indiana.

May 17 Numbers are down for tonight's show in Louisville, Kentucky (the home of Muhammad Ali). Barely 2,000 fans attend the gig at the 4,500-capacity Convention Center. Nonetheless, reports from this and most other gigs on this run state clearly that AC/DC blew away UFO, who are billed as co-headliners.

May 18–20 Crowd numbers improve as the band plays in Springfield, Illinois; and Dayton and Cleveland, Ohio. While staying at the Bel-Air Motel in Springfield, Malcolm, Angus, and Bon mingle with some fans who have driven the hundred miles from St Louis but failed to get tickets for the gig, so have set up camp in the car park of the Bel-Air. One über-fan, Trace Rayfield, is even invited up to Scott's room for a beer. The band slip them backstage passes for that night's show. Clearly, their claim to be a band of the people is much more than hype.

May 22 Bon Scott nurses a bottle of whiskey for much of tonight's gig at the 2,000-seat Tennessee Theatre in Nashville, before eventually smashing it at the conclusion of 'The Jack'. Michigan group Brownsville Station—of 'Smoking In The Boys Room' fame—open the show.

This is the final hurrah for AC/DC's manager, Michael Browning, who is sacked by the band immediately after the show. They cite various business disagreements as their reason—it doesn't help that Browning was heavily involved in the decision to replace Vanda & Young with 'Mutt' Lange (even though the huge commercial returns to come from that partnership could also be attributed, in part, to Browning).

Browning has sensed the band had a change in mind for some time. 'I knew I was screwed,' he later writes in his memoir. 'My radar had been correct; something had been brewing, probably from the time Peter Mensch had a post-meeting word in Malcolm's ear.'

Mensch, who has been looking after the high-flying Aerosmith, swiftly takes over as AC/DC's manager; he will work with the band for several decades (and later marry one-time British MP Louise Bagshawe).

Probable setlist: 'Live Wire' / 'Problem Child' / 'Sin City' / 'Bad Boy Boogie' / 'The Jack' / 'High Voltage' / 'Riff Raff' / 'Rocker' / 'Whole Lotta Rosie'.

May 23–25 Twenty-five hundred fans attend the band's show at the University of Tennessee. AC/DC then stage a two-night stand at the Agora Ballroom, a venue in the basement of an old hotel in Atlanta, Georgia, where tickets range from $4.50–$5.50.

May 27 AC/DC appear toward the bottom of a bill for a festival at the 55,000-capacity Tangerine Bowl in Orlando, Florida. The line-up features Boston, The Doobie Brothers, and Poco—AC/DC are very clearly the odd band out. Regardless, Angus is in overdrive:

during his extended solo, he and Bon race across the football field to the top level of the Bowl then back to the stage via the fifty-yard line.

Before their set, Bon speaks with Neal Mirsky from WDIZ in Florida. Asked if he's been to Miami before, he reveals that the band spent five weeks there working on the songs for *Highway To Hell*. 'It's God's waiting room, I think,' he laughs. He goes on to joke about how he's looking forward to the album making him a million dollars.

'Then you'll retire?' Mirsky asks.

'Oh, no, I've still got a lot of debts to pay.'

Asked whether he has a preference for big outdoor shows like that at the Tangerine Bowl, or club gigs, Bon insists, 'I don't care. Here or two hundred people, doesn't matter, long as it's kicking on.'

May 31 The band return to the UFO tour, for a show at the Shea's Buffalo Theatre in Buffalo, New York. UFO haven't made it to the gig, however, as they've been detained at the Canada/US border, so AC/DC play two sets. Angus and Bon do their usual lap of the venue while playing 'Let There Be Rock'.

June 1 UFO headline this show at the 2,500-capacity Auditorium Theater in Rochester, New York, but many in the crowd leave after AC/DC's blistering set.

June 3 Another festival gig, this time at Davenport, Indiana: the Mississippi River Jam II. Also on the bill are Heart, Nazareth, and UFO, but only 12,500 tickets are sold, leaving the 35,000-seat venue very empty. Still, Angus and Bon race into the crowd with the sun beating down on them, stirring the audience into action.

While they'd clearly prefer to be the headliner, Malcolm believes that they can get a lot done in a short set. 'I can't stand those bands that take two hours to warm a crowd up. We got all the time we need when we play second to the headliner.'

June 4 During a show at the Bradley University in Peoria, Illinois, Bon Scott encourages the audience to move closer to the stage, resulting in what one punter calls 'a tangled mass of humanity'. Security insists that the audience sits down, though that doesn't last long.

June 6 From the opening 'Riff Raff' onward, AC/DC have the crowd at the

"*We feel we don't need to start slow and build up our set, so we just go on without any soundchecks or warm-ups and play as loud and hard as we can.*"

MALCOLM YOUNG TO *CLASSIC ROCK*, 2001

"*We're not too concerned with being very artistic or sounding pretty ... we just want to make the walls cave in and the ceilings collapse. Nice clothes and fancy guitars can carry you only so far.*"

BON SCOTT TO ANDY SECHER,
SUPER ROCK, JUNE 1979

5,200-capacity County Fieldhouse in Erie, Pennsylvania, eating out of their hands—much to the chagrin of UFO, who are once again headlining.

June 7 Angus's 'Let There Be Rock' showcase now runs to something like fifteen minutes, as he all the while does his best dying bug; that is, playing furiously while spinning on his back. Tonight's gig is at the Ag Hall in Allentown, Pennsylvania. The 4,200-seat venue is pretty much full.

June 8 AC/DC (and UFO) fill the 12,500-capacity Capitol Center in Landover, Maryland—tickets are a steal at $5. A nude woman somehow makes her way to the top of the PA stack while AC/DC are playing. She is led away, much to the crowd's dismay.

June 9 A reporter from *Super Rock* magazine, Andy Secher, witnesses the AC/DC blitzkrieg at the Palladium in New York. 'The members of AC/DC are as volatile as their music,' he writes, 'coming across as a mixture of street punks and stand-up comics.'

   Malcolm sings his brother's praises, making the point that his playing is as good as his onstage antics. 'Angus is a fantastic guitarist,' he says. 'I don't think there is another guitarist in the world who can play with as much power and control.'

June 10 Angus and Bon again somehow make their way to the balcony during their set at the Palace Theater in Albany, New York—still playing all the while.

June 12 AC/DC manage to fill the 2,800-seat Massey Hall in Toronto, Canada, even though their road buddies Cheap Trick are playing across town on the same night.

June 15 After a pair of shows in Pittsburgh, Pennsylvania, and Poughkeepsie, New York, AC/DC pack the 3,000-capacity Tower Theater in Philadelphia, once again double-heading with UFO. Early in their set, a fan throws a sparkler onto the stage, setting the drapes on fire. As firemen race to extinguish the blaze, Angus keeps playing, seemingly indifferent to the chaos. He and Bon then head up the aisle of the Tower, before ending up, once again, in the balcony.

June 20 After the longest break so far on this tour—an epic five days!—AC/DC tag along to another festival date, this time playing with Journey and New England at the

14,000-seat Tarrant County Convention Center Arena in Fort Worth, Texas. More than one fan will later insist that AC/DC 'own' the show; Hirsh Gardner, from the band New England, admits to 'shaking' when the band plays 'Big Balls'. 'Bon and Angus are the down-and-dirty Lennon and McCartney,' he says.

June 21–22 Austin, Texas, is the site of another gig opening for Journey, at the Municipal Auditorium, followed by a show at the HemisFair Arena in San Antonio, Texas. Neither show is especially well attended; the latter draws barely 6,000 fans to a venue that can hold nearly three times that.

June 23–24 During another show opening for Journey, at the Sam Houston Coliseum in Houston, Texas, AC/DC are called back for several encores, despite being the support act. Angus ends the show in his boxers, which are decorated with red hearts.

The following night, at the Memorial Coliseum in Corpus Christi, Angus plays so hard that his knees are covered in blood by the end of the set.

June 26–27 AC/DC play two more shows supporting Journey, in Albuquerque, New Mexico, and Phoenix, Arizona. During the latter gig, at the 7,000-capacity Veterans Memorial Coliseum, Angus leaps onto the shoulders of some members of the crew, who carry him around the venue, playing madly all the while. 'It looked like he was having an epileptic fit,' says one onlooker.

June 29 Tonight, the band are in Denver, Colorado, for their own headlining show at the 1,400-seat Rainbow Music Hall, which they fill. A fresh song appears on their setlist: 'Highway To Hell'. Bon introduces it simply as a 'track from our new album', but it's clear that AC/DC have a new anthem.

Probable setlist: 'Live Wire' / 'Problem Child' / 'Sin City' / 'Bad Boy Boogie' / 'The Jack' / 'High Voltage' / 'Riff Raff' / 'Rocker' / 'Highway To Hell' / 'Whole Lotta Rosie' / 'Let There Be Rock' / 'Dog Eat Dog'.

July 4 AC/DC join a star-laden bill at the Winnebago County Fairgrounds, in Pecatonica, Illinois, that includes Cheap Trick, The Babys, and Molly Hatchet. The crowd is in the vicinity of 50,000. Despite the afternoon heat, Angus and Bon still take a lap of the fairground, much to the crowd's delight.

July 6–7 The band play two more gigs with Cheap Trick, though the venues are smaller: the first is a 5,200-capacity room in Wichita, Kansas; the second an 8,000-seater in Sioux Falls, South Dakota. The latter show includes a rare sight: Angus, Malcolm, and Bon join Cheap Trick on stage when they encore with 'Johnny B. Goode', one of Angus and Malcolm's favourite songs.

Malcolm spends much of the onstage jam trying to find the amp into which his guitar, borrowed from Robin Zander, is plugged. 'I couldn't figure out where my sound was coming from,' he admits afterward. A black scrim is covering the amp, which has been placed under Cheap Trick drummer Bun E. Carlos's drum riser. This live cut will later turn up on *Bun E's Basement Bootlegs, Volume 1: Gigs '79–'94*, as compiled by Carlos.

'There was a common bond,' Carlos states in 2016. 'We were coming up in the same group of bands, we both had a band with a wild guitar player and a cool singer and a solid rhythm section, so we did have a lot in common. We both had a few albums out and neither one of us had a massive hit at that time.'

The band's paths would intersect many times over the next couple of years. 'It was always fun hanging out with those guys,' says Carlos. 'If it was a day off, we'd end up in the hotel bar shooting the breeze and talking about touring and stuff. Jamming with those guys was just a gas.'

July 8–10 Further shows with Cheap Trick, at the Veterans Memorial Auditorium in Des Moines, Indiana, and the Civic Auditorium Arena in Omaha, Nebraska. Members of AC/DC again join Cheap Trick for the encore at the second gig. The crowd is unsure what's more exciting: the dying-bug antics of Angus, or Cheap Trick's Rick Nielsen wrestling with a five-neck guitar and flicking plectrums into the crowd like mini Frisbees. Bon Scott, meanwhile, hoists Cheap Trick's Robin Zander onto his shoulders, Angus style, much to the singer's surprise. Clearly, Cheap Trick are among the few bands AC/DC respect as peers.

Interestingly, years later, Nielsen reveals that he and his wife tried to emigrate to Australia in the early 1970s. 'I'd be in The Angels or AC/DC right now if that happened,' he says.

Mid-July In a break between US dates, AC/DC travel to Holland, where they record a set that is broadcast on *Countdown*. It is at this gig that Angus is introduced to Ellen van Lochem, a golden-blonde Dutch native. At the time, van Lochem is allegedly dating

BON AND ANGUS BRING THE THUNDER TO THE OAKLAND COLISEUM AT THE MONSTERS OF ROCK FESTIVAL. 'YOU'RE ALL SINNERS,' SCOTT TELLS THE 60,000 CROWD. 'ISN'T IT GREAT?'

the vocalist of Dutch band Normaal, who open that night for AC/DC. They are an odd couple—van Lochem is a full six inches taller than the diminutive rocker, for one thing, and Angus isn't fluent in Dutch—but theirs is a match built to last. Ellen will become quite a strong presence on the road, tending to such things as the ironing of Angus's uniform before he plays.

July 19 After a few days of downtime, the band hit the road again, sharing the bill with Mahogany Rush at the San Diego Sports Arena. Much of the 5,000-strong crowd leave after the opening band's set, having not seen AC/DC before. Those who stay, however, are treated to Angus and Bon in full flight.

July 21 The band return to Oakland Coliseum for a third time, for yet another Bill Graham Monsters Of Rock / Day On The Green concert extravaganza. They're on a bill that features Ted Nugent, Aerosmith, Mahogany Rush, and St Paradise—all of these bands (and now AC/DC, too) are managed by the powerful US firm Leber-Krebs. The concert draws 60,000 punters paying between $12.50 and $15—not bad value for money, all things considered.

> **It was always fun hanging out with those guys. If it was a day off, we'd end up in the hotel bar, shooting the breeze and talking about touring and stuff. Jamming with those guys was just a gas.**
>
> CHEAP TRICK'S BUN E CARLOS TO *ULTIMATE CLASSIC ROCK*, 2017

'Lovely day today, isn't it, hey?' Scott announces in his raw Aussie accent, one song in. He's already worked up a fair sweat, probably not helped by the spray-on jeans he's wearing. He shrugs off his sleeveless denim jacket and goes topless for the rest of the set, strutting confidently around the stage like some kind of rock'n'roll rooster.

Angus, despite going absolutely full-bore from song one, duck-walking like a man not quite in control of his limbs, leaves his uniform on for a few numbers—at least until his extended performance piece on 'Bad Boy Boogie', during which he, too, opts to go topless. It's a big hit with the late-afternoon crowd.

One fan holds up a homemade poster of Angus's Gibson guitar and his schoolboy cap—a clear sign that the band are connecting with American audiences. Beach balls bounce around the crowd as they play.

'You're all sinners,' Scott slurs during a slow-burning moment in 'Sin City'. 'Isn't it great?'

Angus decides to test out his wireless guitar rig mid-set and races way off into the nosebleed sections of the Coliseum during an extended 'Rocker'. The crowd cheers his every move. On stage, now well used to their lead guitarist's tendency to wander, Williams, Rudd, and Malcolm lock into a hard-driving groove. After several minutes, Angus reappears atop Scott's shoulders, then finally brings 'Rocker' to a thunderous finale perched atop Williams's speaker stack. An equally thunderstruck 'Dog Eat Dog' wraps up a solid afternoon's work for the band.

The YouTube video of this show has been watched almost three million times—ample proof that it's one of the more popular, and inspired, AC/DC performances of the decade.

Setlist: 'Live Wire' / 'Problem Child' / 'Sin City' / 'Highway To Hell' / 'Bad Boy Boogie' / 'The Jack' / 'Rocker' / 'Dog Eat Dog'.

July 27 *Highway To Hell* is released. According to Angus, it was a struggle to get the label to accept the title; executives there thought it hinted at devil worship. But the band relate to the phrase: to them, it describes the hard life they've been living, the years of constant grind to get to this point they've reached, poised on the brink of world domination.

The album becomes their first LP to crack the US Top 100. In his review for *Rolling Stone*, Greg Kot nominates 'Shot Down In Flames' as the album's 'prize moment', although, in his view, the complete album is a huge leap forward for the band. 'The songs are more compact, the choruses fattened by rugby-team harmonies.'

In the UK, while the album is a hit—peaking at #8 and charting for forty weeks—the press remains a little sniffy toward this band of Aussie upstarts. 'The Greatest Album Ever Made,' reads the *NME*'s headline, under which is printed, in much smaller type, '(In Australia)'. A promotional poster is made using the album's front cover, devil's horns protruding from Angus's cap, the others in the band either chuckling (Bon), scowling (Malcolm), or somewhere in between (Williams and Rudd). 'AC/DC burning a Highway to Hell,' the poster announces.

By the end of August, *Highway To Hell* has reached a US chart peak of #17. As of 2018, the album has sold seven million copies in the USA and close to two million units elsewhere in the world, and is ranked at #200 on *Rolling Stone*'s '500 Greatest Albums Of All Time'.

Writing in *1001 Albums You Must Hear Before You Die*, Claire Stuchbery calls *Highway To Hell* the rarest of beasts: an album on which almost all of the tracks could stand tall as singles. 'AC/DC have come pretty close,' she writes. 'The album serves as a celebration of sin [while] lyrically, it is an ode to sex.'

FOLLOWING PAGES: *HIGHWAY TO HELL* IS THE ALBUM THAT PAVES THE WAY FOR AC/DC'S REMARKABLE COMMERCIAL SUCCESS IN THE 1980s, GOING ON TO SELL IN EXCESS OF NINE MILLION COPIES.

"*Just because you call an album* **Highway To Hell** *you get all kinds of grief. All we'd done is describe what it's like to be on the road for four years … when you're sleeping with the singer's socks two inches from your nose, that's pretty close to hell.*"

ANGUS YOUNG TO *GUITAR WORLD*, 2000

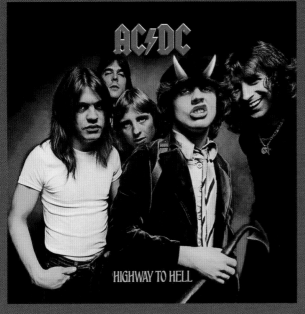

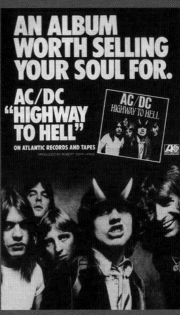

July 28 The band play a short, sharp, six-song set at the humbly titled World Series Of Rock festival at the Cleveland Municipal Stadium, appearing second on the bill alongside Aerosmith, Ted Nugent, Journey, Thin Lizzy, and Scorpions. (The Rolling Stones headlined the festival the year before, drawing 82,000 fans to what was reportedly the first rock show ever to gross more than $1 million.)

Scott, his tatts on full and proud display, doesn't even bother with a shirt, introducing 'The Jack' with a wink as a 'love song'. Angus pulls off one of his finest-ever dying-bug routines during what is now a ten-minute-plus 'Bad Boy Boogie', clearly intent on blowing away the other, higher-profile acts. His antics are feverish enough to get much of the afternoon crowd on their feet. Duly inspired, he drops his guitar, then sheds his tie and shirt and plays on in shorts and sneakers, dripping sweat. He ends the set with yet another blazing solo, playing while perched atop his amplifier, doing a pretty fair Statue of Liberty. A sign held high by fans down front reads simply, 'AC/DC T.N.T. ROCK'N'ROLL'.

This is the last World Series Of Rock to be staged in Cleveland, following five shootings (including one fatality), dozens of robberies, and numerous reports of violence—much of it on the night before the show, when eager fans lined up for the best spots. A second show, scheduled to take place three weeks later, is cancelled.

Setlist: 'Live Wire' / 'Problem Child' / 'Sin City' / 'Bad Boy Boogie' / 'The Jack' / 'Rocker'.

July 29 The band pack the 5,000-seat Mesker Field in Evansville, Indiana.

July 31 Prior to their set at the Allen County War Memorial Coliseum, in Fort Wayne, Indiana, supporting Ted Nugent (hot off his *Double Live Gonzo*, a three-million-seller in North America) and Scorpions, Bon and Angus put in an appearance at local station WXKE, spinning 'Highway To Hell' and 'Shot Down In Flames'.

August 1–3 AC/DC play three more large-scale shows with Nugent and Scorpions (who are running hot with their album *Lovedrive*, a gold record in North America), first at the 18,000-capacity Market Square Arena in Indianapolis, Indiana, followed by the Riverfront Coliseum in Cincinnati, Ohio, and then the Pittsburgh Civic Arena. By now, 'Highway To Hell' has become a keeper in their set, and is starting to receive some radio airplay.

'We're beginning to make an impact there at last,' Scott tells *Record Mirror*. '[But] I reckon we'll still have to push a bit harder to get to the top of the hill.'

August 4 When AC/DC open for Nugent at New York's Madison Square Garden, a fight breaks out between punters, some of whom throw chairs and climb to the top of the pile to get a better view of the band; others allegedly set their chairs on fire. Even the sight of Nugent entering the stage astride a six-metre-high Marshall amp can't really compete with the Angus and Bon show.

Afterward, Scott sets Andy Secher, a reporter from *Hit Parader*, straight. 'Give us a year or two and we'll sell this place out ourselves,' he says. 'We've got the talent and we work harder than anyone.'

Setlist: 'Live Wire' / 'Problem Child' / 'Sin City' / 'Highway To Hell' / 'Bad Boy Boogie' / 'The Jack' / 'Rocker' / 'Whole Lotta Rosie'.

August 5 The Ted Nugent–AC/DC roadshow ends with a gig at the 20,000-seat Spectrum Arena in Philadelphia. Angus does his usual lap of honour, emerging in the concourse section of the venue, among the merchandising and food stalls, astride a roadie's shoulders.

August 18 Back in the UK following a show the night before in Bilzen, Belgium, the band make their Wembley debut as part of a triple-header also featuring The Stranglers, Nils Lofgren, and headliners The Who—who are breaking in new drummer Kenney Jones—playing to a crowd reported to be as large as 80,000. AC/DC—billed as 'special guests'—play during the late afternoon, and, despite the unfamiliar timeslot and technical hassles, still manage to stir up the crowd.

'Only AC/DC really manage to move the audience,' *Melody Maker*'s Harry Doherty reports. But it's hard work for the group. A malfunctioning PA shuts down suddenly during 'Whole Lotta Rosie' and sets off a rowdy response from the crowd, many of whom are here to see AC/DC. 'Turn the fucking thing on!' one punter screams during the outage; the band continue to play, even though they can barely project beyond the first few rows. Finally, the PA roars back into life during 'Rocker'; the crowd yells its approval, and the pissed-off, fired-up band power on to a huge finale.

The malfunction will become the source of many rumours. Perhaps AC/DC are the victims of sabotage; could an envious headliner's crew be to blame? Despite the

FOLLOWING PAGES: AC/DC'S SET AT WEMBLEY STADIUM ON AUGUST 18 IS A STANDOUT GIG, EVEN THOUGH A MALFUNCTION CAUSES SOME HASSLES. A RUMOUR SPREADS THAT AN ENVIOUS HEADLINER MAY HAVE SABOTAGED THEIR EQUIPMENT.

"The audience left no doubt as to their partiality for AC/DC. This could be just the break the band needed to finally push their point home to Britain."

HARRY DOHERTY, *MELODY MAKER*, AUGUST 1979

problems, Stranglers frontman J.J. Burnel later reports, 'They were awesome. And it was solid packed.'

Meanwhile, on the day of the gig, *Highway To Hell* makes its first impression on the UK album chart, becoming the first AC/DC album to crack the Top 10, reaching #8. It will stick to the charts for forty weeks.

Setlist: 'Live Wire' / 'Shot Down In Flames' / 'Walk All Over You' / 'Bad Boy Boogie' / 'The Jack' / 'Highway To Hell' / 'Whole Lotta Rosie' / 'Rocker' / 'If You Want Blood (You've Got It)'.

August 20–21 The band undertake a two-night stand at the Olympic Ballroom in Dublin. They are now alternating the tracks 'Sin City' and 'Dog Eat Dog' with 'Walk All Over You' and with 'Let There Be Rock', but the bulk of their setlist is cast in stone.

August 23–24 Another two-night stand, this time at Belfast's Ulster Hall.

August 27 Tonight show is a warm-up for their next big festival date, for which AC/DC fill the Theatre De Verdure in Aix-Les-Bains, France.

September 1 AC/DC again work with The Who, this time at the Open Air Festival in Zeppelin Feld, Nuremburg—site of the notorious Nazi rallies of the 1930s—along with Cheap Trick, Molly Hatchet, Nils Lofgren, Miriam Makeba, and Scorpions, pulling a crowd of 60,000. Rain pours throughout the show. Angus stands at the side of the stage while The Who play, watching Pete Townshend closely, in a rare show of respect toward another act. Afterward, in the hotel bar, Townshend shakes his head and tells Angus and the band, 'Oh well, you've done it again, you fuckers. You stole the show.' Bon Scott allegedly replies, 'That's right, Pete. So what the fuck are you going to do up there—fucking sleep?' He then asks reformed boozer Townshend to buy him a drink, rubbing his nose in it just a little more.

On the same day, the single 'Highway To Hell' sneaks into the UK chart, reaching #56 at the start of a four-week chart run.

September 5 The first US show of a two-month run is staged at the Oakland Auditorium in California. All the seats have been removed from the 6,400-capacity room—possibly as a reaction to the chaos at the August 4 show with Nugent—which enables the crowd to loosen up considerably. 'This concert was wild,' one fan recalls. 'I could not hear for two days.'

During some of these gigs, AC/DC play 'Walk All Over You' rather than 'Hell Ain't A Bad Place To Be'; 'If You Want Blood (You've Got It)' also features on a few nights. The rest of the setlist is: 'Live Wire' / 'Shot Down In Flames' / 'Sin City' / 'Problem Child' / 'Bad Boy Boogie' / 'The Jack' / 'Highway To Hell' / 'High Voltage' / 'Whole Lotta Rosie' / 'Rocker' / 'Let There Be Rock'.

The shows on this US tour vary in size from 2,000- to 10,000-seaters. Many of the gigs are staged by powerful US promoter Bill Graham—an incredibly handy man for AC/DC to have in their corner.

September 7–9 The band fill the 2,000-capacity Santa Cruz Civic Centre. When Bon hikes Angus onto his shoulders for a quick lap of the room, one of several bikers in the crowd punches the singer in the mouth. 'We're never going to play Santa Cruz again,' Scott says from the stage, through a split lip.

The following morning, in an interview with local station KSJO 92.3, Angus laughs off the incident, even if his response is unintentionally prescient: 'Don't worry about Bon; he's already got his coffin ordered.' The band remain true to their word, though, and never return to Santa Cruz.

There's no such drama the following night, when they pack the 2,000-capacity Warnors Theatre in Fresno, California.

September 9 Tonight's show at the San Diego Sports Arena only draws 2,500 fans, barely half-filling the venue.

September 10 A show at the Long Beach Arena in California is covered by the *LA Times*. Angus is singled out for some high praise; the writer, Don Snowden, goes as far as to say that AC/DC are 'strictly a one-man show, with other members simply doing their job and staying out of Angus's way'. For Snowden, however, the band's appeal fades as their hour-long set continues. 'AC/DC's dedication to the primeval stomp sustained my interest for about 20 minutes, but the utter lack of variety and Angus's increasingly excessive guitar solos ultimately registered as boring in the extreme.' The 6,000-capacity venue is only about three-quarters full, despite a reasonable ticket price of $6.50–7.50.

September 13 Molly Hatchet open for AC/DC at the Civic Centre Arena in Amarillo, Texas—as they will on several more dates of this US run.

September 14 Next stop is Lubbock, Texas, the home of Buddy Holly—a fact that wouldn't have been lost on Angus and Malcolm Young, both of whom are big admirers of the rock'n'roll great. AC/DC open for Aerosmith, who are about to release *Night In The Ruts*. During 'Rocker', Angus does his usual lap of the room (the venue is the 3,000 capacity Memorial Auditorium), leaving a deep impression on the crowd and the headliner.

Years later, while inducting AC/DC into the Rock and Roll Hall of Fame, Steven Tyler asks, of Angus, 'How did such big balls get in such short pants?'

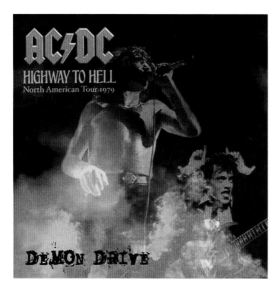

DEMON DRIVE IS A BOOTLEG OF A WILD SHOW FROM THE BAND'S 1979 AMERICAN TOUR TO PROMOTE HIGHWAY TO HELL.

September 15–21 Continuing the Texas leg of the tour, the band play the Chaparral Center in Midland, Scott slugging from a bottle of booze as they play. AC/DC are headlining the show, but the 7,500-seat room is only half-full. Scott also appears to be more than a little loose during the next night's gig at the Civic Center in El Paso, where he's seen stumbling about the stage.

More well-received gigs follow at the Convention Center in McAllen, the Memorial Coliseum in Corpus Christi, and the Music Center in Houston, all 2,000–3,000-seaters. On September 21, after a typically frenetic show at the Convention Center Arena in Dallas, Texas, the band members head to Sound Warehouse for a late-night record-signing.

September 22 AC/DC fill the 7,000-capacity HemisFair Arena in San Antonio, Texas. For the moment, Bon has delegated the task of piggybacking Angus around the venue to a diligent roadie. He's got more pressing concerns, such as the attention of the Heathen Girls—groupies who stick like glue to the singer whenever AC/DC tour North America. During AC/DC's set, Molly Hatchet guitarist Dave Hlubek appears on stage dressed as a schoolboy; clearly, relations between the two bands are strong.

September 24–28 The *Highway To Hell* tour powers on, with gigs in Beaumont,

Texas; then Memphis, Tennessee; and across the state in Johnson City, with Sammy Hagar opening, where they all but fill the 8,500-seat Freedom Hall Civic Center.

September 29 During AC/DC's encore at the 12,000-seat Charlotte Coliseum, members of Molly Hatchet join them for a thunderous 'Let There Be Rock'. Roof is duly raised.

September 30–October 3 Further shows follow in Greenville, South Carolina; Knoxville, Tennessee; and Greensboro, North Carolina. Blackfoot and Mother's Finest are the supports.

October 5 The band return to their happy rocking ground of Jacksonville, Florida, which remains so even though the 11,500-capacity Veteran's Memorial Coliseum is only three quarters full. Still, this is a city they'll play upward of ten times during their career.

October 6–13 The next run of shows takes AC/DC to Birmingham, Alabama; Orlando, Florida; Dothan, Alabama; Atlanta, Georgia; Norfolk, Virginia; and Wheeling, West Virginia. Most of the venues in these cities remove the seats and sell only general admission tickets, turning their lower levels into seething mosh-pits, although that's not the case at the Fox Theatre in Atlanta, where the ushers try their best to enforce the venue's stay-seated policy. Key word: *try*.

> **"We'd like the security down the front here to fuck off. We're having a rock'n'roll concert, and they ain't rock'n'roll."**
>
> BON SCOTT, INTRODUCING 'HIGHWAY TO HELL' AT THE ARAGON BALLROOM, OCTOBER 1979

October 14 The band's show in Huntington, West Virginia, is briefly halted when a crowd surge results in some stage-front pileups. There are no reported injuries, however.
  Setlist: 'Live Wire' / 'Shot Down In Flames' / 'Hell Ain't A Bad Place To Be' / 'Sin City' / 'Problem Child' / 'Bad Boy Boogie' / 'The Jack' / 'Highway To Hell' / 'High Voltage' / 'Whole Lotta Rosie' / 'Rocker' / 'If You Want Blood (You've Got It)' / 'Let There Be Rock'.

October 16–19 The band hit Towson, Maryland; Buffalo, New York; Cleveland, Ohio; and Chicago, Illinois—where they fill the Aragon Ballroom—like the proverbial hurricane. Bon Scott spars with some heavy-handed bouncers in Towson, dedicating

'The Jack' to 'the security, because they're such a bunch of arseholes'. Several bootleg recordings capturing Scott's verbal barrage will later surface, one titled *The Ecstasy Of Mr S* and another called *Demon Drive*.

The authorities in Towson subsequently ban rock concerts due to the proliferation of broken bottles and debris outside the venue, which resembles a bombsite at the end of the night. This gig provides some punters' first exposure to AC/DC; many have been drawn to it by the success the opening act, Pat Travers, has been having with a song called 'Boom Boom (Out Go The Lights)', but most of them leave as dedicated AC/DC fans.

Setlist: 'Live Wire' / 'Shot Down In Flames' / 'Hell Ain't A Bad Place To Be' / 'Sin City' / 'Problem Child' / 'Bad Boy Boogie' / 'The Jack' / 'Highway To Hell' / 'High Voltage' / 'Whole Lotta Rosie' / 'Rocker' / 'If You Want Blood (You've Got It)' / 'Let There Be Rock'.

October 20 Angus drops trou' and moons the faithful squeezed into Ohio's Toledo Sports Arena. Clearly, he doesn't have the same concerns about being arrested in the USA as he does in the UK and Australia.

October 21 Tonight's concert at the 9,000-seat St John Arena in Columbus, Ohio, is Bon Scott's final US show. *Highway To Hell* is now a gold record in North America, its sales having exceeding 500,000 copies. It will hit a chart peak of #20 on October 27, while the single of the album's title track reaches #47. The nation's #1 is currently Led Zeppelin's *In Through The Out Door*, with the dreaded Eagles and their *Long Run* at #2.

October 26 Back in the Old Dart, the support for AC/DC show at the Mayfair Ballroom in Newcastle is a bunch of up-and-comers named Def Leppard, who are also working with producer 'Mutt' Lange. Many years later, Leppard's Joe Elliott will feature on Brian Johnson's Sky Arts TV show about car nuts, *Life On The Road*.

The gig itself has had to be rescheduled from the night before because a fire broke out in the venue during AC/DC's soundcheck.

October 27–28 The band stay at the Albany Hotel in Glasgow while undertaking a two-night stand at the Apollo Theatre, again with Def Leppard in support. 'I've been in bigger jail cells than this room,' Bon grumbles.

October 29–30 Another two-night stand, this time at the Apollo Theatre in Manchester. A recording of the October 29 show—all eighty-six rockin' minutes of it—will later appear on a bootleg with the highly imaginative title *Apollo Theatre Manchester October 29 1979*.

   Setlist: 'Live Wire' / 'Shot Down In Flames' / 'Hell Ain't A Bad Place To Be' / 'Sin City' / 'Problem Child' / 'Bad Boy Boogie' / 'The Jack' / 'Highway To Hell' / 'Girl's Got Rhythm' / 'Whole Lotta Rosie' / 'Rocker' / 'If You Want Blood (You've Got It)' / 'Let There Be Rock'.

November 1–4 Who needs a two-night stand when you can stay for four? The band settle into London's Hammersmith Odeon for four shows, the second of which is recorded for the BBC's *In Concert* series. An eleven-track 'album' is pressed purely for BBC use, and yet after the show, which is broadcast on January 7 1980, a few rogue copies once again find their way onto the bootleg market, one of them going by the name *Angus Cha Cha*. Another is titled *Bon Scott Forever*.

   A full bootleg of one of the Hammersmith gigs, known as *Tropical Prison*, will also do the rounds. On it, Bon can be heard juicing up the lyrics of 'Highway To Hell', shouting, *'Nobody's going to fuck me around.'*

   Track listing: 'Live Wire' / 'Shot Down In Flames' / 'Hell Ain't A Bad Place To Be' / 'Sin City' / 'Walk All Over You' / 'The Jack' / 'Highway To Hell' / 'Girls Got Rhythm' / 'High Voltage' / 'If You Want Blood (You've Got It)' / 'Let There Be Rock'.

November 5–6 The band's thing for 'mini-residencies' continues, this time over two nights at the Empire in Liverpool.

November 8–9 Angus takes to the upper balcony at Bingley Hall in Stafford during his extended solo. The crowd goes gaga, as usual. The following night, before heading to the continent for even more touring, the band fill the De Montfort Hall in Leicester.

November 11 Another UK band on the rise, Judas Priest, open for AC/DC at the 5,500-capacity Forest National in Bruxelles, Belgium, and will go on to do so at many other concerts on the band's subsequent run of European dates. Singer Rob Halford is a convert, making a point of watching AC/DC's sets from the side of the stage, 'Because of their energy and their power and their love of what they did.'

November 13–21 More shows follow in the Germany cities of Koln, Hannover, Essen, Regensburg, Wurzburg, Passau, Offenbach, and Dortmund, in venues varying in capacity from 2,000 to 5,000.

November 22–December 4 Germany is clearly a key target for the band, as they play nine more gigs in the country during this period, in Bremen, Hamburg, Regensburg, Ravensburg, Hof, Munich, Ludwigshafen, Nuremburg, and Berlin, along with a show in the Swiss capital of Bern on November 25. For the final date on this leg of the tour, the band's venue in Berlin is upgraded to the 5,000-seat Eissportahalle.

December 6–15 An extended run of French dates ensues, with stops in Metz, Reims, Lille, Grenoble, Lyon, Clermont-Ferrand, Montpellier, Nice, and Paris. Arriving in the capital, Angus is a tad disappointed by the Bastille: 'I'd like them to rebuild it.'

A film crew follows the band, shooting footage that will eventually surface in the 1980 concert movie *Let There Be Rock*. It is originally intended purely as promo material, but after being given the OK by band manager Peter Mensch, the filmmakers, Eric Dionysius and Eric Mistler, borrow money left, right, and centre to finance a full-length concert movie. Ultimately, a crew of forty people will be involved in the production.

As the cameras roll, Angus and Malcolm are caught tuning up backstage, ever-present ciggies in their mouths, seemingly immune to everything, and everyone, around them.

Angus looks up when asked about his bandmates. 'Phil, he's good, except he keeps picking his nose and flicking it at me with his drumstick. Gets a bit out of hand, but you learn to duck. Cliff? He's like Phil, you know, always swinging the bass; you gotta learn to duck him, too, keep dodging the guitar. Bon's very different, too, he's a very individual person. What can I say? He's a lunatic, but he's great.'

Bon then talks about Angus. 'I think he's kind of crazy. The first night I saw the band was at a club back in Australia … I stood there and there's this little guy in a school uniform, bag on his back, going crazy. I laughed for about half an hour. I still laugh. I think he's great.'

In an effort to display the non-musical sides to the guys in the band, Malcolm is filmed kicking around a soccer ball, Angus while sketching, Rudd driving a Porsche,

> **"*He's my height, the same size — I can look him in the eye. The notorious Young brothers.*"**
>
> ANGUS ON MALCOLM, DURING THE FILMING OF *LET THERE BE ROCK*

ONE OF THE FINAL STUDIO SHOOTS TO FEATURE BON SCOTT, CAMDEN, LONDON, AUGUST 1 1979. HE AND THE BAND HAVE COME A HELL OF A LONG WAY SINCE 1974.

and Cliff at the controls of a World War I–era plane. The original plan for Bon is to film him riding a motorbike, but when that falls through, the crew take him to Versailles and decide to shoot him while dancing on a frozen lake. The ice begins to crack while Scott is horsing about, however, and he beats a hasty retreat.

The concert film will be released in the UK on September 1 1980 and in the USA two weeks later. Oddly, it's not released in Australia until late 1981. In a retrospective review, ultimaterockclassic.com declares, 'The energy Scott and his bandmates, particularly lead guitarist and human tornado, Angus Young, put out … simply must be seen to be believed.'

December 17–21 AC/DC return to their London 'home', the Hammersmith Odeon, with further UK shows following in Brighton and Birmingham—their final gigs of an incredibly lively and productive year. For these shows, they reintroduce the songs 'It's A Long Way To The Top' and 'Baby, Please Don't Go' into their set, having not played either for some time. (The first of two shows in Birmingham, at the Odeon Theatre on December 20, is bootlegged.)

Asked after the gig about his state of mind, Bon is in high spirits. 'I'm thirty-three, [but] you're never too old to rock'n'roll.'

Late December Scott returns to Sydney to spend Christmas with family and friends; he jumps on stage at a gig staged at suburban Sydney venue the Family Inn, jamming with the band Swanee. One of the songs he sings is Chuck Berry's 'Back In The USA'.

AC/DC, meanwhile, sneak into *Creem* magazine's 'Top 25 Groups' reader's poll, coming in at #20, outranking Fleetwood Mac and Judas Priest but lagging well behind the #1 and #2 acts, Led Zeppelin and Cheap Trick. *Highway To Hell* is #16 in the magazine's Albums Of The Year chart. (Led Zep, again, top the poll, with *In Through The Out Door*.)

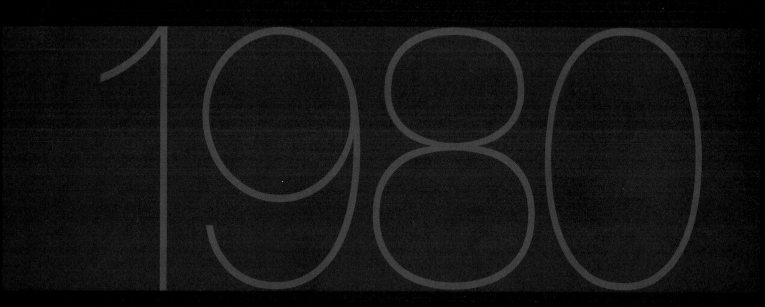

*Work begins on the album that will become
Back In Black; Bon Scott is found dead on
a London back street, and the music world
mourns his demise; Malcolm and Angus Young
contemplate the band's future.*

January 16–23 After a few weeks off over Christmas and New Year, the band undertake another whistle-stop tour of France, with gigs in Poitiers, Bordeaux, Toulouse, Rouen, Nantes, Brest, and Le Mans. The *Highway To Hell* LP is well represented in their setlist; they now play 'Shot Down In Flames', 'Highway To Hell', and 'Girls Got Rhythm', alongside the usual standards.

January 25 On stage at the 1,500-capacity Mayfair Ballroom in Newcastle, Bon is in a talkative mood, flashing back to the problems they had the year before, when a fire broke out during their soundcheck and caused the gig to be rescheduled. 'We're gonna hope the place doesn't burn down until we're finished,' he says, as they launch into 'Shot Down In Flames', which elicits a football-style chant from the crowd. He then playfully introduces 'Hell Ain't A Bad Place To Be', slurring noticeably, as 'a song from the new album about Newcastle'. 'The Jack' is one big sing-along, Scott conducting the crowd as they chant, 'She's got the jack!' It's all good, dirty fun.

This is the last Bon Scott show to be recorded, bootlegged as *Nearing The End Of The Highway*. His voice is raw; he screams the lyrics to the opener 'Live Wire' and rasps his way through the rest of the gig. The rest of the band are in prime form, however; Angus's soloing on 'Shot Down In Flames', in particular, is red hot. He opens 'Problem Child' with a tasty few minutes of lean, bluesy guitar, the crowd with him all the way, before his bandmates crash into the song with the force of a Sherman tank. Malcolm has the opening riff for 'Highway To Hell' crafted to perfection; it's a dazzling blast of rock and rhythm, powerful enough to dislodge fillings.

Setlist: 'Live Wire' / 'Shot Down In Flames' / 'Hell Ain't A Bad Place To Be' / 'Sin City' / 'Problem Child' / 'Bad Boy Boogie' / 'The Jack' / 'Highway To Hell' / 'Girls Got Rhythm' / 'High Voltage' / 'Whole Lotta Rosie' / 'Rocker' / 'T.N.T.' / 'Let There Be Rock'.

January 26 Bon Scott's final show with the band—on Australia Day, no less—is a rescheduled gig at the Gaumont in Southampton. Sporting new red trainers, he appears to be in top form, both physically and vocally; his hair's a little shaggier than usual, but he's as buff and brawny as ever. And his skin-tight jeans leave absolutely nothing whatsoever to the imagination.

February 2 'Touch Too Much' is the second single from the *Highway To Hell* LP to hit the UK singles chart, reaching #29 (and #13 in Germany). On the B-side are in-concert

takes of 'Live Wire' and 'Shot Down In Flames'. A performance video is also released of the band in full steam while rehearsing for their 1978–79 tour. Upon hearing 'Touch Too Much', a youthful Axl Rose, a massive fan of the band, will declare it to be his favourite AC/DC track.

February 7 The band rock 'Touch Too Much' on *Top Of The Pops*. Or attempt to, as miming isn't their natural domain. A less-than-ideal situation is made even trickier when it's decided that Angus can only be filmed from the waist up (his gyrations are considered far too racy for the audience). Oddly, Scott's open shirt, with his chest on full and proud display, causes no such concerns.

It's the usual mixed bag of a *Top Of The Pops* line-up: also on the show are The Tourists, Cliff Richard, The Boomtown Rats, Joe Jackson, and Buggles, whose Trevor Horn is tasked with introducing AC/DC.

Bon, meanwhile, returns to the Hammersmith Odeon, but not to play; rather, he's cheering on his buddies in UFO as they stage their own three-night run at the venue. He is photographed backstage—perhaps the last time his photo is taken.

Members of UFO will later admit that heroin was among their after-show indulgences, with AC/DC's manager Peter Mensch subsequently speaking out about the negative influence he felt this environment had on Scott. Alas, his bandmates, being younger than Scott, are hardly in a position to give him lifestyle lectures, or to stage any sort of intervention, if one is required.

February 9 AC/DC play 'Beating Around The Bush' on a Spanish TV show called *TV Applauso*, as well as 'Girls Got Rhythm'. The intro from host Silvia Tortosa lays it on the line: 'Today on *TV Applauso*, we receive a new group in Spain: AC/DC. They're Australian and are considered one of the best rock bands of the last generation … today, for the first time in Spain, AC/DC!'

Angus is in full flight—his cap goes flying after 'Beating Around The Bush''s opening riff—but Bon isn't at his best. He's unkempt, his unruly hair falling into his eyes, his skin pale. He looks tired, drained. Angus powers on, delivering a near-perfect dying bug as the opening song reaches its explosive climax, and breaking into a duck walk during

'TOUCH TOO MUCH' IS AC/DC'S FINAL SINGLE TO BE RELEASED DURING BON SCOTT'S LIFETIME.

239

'Girls Got Rhythm'. The seated audience, an odd assortment of Spaniards both young and old, clap politely.

February 13 At London's Scorpion Studios, Scott records a new version of 'Ride On' with his French buddy Bernie Bonvoisin and his band Trust, transforming it into an even bluesier, even more sinewy cut than the stellar original (from *Dirty Deeds*). It's a standout of the popular AC/DC bootleg *Ride On, Bon!*, which compiles live cuts, curios, and TV performances, dating from the period 1976–80.

It is also during February that Angus marries his partner, Ellen. Malcolm married his girlfriend, O'Linda, a former Alberts employee, just before Christmas. O'Linda was a colleague and close friend of Fifa Riccobono from Alberts, an AC/DC insider and confidante.

February 15 Scott drops by a rehearsal studio in London, where Malcolm and Angus are working on instrumental versions of new songs 'Have A Drink On Me' and 'Let Me Put My Love Into You'. Rather than sing or work on any lyrical ideas, Scott plays drums—an unintentionally poignant gesture, given that he'd originally offered his services to the band as a drummer.

February 18–19 Having recently separated from girlfriend Silver Smith, Bon is now living with a new partner, a Japanese woman named Anna Baba. He spends the night of February 18 with a friend, Alistair Kinnear, drinking at a club called the Music Machine. Unable to get the drunken singer upstairs to his flat, Kinnear covers him with a blanket and leaves him in the back seat of a friend's Renault 5, parked in Overhill Road in East Dulwich, to sleep off his bender.

Sometime during the night, Scott vomits and chokes to death. Kinnear finds the singer's lifeless body the next day.

Scott is rushed to Kings College Hospital in Camberwell, but is pronounced dead on arrival. Kinnear calls Silver Smith; Anna Baba phones Angus, who is shocked beyond belief. He pulls himself together and calls Malcolm, who contacts tour manager Ian Jeffery.

Jeffery asks Malcolm if he is joking.

'Would I fucking joke about a thing like that?'

Manager Peter Mensch travels to the hospital to identify the body, while Malcolm takes on the job of calling Scott's parents with the awful news.

'Someone had to call them, and it was better coming from one of the band than from the newspaper,' he later recalls to VH-1's *Behind The Music*. 'Most difficult thing I've ever had to do; hope I never have to do anything like that again.

'In Britain, they made [Bon's death] a bit of a joke almost, you know. We've never forgiven them for that. All we were concerned about was Bon's parents— they're really nice people, they don't need this shit.'

Over time, there would be almost as many conspiracy theories surrounding Scott's death as there are regarding Jim Morrison's mysterious demise several years earlier. But his death certificate, issued on February 22, states clearly that Scott died as a result of 'acute alcohol poisoning', a 'death by misadventure'.

The press keeps the news simple.

'Bon Scott Dead,' reads one headline. 'What now for AC/DC?'

'Aussie Rock Star DEAD,' screams Australian rag the *Daily Mirror*.

'Rock Star, Left In Car "To Sober Up", Found Dead,' reads another daily.

'Singer of the rock group AC/DC was found dead last night in a parked car in South London,' the first US radio coverage of his death announces. 'Scotland Yard said the body of thirty-year-old Bon Scott was discovered by a friend who had left him in a car a few hours earlier to sober up after a day's drinking.'

Bernard Bonvoisin, whom Scott had called and invited to the Music Machine on the night of his death, later admits that hearing the news is like 'a big blow from an iron bar to the head'. He finds it impossible to believe that his buddy is gone; wasn't Bon bulletproof? Then Bonvoisin goes to Scorpion Studios, where he once recorded with Scott. As soon as he walks in, the reality of it hits him like a thunderbolt. Scott really is dead. 'I saw the faces of the guys in the studio … I sat down and cried.'

'I was sad for Bon,' Angus says. 'I didn't even think about the band. We'd been with Bon all that time; we'd seen more of him than his family did.'

A few days after Scott's death, Angus speaks to Bruce Elder, an Australian journalist currently based in London. 'Who in the band was closest to Bon?' Elder asks, to which Angus replies, 'We all were. You see, we were on the road for ten or eleven months every year, and the rest of the time we were in the studio recording the next album. We were all close to Bon.'

The Australian music industry is in a state of shock. *Countdown* host Molly Meldrum is crushed by the news. He and Scott had been close since the time of The Valentines; he and *Countdown* have been massive supporters of AC/DC. *Countdown* funded the

FOLLOWING PAGES: A LIVE VERSION OF 'WHOLE LOTTA ROSIE' WAS THE BAND'S FIRST RELEASE AFTER BON SCOTT'S DEATH; SCOTT LIGHTS UP AT NORTH ALTONA TECHNICAL HIGH SCHOOL, JULY 1975.

He looked fantastic, he was looking after himself. I said, 'We're just about ready for you, Bon, maybe next week sometime.' He went out, just for a drink, maybe to clear his head, and then he was looking forward to getting into his writing. He had it all ahead of him.

MALCOLM YOUNG ON THE LAST TIME HE SAW BON SCOTT, *BEHIND THE MUSIC*

videos for 'It's A Long Way To The Top' and 'Jailbreak'—clips that helped establish the band across Australia and beyond—and traced their every step in the UK and America.

'Earlier this week, there was some very, very sad news for ... the Australian rock scene, and that was the death of one of, in my mind, the greatest Australian rock'n'rollers we've had over the past ten years ... Bon Scott,' Meldrum announces on the February 24 episode of the show. 'Not only was he a friend of mine ... but I think it's a great blow to Australian industry and to AC/DC.'

Meldrum goes on to document how close the band has been to becoming 'one of the world's top supergroups'. Fumbling around for words, he adds, 'I mean, what can you say, except that we at *Countdown* owe Bon and the boys a lot.' He then plays the classic 'Jailbreak' clip in Scott's honour, followed by 'Show Business', and hints that the show might just go on for AC/DC, even though no announcement has yet been made to their future.

Scott's body is embalmed and returned to Fremantle, Western Australia, where he is cremated and his ashes sprinkled in various favourite sites around his hometown. His grave marker, in Fremantle Cemetery, reads, in part, 'Close to our hearts, he will always stay, loved and remembered every day.' His gravesite will become one of the most visited in Australia. (A statue of Scott now stands in the middle of Fremantle—another must-see site on any Bon Scott–AC/DC pilgrimage.)

At the service, Malcolm and Angus, who are devastated by their bandmate's death, ask Scott's parents, Chick and Isa, what they should do: would it be best to end the band, as a mark of respect for Bon?

'Keep going,' the Scotts tell them. 'That's what Bon would have wanted.'

It's their support that inspires the next chapter of the AC/DC story.

> **"Bon was a gypsy, a vagabond, a buccaneer, a bad boy and a rock'n'roll outlaw. He was truly a street poet, documenting in lyric and performance all that he thought, felt, and cared about life. He was the only other singer I ever invited to sing with the Tatts—whenever he felt like it."**
>
> ANGRY ANDERSON OF ROSE TATTOO TO THE *AUSTRALIAN*, 2006

WHEN BON SCOTT DIES, ANGUS AND MALCOLM HAVE NO IDEA WHETHER TO CONTINUE THE BAND, BUT A CHANCE CONVERSATION WITH BON'S PARENTS HELPS THEM PLAN THEIR FUTURE.

SELECTED DISCOGRAPHY

CHARTING SINGLES

'Can I Sit Next To You, Girl' /
'Rockin' In The Parlour'
First charted: 26/8/74 (Australia)
Weeks on chart: 10
Highest position: #50

'Baby, Please Don't Go' / 'Love Song'
First charted: 31/3/75 (Australia)
Weeks on chart: 18
Highest position: #20

'High Voltage' / 'Soul Stripper'
First charted: 21/7/75 (Australia) /
28/6/80 (UK)
Weeks on chart: 22 (Australia) / 3 (UK)
Highest position: #10 (Australia) / #48 (UK)

'It's A Long Way To The Top (If You Wanna
Rock'n'roll)' / 'Can I Sit Next To You, Girl'
First charted: 22/12/75 (Australia) /
28/6/80 (UK)
Weeks on chart: 19 (Australia) / 3 (UK)
Highest position: #9 (Australia) / #55 (UK)

'T.N.T.' / 'I'm A Rocker'
First charted: 8/3/76 (Australia)
Weeks on chart: 18
Highest position: #19

'Jailbreak' / 'Fling Thing'
First charted: 28/6/76 (Australia)
Weeks on chart: 19
Highest position: #10

'Dirty Deeds Done Dirt Cheap' /
'RIP (Rock In Peace)'
First charted: 18/10/76 (Australia) /
28/6/80 (UK)
Weeks on chart: 18 (Australia) / 3 (UK)
Highest position: #29 (Australia) /
#47 (UK)

'Love At First Feel'
First charted: 14/2/77 (Australia)
Weeks on chart: 9
Highest position: #63

'Dog Eat Dog' / 'Carry Me Home'
First charted: 18/4/77 (Australia)
Weeks on chart: 5
Highest position: #60

'Let There Be Rock' / 'Problem Child'
First charted: 6/2/78 (Australia)
Weeks on chart: 6
Highest position: #82

'Rock'n'roll Damnation' / 'Sin City'
First charted: 17/7/78 (Australia) /
10/6/78 (UK)
Weeks on chart: 8 (Australia) / 9 (UK)
Highest position: #83 (Australia) /
#24 (UK)

'Highway To Hell' / 'If You Want
Blood (You've Got It)'
First charted: 3/9/79 (Australia) /
1/9/79 (UK) / 8/12/79 (USA)
Weeks on chart: 20 (Australia) /
4 (UK) / 9 (USA)
Highest position: #24 (Australia) /
#56 (UK) / #47 (USA)

'Touch Too Much' / 'Live Wire' (live) /
'Shot Down In Flames' (live)
First charted: 2/2/80 (UK)
Weeks on chart: 9 (UK)
Highest position: #29 (UK)

'Whole Lotta Rosie' (live)
First charted: 28/6/80 (UK)
Weeks on chart: 8 (UK)
Highest position: #36 (UK)

ALBUMS

HIGH VOLTAGE (original Australian album)
Track listing: 'Baby, Please Don't Go' / 'She's Got Balls' / 'Little Lover' / 'Stick Around' / 'Soul Stripper' / 'You Ain't Got A Hold On Me' / 'Love Song' / 'Show Business'
First charted: 10/3/75 (Australia)
Weeks on chart: 39
Highest position: #14 (Australia)

T.N.T. (original Australian album)
Track listing: 'It's A Long Way To The Top (If You Wanna Rock'n'roll)' / 'Rock'n'roll Singer' / 'The Jack' / 'Live Wire' / 'T.N.T.' / 'Rocker' / 'Can I Sit Next To You, Girl' / 'High Voltage' / 'School Days'
First charted: 5/1/76 (Australia)
Weeks on chart: 30
Highest position: #2

HIGH VOLTAGE (international album)
Track listing: 'It's A Long Way To The Top (If You Wanna Rock'n'roll)' / 'Rock'n'roll Singer' / 'The Jack' / 'Live Wire' / 'T.N.T.' / 'Can I Sit Next To You, Girl' / 'Little Lover' / 'She's Got Balls' / 'High Voltage'
First charted: 30/5/81 (USA)
Weeks on chart: 39
Highest position: #146 (USA)

DIRTY DEEDS DONE DIRT CHEAP
Track listing (Australia): 'Dirty Deeds Done Dirt Cheap' / 'Ain't No Fun (Waiting 'Round To Be A Millionaire)' / 'There's Gonna Be Some Rockin'' / 'Problem Child' / 'Squealer' / 'Big Balls' / 'R.I.P. (Rock In Peace)' / 'Ride On' / 'Jailbreak'
Track listing (international): 'Dirty Deeds Done Dirt Cheap' / 'Love At First Feel' / 'Big Balls' / 'Rocker' / 'Problem Child' / 'There's Gonna Be Some Rockin'' / 'Ain't No Fun (Waiting 'Round To Be A Millionaire)' / 'Ride On' / 'Squealer'
First charted: 4/10/76 (Australia) / 30/5/81 (USA)
Weeks on chart: 24 (Australia) / 55 (USA)
Highest position: #5 (Australia) / #3 (USA)

LET THERE BE ROCK
Track listing (Australia): 'Go Down' / 'Dog Eat Dog' / 'Let There Be Rock' / 'Bad Boy Boogie' / 'Problem Child' / 'Overdose' / 'Crabsody In Blue' / 'Hell Ain't A Bad Place To Be' / 'Whole Lotta Rosie'
Track listing (international): 'Go Down' / 'Dog Eat Dog' / 'Let There Be Rock' / 'Bad Boy Boogie' / 'Problem Child' / 'Overdose' / 'Hell Ain't A Bad Place To Be' / 'Whole Lotta Rosie'
First charted: 4/4/77 (Australia) / 5/11/77 (UK) / 15/10/77 (USA)
Weeks on chart: 20 (Australia) / 5 (UK) / 17 (USA)
Highest position: #19 (Australia) / #17 (UK) / #154 (USA)

POWERAGE
Track listing (Australia and USA): 'Rock'n'roll Damnation' / 'Down Payment Blues' / 'Gimme A Bullet' / 'Riff Raff' / 'Sin City' / 'What's Next To The Moon' / 'Gone Shootin'' / 'Up To My Neck In You' / 'Kicked In The Teeth'
Track listing (Europe): 'Rock'n'roll Damnation' / 'Gimme A Bullet' / 'Down Payment Blues' / 'Gone Shootin'' / 'Riff Raff' / 'Sin City' / 'Up To My Neck In You' / 'What's Next To The Moon' / 'Cold Hearted Man' / 'Kicked In The Teeth'
First charted: 26/6/78 (Australia) / 20/5/78 (UK) / 23/9/78 (USA)
Weeks on chart: 16 (Australia) / 9 (UK) / 17 (USA)
Highest position: #22 (Australia) / #26 (UK) / #133 (USA)

IF YOU WANT BLOOD, YOU'VE GOT IT
Track listing: 'Riff Raff' / 'Hell Ain't A Bad Place To Be' / 'Bad Boy Boogie' / 'The Jack' / 'Problem Child' / 'Whole Lotta Rosie' / 'Rock'n'roll Damnation' / 'High Voltage' / 'Let There Be Rock' / 'Rocker'
First charted: 11/12/78 (Australia) / 28/10/78 (UK) / 17/2/79 (USA)
Weeks on chart: 15 (Australia) / 59 (UK) / 14 (USA)
Highest position: #37 (Australia) / #13 (UK) / #113 (USA)

HIGHWAY TO HELL
Track listing: 'Highway To Hell' / 'Girls Got Rhythm' / 'Walk All Over You' / 'Touch Too Much' / 'Beating Around The Bush' / 'Shot Down In Flames' / 'Get It Hot' / 'If You Want Blood (You've Got It)' / 'Love Hungry Man' / 'Night Prowler'
First charted: 15/10/79 (Australia) / 18/8/79 (UK) / 10/11/79 (USA)
Weeks on chart: 15 (Australia) / 40 (UK) / 83 (USA)
Highest position: #13 (Australia) / #8 (UK) / #17 (USA)

Sources
www.billboard.com
www.officialcharts.com

NOTES AND SOURCES

ACKNOWLEDGEMENTS
A huge thanks to Tom Seabrook and Nigel Osborne at Jawbone Press, not only for getting on board, but for sharing this creative journey from page one onward. Big thanks also to the following people who contributed to this book: Glenn A. Baker, Herm Kovac, Neil Litchfield, Philip Morris (itsalongway.com.au/philip-morris.html), Tim Petts, Graeme Webber (graemewebber.com.au), Frank White, and Andrew Witner. And a hefty shout-out to the staff at the National Archive of Australia, who dug very deep.

BOOKS
Jim Barnes, Stephen Scanes *The Book: Top 40 Research 1956–2010*, Scanes Music Research, 2011

Michael Browning *Dog Eat Dog*, Allen & Unwin, 2014

Toby Creswell, Craig Mathieson, John O'Donnell *The 100 Best Australian Albums*, Hardie Grant Books, 2010

Robert Dimery *1001 Albums You Must Hear Before You Die*, Quintet Publishing, 2005

Murray Engleheart, Arnaud Durieux *AC/DC: Maximum Rock & Roll*, Harpercollins, 2006

Mark Evans *Dirty Deeds: My Life Inside And Outside AC/DC*, Allen & Unwin, 2011

David Kent *Australian Chart Book 1970–1992*, David Kent, 1993

Ian McFarlane *Encyclopedia Of Australian Rock and Pop*, Allen & Unwin, 1999

Dave McAleer *The Warner Guide To US & UK Hit Singles*, Carlton/Little, Brown, 1994

Philip Morris *It's A Long Way: From Acca-Dacca To Zappa 1969–1979*, Echo Publishing, 2015

Bob Rogers with Denis O'Brien *Rock 'n' Roll Australia*, Burbank Production Services, 2008

John Tait, Vanda & Young *Inside Australia's Hit Factory*, New South Books, 2010

Irene Thornton *My Bon Scott*, Pan Macmillan, 2014

Clinton Walker *Highway To Hell: The Life & Death Of AC/DC Legend Bon Scott*, Pan Macmillan, 1994

ARTICLES
Cameron Adams '10 Of The Most Amazing AC/DC Moments', news.com.au, April 15 2014

Ellen Aman 'Get Out The Earplugs For Kiss Concert', *Lexington Leader*, December 16 1977

Laura Armitage 'Forty Years Since AC/DC Played Year 12 Formal At Ivanhoe Grammar For $240', *Herald-Sun*, May 7 2015

Geoff Barton 'AC/DC High On Orange Smarties', *Sounds*, May 22 1976

Geoff Barton 'AC/DC: The Fastest Knees In The West', *Sounds*, June 12 1976

Geoff Barton 'Same Old Song And Dance (Bot So What?)', *Sounds*, November 20 1976

Geoff Barton 'A Long Way To The Top: How AC/DC Conquered The World From The Back Of A Van', *Classic Rock*, August 2016

Lachlan Bennett 'Memories Of AC/DC Concerts In Queenstown, Devonport', *The Advocate*, November 20 2017

Tom Beaujour 'AC/DC's Angus Young Discusses Bon Scott And The *Bonfire* Box Set', *Ultimate Classic Rock*, December 1 2011

Joe Bonomo 'The Night AC/DC Stormed Cbgbs', salon.com, November 5 2017

Robert Brinton 'Spanish Fly', *Disc*, April 21 1973

David Brown 'The Dirtiest Group In Town', *Record Mirror*, November 13 1976

Alesha Capone 'High Voltage For AC/DC Anniversary At St Albans Secondary College', *Herald-Sun*, March 4 2016

Roy Carr 'Is Britain Ready For The Human Kangaroo?', *NME*, October 16 1976

Paul Cashmere 'AC/DC's First Setlist From 40 Years Ago', noise11.com, December 31 2013

Tony Catterall 'Magnificent Assault On Eardrums', *Canberra Times*, December 13 1976

John Conroy 'Vintage Voltage: When AC/DC Rocked Albury', *Border Mail*, February 11 2010

Caroline Coon 'Live Review', *Melody Maker*, May 8 1976

Ian Cross 'Tiny Angus Is Cult Figure', *Canberra Times*, December 14 1978

Giovanni Dodomo 'Destroy Your Brain With AC/DC', *Sounds*, May 15 1976

Harry Doherty 'AC/DC Marquee London', *Melody Maker*, August 21 1976

Harry Doherty 'Current Affairs: Harry Doherty Travels To Cardiff To See How AC/DC Are Steadily Working Their Way To The Top', *Melody Maker*, March 5 1977

Harry Doherty 'The Who / The Stranglers / AC/DC / Nils Lofgren, Wembley Stadium—Close Encounters Of The Wembley Kind', *Melody Maker*, August 25 1979

Malcolm Dome 'AC/DC's First British Gig', *Classic Rock*, April 23 2014

Bethan Donnelly, *Villawood Migrant Hostel*, phansw.org.au/wp-content/uploads/2012/09/BethanDonnelly2008.pdf

Patrick Donovan 'For A Piper, It's A Long Way To The Top From The Back Of A Flatbed Truck', *The Age*, February 13 2010

Bruce Elder 'AC/DC By Name And Nature', *The Age*, January 29 2010

Christie Eliezer 'AC/DC Spray Their Piece', *RAM*, December 11 1976

Paul Elliott 'AC/DC: Cash For Questions', Q, September 2003

Luis Feliu 'More Than A Little Sunburn', *Canberra Times*, December 1 1978

John Finley 'Kiss, Kiss, Bang, Bang, At Fairgrounds Concert', *Courier-Journal*, December 11 1977

Ian Flavin 'AC/DC Hiding From A Gunman', *Rock Star*, March 5 1977

David Fricke 'AC/DC Shrug Off A Death And Rock On', *Rolling Stone*, October 30 1980

Bob Granger 'The Lusts Of AC/DC—Band Bids For Supreme Punkdom', *RAM*, September 20 1975

Andy Greene 'Readers' Poll: The 10 Best AC/DC Songs', *Rolling Stone*, October 15 2014

Andy Greene '10 Classic Albums Rolling Stone Originally Panned', *Rolling Stone*, July 25 2016

Kory Grow 'Metallica's Lars Ulrich: My 15 Favourite Metal And Hard Rock Albums', *Rolling Stone*, June 22 2017

Kory Grow 'Hipgnosis' Life In 15 Album Covers', *Rolling Stone*, May 2 2017

Michelle Hoctor 'It's A Long Way To The Top… From AC/DC's Early Days In Corrimal', *Illawarra Mercury*, February 5 2010

Ira Kaplan 'AC/DC's High-Voltage Sonic Assault', *Rolling Stone*, November 16 1978

Howie Klein 'AC/DC Hit California', *New York Rocker*, November 1977

Julie Kusko 'A Family Reunion For The Easybeats', *Australian Women's Weekly*, October 15 1969

Dave Lewis 'Sex + Drugs + Rock & Roll = AC/DC?', *Sounds*, May 20 1978

Melissa Locker 'Catching Up With Cheap Trick's Rick Nielsen, 35 Years After *Live At Budokan*', *Time*, May 3 2013

Vince Lovegrove 'Australian Music To The World' youtube.com/watch?v=g3lkdpoexwq

Vince Lovegrove 'Fraternity: 5+1+1=7 More Than Just A Pop Group', *Go-Set*, September 18 1971

Neil Mursky 'Interview With Bon Scott', WDIZ Orlando Florida, May 1979 www.youtube.com/watch?v=lgK3yXpyiTQ&t

Dave Mustaine 'The Record That Changed My Life', *Guitar World*, January 15 2014

Phil McNeill 'I Wallaby Your Man', *NME*, May 8 1976

Georgina Mitchell 'Cheap Trick's Rick Nielsen "Would Be In The Angels Or AC/DC Right Now" If Plan To Move To Australia Had Gone Ahead', *Newcastle Herald*, September 19 2014

Tony Moore 'Cloudland: Inside Brisbane's Dead Queen Of The Ballrooms', *Brisbane Times*, May 3 2017

Ed Nimmervoll 'AC/DC', *Juke*, June 4 1975

Anthony O'Grady 'Australia Has Punk Rock Bands Too, You Know', *RAM*, April 19 1975

Anthony O'Grady 'Gonna Be A Rock'n'roll Singer, Gonna Be A Rock'n'roll Band', *RAM*, April 23 1976

Anthony O'Grady 'AC/DC Would Really Like To Be As Successful Here As They Are In England, But … ', *RAM*, July 14 1978

Irving Sealey 'AC/DC The Lusty Boys From Down Under', *Rock Gossip #1*, 1979

Andy Secher 'Plug Into AC/DC', *Super Rock* Vol. 3 #1, 1979

Sylvie Simmons 'AC/DC Celebrate Their Quarter Century', *Mojo*, December 2000

David Sinclair 'AC/DC: Phew! Got Away With It, Readers!', Q, December 1990

Daniela Soave 'Kerrang! Whang! Crunch! It's AC/DC!', *Sounds*, August 18 1979

Tony Stewart 'Review Of Hammersmith Odeon Show', *NME*, November 20 1976

Phil Sutcliffe 'More Songs About Humping And Booze', *Sounds*, July 24 1976

Phil Sutcliffe 'The Dirtiest Story Ever Told', *Sounds*, August 28 1976

Phil Sutcliffe 'AC/DC: Let There Be Rock', *Sounds*, October 22 1977

Phil Sutcliffe 'AC/DC: Sex, Snot, Sweat And School Kids', *Sounds*, October 29 1977

Phil Sutcliffe 'No Cord Wonder', *Sounds*, November 12 1977

Mick Wall *AC/DC: The Making Of Highway To Hell*, teamrock.com, November 6 2013

Matt Wardlaw 'AC/DC's Cheap Trick Connection: Malcolm Young Was The "Main Man"', ultimateclassicrock.com, 2016

Philip Wilding 'The Story Behind The Album: AC/DC's Back In Black', *Classic Rock*, January 2001

Matthew Wilkening 'How AC/DC Brought Their Live Show To The Studio With Let There Be Rock', ultimateclassicrock.com

Matthew Wilkening 'Top 10 Bon Scott AC/DC Songs', ultimateclassicrock.com

Matthew Wilkening '10 Surprising Things We Learned During AC/DC's "Ask Us Anything" Session', ultimateclassicrock.com

Emma Young Lost Perth's AC/DC Memories: '3 Hours Straight And Angus Was Cranking', *Sydney Morning Herald*, November 30 2015

Bernard Zuel 'Albert Productions, The Label Behind AC/DC, Rocks Up 50 Years', *Sydney Morning Herald*, August 10 2014

'AC/DC Creates Another Rock Concert Riot', *TV Week*, March 27 1976

'AC/DC Madness', *Juke*, October 14 1978

'AC/DC Nipped', *Juke*, June 25 1975

'AC/DC Score Heavy Overseas Workload', *RAM*, April 9 1976

'AC/DC To Export An Album', *TV Times*, February 7 1976

Australian Women's Weekly, October 6 1976

Best, December 1979

'Classic Albums Revisited: Dirty Deeds Done Dirt Cheap', *Defending Axl Rose* (Blog), July 30 2012

'Easybeats In Hysterical Farewell', *Canberra Times*, July 11 1966

'George Young Interview', *Let There Be Light*, issues 5 and 6, February/December 1993

'Great Moments In Rock Criticism', *Spin*, September 1987

'Interview With Bernie Bonvoisin Of Trust', *Energy Paris*, November 1982

'Phil Rudd Interview: KISS Were Like A Cartoon Band', skiddle.com, September 7 2017

Riff, May 2003

'Sharpies: The Mulleted Rocker Kids Of 70s Australia', dangerousminds.net, June 24 2013

'The Easybeats', *Good Neighbour*, June 1 1967

'Treble Exposure', *Record Mirror*, June 3 1978

WEBSITES

ac-dc.net
acdccollector.com

highwaytoacdc.com
rockmine.com/Pistols/SexDates.html

rockshowvideos.com/rocksuperbowl4.html
superseventies.com/creem.html

VIDEO

'Angus And Malcolm Young On How They Founded AC/DC', youtube.com/watch?v=Gwb-SNVb4Vo.

'Angus Talks About Playing In AC/DC', September 16 2016, acdc.com

'Angus Young On Why He Admires Chuck Berry So Much', youtube.com/watch?v=IMM_fGl3gpA.

Blood & Thunder: The Sound Of Alberts, 2015 (Beyond International/Bombora Film & Music Production Company, 2015)

'Bon Scott, The Classic 1978 Interview', youtube.com/watch?v=-7Yuo-QoQi0

Countdown interview en route to London, 1976, youtube.com/watch?v=YQIQJMhcAQU

Countdown interview with Bon Scott in London, 1977, youtube.com/watch?v=-M-0S6B-3Zw

'Funny Angus Young [Talks] About AC/DC's First Singer', youtube.com/watch?v=GFSUySHjjzY.

'Show Business' video, youtube.com/watch?v=dvFxTpnxk8s

Excerpts from the concert film *Let There Be Rock*, youtube.com/watch?v=cXS4fdof_-A, youtube.com/watch?v=OhUQzFNwV7I

Spanish TV show *Applauso*, 1980, https://www.youtube.com/watch?v=SkpxBxlOhQA

PHOTO CREDITS

The photographs in this book came from the following sources, and we are grateful for their help. All efforts have been made to trace original copyright holders, but if you feel there has been a mistaken attribution, please contact the publisher.

Front cover Michael Ochs Archives/Getty Images; **front flap** Graeme Webber **7** Philip Morris; **14** *Burwood* courtesy of Neil Litchfield; *George and Margaret* Glenn A. Baker; **22** Philip Morris; **23** Glenn A. Baker; **26**, **30**, **34**, **38**, **42**, **46**, **47**, **51** Philip Morris; **62** Andrew Wittner; **74**, **78**, **82** Philip Morris; **86**, **87** Graeme Webber; **90**, **91** Philip Morris; **99** Graeme Webber; **107** Philip Morris; **111** Martyn Goddard/Corbis/Getty Images; **119** Dick Barnatt/Redferns/Getty Images; **122**, **131** Michael Putland/Getty Images; **146** Glenn A. Baker; **150**, **151** Tim Petts; **158** Bob King/Redferns/Getty Images; **171** Waring Abbott/Getty Images; **174** Michael Ochs Archives/Getty Images; **178**, **179** Jay Good/Frank White Photo Agency; **199**, **206** Ron Pownall/Frank White Photo Agency; **211** *both images* Philip Morris; **219** Larry Hulst/Michael Ochs Archives/Getty Images; **226** Andre Csillag/REX/Shutterstock; **227** Richard Young/REX/Shutterstock; **234** Fin Costello/Redferns; **243** Graeme Webber; **245** Michael Ochs Archives/Getty Images. Memorabilia selected from the author's collection and the Balafon Image Bank.

INDEX

254

ALSO AVAILABLE IN PRINT AND EBOOK EDITIONS FROM JAWBONE PRESS